China Unbound

"No historian has so sure a touch in exploring our ethnocentrism and pointing the ways around it. These essays are a rich mosaic of Cohen's historiographical thinking over four decades. With their fresh perspectives on the risks and opportunities of the historian-as-outsider, they challenge us to think more deeply about our craft and about China."

Philip A. Kuhn, Harvard University

In this absorbing volume by one of the leading experts on modern Chinese history and historiography, Paul Cohen consistently argues for fresh ways of approaching the Chinese past, training his critical spotlight alternately on Western historians, Chinese historians, and the history itself.

The book provides a persuasive critique of older approaches to nineteenth- and twentieth-century China and offers powerful reinterpretations of such diverse topics as the Boxer uprising, American China historiography, nationalism, popular religion, and reform. In an important introductory essay, Cohen also revisits the "China-centered approach," raising searching questions concerning its applicability to recent areas of scholarly interest.

While maintaining the view that culture is important, the author cautions that the claims of Western and Chinese cultural difference, when overstated, can easily lead to cultural stereotyping and caricaturing. To offset this tendency, he repeatedly foregrounds common elements in the thinking and behavior of Chinese and non-Chinese, confident that by subverting parochial perspectives that continue to cordon China off in a realm by itself, historians can render its history intelligible, meaningful, and even important to people in the West.

This book will be essential reading for all scholars and students with an interest in Chinese studies and history.

Paul A. Cohen is Edith Stix Wasserman Professor of Asian Studies and History, Emeritus, Wellesley College and an Associate at the Fairbank Center for East Asian Research at Harvard University. He has published widely on Chinese history, including the award-winning *History in Three Keys: The Boxers as Event, Experience, and Myth* (1997) and *Discovering History in China: American Historical Writing on the Recent Chinese Past* (1984).

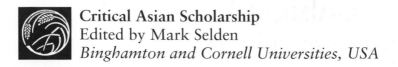

Critical Asian Scholarship
Edited by Mark Selden
Binghamton and Cornell Universities, USA

The series is intended to showcase the most important individual contributions to scholarship in Asian studies. Each of the volumes presents a leading Asian scholar addressing themes that are central to his or her most significant and lasting contribution to Asian studies. The series is committed to the rich variety of research and writing on Asia, and is not restricted to any particular discipline, theoretical approach or geographical expertise.

Southeast Asia
A testament
George McT. Kahin

Women and the Family in Chinese History
Patricia Buckley Ebrey

China Unbound
Evolving perspectives on the Chinese past
Paul A. Cohen

China Unbound

Evolving perspectives on
the Chinese past

Paul A. Cohen

RoutledgeCurzon
Taylor & Francis Group

LONDON AND NEW YORK

First published 2003
by RoutledgeCurzon
11 New Fetter Lane, London EC4P 4EE

Simultaneously published in the USA and Canada
by RoutledgeCurzon
29 West 35th Street, New York, NY 10001

RoutledgeCurzon is an imprint of the Taylor & Francis Group

© 2003 Paul A. Cohen

Typeset in Sabon by Taylor & Francis Books Ltd
Printed and bound in Great Britain by MPG Books Ltd, Bodmin

British Library Cataloguing in Publication Data
A catalogue record for this book is available from the British Library

Library of Congress Cataloging in Publication Data
Cohen, Paul A.
China unbound: evolving perspectives on the Chinese past /
Paul A. Cohen.
(Critical Asian scholarship)
Includes bibliographical references and index.
1. China–History–19th century. 2. China–History–19th
century–Historiography. 3. China–History–20th century.
4. China–History–20th century–Historiography. I. Title.
II. Series.
DS755.2 .C64 2003
951'.035'072–dc21
2002151642

ISBN 0–415–29822–9 (hbk)
ISBN 0–415–29823–7 (pbk)

For Elizabeth

Contents

Illustrations

Acknowledgments

When Routledge first invited me to put together a book of my writings for its new Critical Asian Scholarship series, I was both flattered and hesitant. Flattered, because the initial group of invitees was very small and (as I soon discovered) included such esteemed scholars as Patricia Ebrey and the late George Kahin. Hesitant, in part, because it would mean an interruption of the work I was then (and am still) engaged in on the problem of national humiliation in twentieth-century China, and also, in part, because preparing such a volume would inevitably mean confronting certain intellectual issues that had for some time been a nagging source of unease in my work. As I began to think about what to include in such a book and how, in an introductory essay, I might address and work through the issues just alluded to, the unease gradually abated and I became increasingly enthusiastic about the multiple challenges the project offered.

Two people who were particularly important in moving me forward in this process were Mark Selden and Elizabeth Sinn. Having had as a mentor in graduate school John Fairbank, whose gifts as a nurturer of successful manuscripts were legendary, I held Mark Selden, the editor of the Critical Asian Scholarship series, to an impossibly high standard. Mark, doing the impossible, met this standard at every step of the way. As an experienced volume editor, he exercised exceptionally good judgment in helping me decide what to include (and not include) in the book. His detailed comments on all of the chapters, save the three (Chapters 1, 2, and 7) that had been previously published in English and that I was unwilling to change except in regard to mechanical matters (such as converting the romanization of Chinese names and terms from Wade-Giles to *pinyin*), were unfailingly constructive, all the more remarkable because his specific interests and starting point for approaching history tend (with some exceptions) to be quite different from mine. Mark's comments covered everything from style and word choice to weaknesses or illogicalities in my argument to bibliographical lacunae. He pushed me especially hard on the introductory essay, which he rightly judged to be critical to the success of the volume as a whole. The finished piece benefited greatly from his many specific suggestions, insightfulness, and tireless prodding.

Elizabeth Sinn was at the outset a good deal more excited by the idea of this book than I was and did much to overcome my initial misgivings. Beyond this, she read through multiple versions of several of the chapters, pointing out ambiguities and infelicities in the writing, lapses in documentation, and places where the analysis was in clear need of sharpening. Knowing the author well, including his very considerable capacity for defensiveness, Elizabeth navigated with practiced adroitness the treacherous border area between criticism and encouragement, for which I thank her with warm affection.

Elizabeth Perry, who had recently compiled a book of her own writings, shared her experience concerning the nature of the process. John Ziemer drew on his years of work in publishing to guide me through the thickets of copyright practice, indicating when permission was required and when it was not. Lisa Cohen prepared most of the photographs and all of the digitized images for the book's illustrations. Craig Fowlie of Routledge responded promptly to my periodic queries and graciously offered the services of his office in applying for reprint permissions. My thanks to all of these individuals for their generous help.

The author and publisher would like to thank the following for granting permission to reproduce material in this work:

- The Harvard University Asia Center for permission to reprint pp. vii–xii, 3–7, 87–90, 143–53, 239–43, 279–80, 294, 306–7, 317–18 from Paul A. Cohen, *Between Tradition and Modernity: Wang T'ao and Reform in Late Ch'ing China*, paperback edition, Harvard East Asian Monographs, 133 (Cambridge, Mass.: Harvard University Council on East Asian Studies, 1987), original edition © 1974 and paperback edition © 1987 by the President and Fellows of Harvard College.
- The University of Michigan for permission to reprint the article "Remembering and Forgetting National Humiliation in Twentieth-Century China," by Paul A. Cohen, which appeared in *Twentieth-Century China* 27.2 (April 2002), pp. 1–39.
- The Columbia University Press for permission to reprint Chapter 2 ("Moving Beyond 'Tradition and Modernity'") from Paul A. Cohen, *Discovering History in China: American Historical Writing on the Recent Chinese Past* (original edition © 1984), pp. 57–96, 205–13, and "Preface to the Second Paperback Edition" from the 2nd paperback edition of this book (1997), pp. ix–xxvii.
- The British Library for permission to reproduce Figure 8.4.

Introduction
China unbound

Putting together a volume of my writings, spanning a publishing career now stretching to almost a half-century,[1] has been fascinating in a number of ways. For one thing, it has involved rereading things that in some cases I hadn't laid eyes on for decades, reminding myself, sometimes happily, sometimes not, of where I was intellectually at various points in my evolution as a historian. For another, it has afforded me the opportunity to play historian to myself, identifying some themes – my teacher Benjamin Schwartz referred to them as "underlying persistent preoccupations"[2] – that have endured from the beginning of my writing life right through to the present, although taking different forms at different times, and others that have emerged at one point or another but weren't there at the outset. In other words, the exercise has enabled me to gain a clearer picture of how my thinking has changed over time and, equally important, how it hasn't.

Although most of my scholarly work has focused on the nineteenth and twentieth centuries and has therefore, almost inevitably, dealt in one way or another with the interactions between China and the West (or a Western-influenced Japan), an abiding concern throughout has been my determination to get inside China, to reconstruct Chinese history as far as possible as the Chinese themselves experienced it rather than in terms of what people in the West thought was important, natural, or normal. I wanted, in short, to move beyond approaches to the Chinese past that bore a heavy burden of Eurocentric or Western-centric preconceptions. An early example of this was my first book, *China and Christianity*, in the preface to which I explicitly distanced myself from the older approach to China missions, with its focus "on missions history, not on Chinese history." With the coming of age of Chinese studies in the postwar era, "the inadequacies of this old Western-centered approach" had become apparent and a new approach had been suggested – the pioneer here was another of my mentors, John Fairbank – that was "more concerned with understanding and evaluating the role played by Christian missions in Chinese history."[3] It was this approach that I adopted in the book.

This was a first step along what has turned out to be a long and tortuous path. In the final chapter of *China and Christianity* I adumbrated the next step: a critical look at the Western impact–Chinese response approach (also closely identified with Fairbank) that had played such an important part in American writing on nineteenth-century China in the immediate postwar decades. "Modern students of Chinese history," I wrote,

> have all too often focused on the process of Western impact and Chinese response, to the neglect of the reverse process of Chinese impact and Western response. The missionary who came to China found himself confronted with frustrations and hostilities which he could hardly have envisaged before coming and which transformed him, subtly but unmistakably, into a *foreign* missionary. His awareness (one might indeed say resentment) of this metamorphosis, together with his fundamental dissatisfaction with things as they were in China...greatly conditioned the missionary's response to the Chinese setting.[4]

The Western impact–Chinese response approach, in other words, oversimplified things by assuming that Chinese–Western interactions in the nineteenth century were a one-way street in which all of the traffic flowed from West to East.[5]

Several years later I wrote an essay in which I scrutinized the impact–response approach more systematically, attempting to identify some of the hidden premises on which it was based. Apart from the assumption of unidirectionality of influence just noted, I pointed to a number of problems inherent in the approach. One was "the tendency, when speaking of the 'Western impact,' to ignore the enigmatic and contradictory nature" of the West itself. This was a point that had been made with particular force by Benjamin Schwartz. Although most Western historians were properly humbled, Schwartz suggested, by the superficiality of their understanding of "non-Western" societies, they viewed the West as home ground, a known quantity. Yet, he cautioned,

> when we turn our attention back to the modern West itself, this deceptive clarity disappears. We are aware that the best minds of the nineteenth and twentieth centuries have been deeply divided in their agonizing efforts to grasp the inner meaning of modern Western development.... We undoubtedly "know" infinitely more about the West [than about any given non-Western society], but the West remains as problematic as ever.[6]

A related source of ambiguity was that the West, even in its modern guise, had changed greatly over time. The West that China encountered during the Opium War and the West that exerted such great influence on Chinese intellectual and political life beginning in the last years of the nineteenth century were both the "modern West." But there were vast differences between the two – differences that Western historians of China regularly overlooked.

Other problems were that the impact–response approach tended to direct attention away from those aspects of nineteenth-century China that were unrelated, or only distantly related, to the Western impact; that it was inclined to assume uncritically that Western-related facets of Chinese history during this period were Chinese responses to the impact of the West when, in fact, they were often responses (however much Western-influenced) to indigenous forces; and, finally, perhaps because of its emphasis on "conscious responses," that the approach seemed to gravitate toward intellectual, cultural, and psychological forms of historical explanation, at the expense of social, political, and economic ones.[7] The upshot was that the impact–response framework, although a decided improvement over earlier approaches that ignored Chinese thought and action entirely, encouraged a picture of nineteenth-century China that was incomplete and suffered unnecessarily from imbalance and distortion.[8] (Other difficulties pertaining to the Western impact are discussed in connection with the thought of Joseph Levenson in Chapter 2.)

The impact–response approach had a built-in tendency to link whatever change was discerned in nineteenth-century China to the impact of the West. As such, it formed part of a broader European and American predisposition in the 1950s and 1960s, when looking at the more recent centuries of Chinese history, to deny the possibility of meaningful endogenous change.[9] Although it was not until the early 1980s that I undertook to examine this issue in a comprehensive way, it is clear to me in retrospect that I was already beginning to move in this direction a decade earlier in my intellectual biography of the late Qing reformer and pioneer journalist Wang Tao.[10] Since Wang Tao spent his entire adult life grappling with complicated questions relating to change, in the course of trying to figure him out I had to confront these questions myself. In the prologues to the four parts of the book, which form the bulk of Chapter 1 of this volume, I touched on a number of broad change-related issues as they pertained to Wang: the relationship between incremental change and revolution, the differences between generational and historical change, the virtue of measuring societal change by internal points of reference, the complex relationship between "tradition" and "modernity," differences between the actual historical past of China and "Chinese tradition," technological change versus value change, the geocultural sources of change in nineteenth- and twentieth-century China, and so on. In much of my discussion of these issues, it later became apparent to me, there was still a residual tendency – even as I was beginning to raise questions concerning it – to overstate the relative importance of Western influence as the key measure of change in late Qing China.[11] The consequences of this, especially as they pertain to the final part of the Wang Tao book, are addressed in the preface to the paperback edition (1987), which is included in Chapter 1.

The gathering discomfort with certain Western-centric tendencies (my own included) that were prefigured in the study of Wang Tao led me in the late 1970s to begin working on a more thoroughgoing critique of the shaping role of these tendencies in postwar American scholarship. The first three chapters of the resulting book, which was entitled *Discovering History in China: American Historical Writing on the Recent Chinese Past* (1984), probed the Western-centric biases of three leading conceptual frameworks: the impact–response approach, the modernization (or tradition–modernity) approach, and the imperialism (or, perhaps more aptly, imperialism–revolution) approach. In the final chapter of the book I identified a new approach in American scholarship – it was really more a collection of discrete characteristics than a single, well-defined approach – which I labeled "China-centered." This approach had emerged around 1970 and, in my judgment, went a long way toward overcoming earlier Western-centric biases. Since the second chapter of *Discovering History in China* ("Moving Beyond 'Tradition and Modernity' ") is reproduced in this book (see Chapter 2), and the preface to the second paperback edition (1997), in which I respond to criticism of the original work, is reprinted in Chapter 7, I will not review the book's contents here. I do, however, want to raise a question that isn't dealt with in either of these chapters: the potential limits of the China-centered approach posed by several recent developments.

The core attribute of the China-centered approach is that its practitioners make a serious effort to understand Chinese history in its own terms – paying close attention to Chinese historical trajectories and Chinese perceptions of their own problems – rather than in terms of a set of expectations derived from Western history. This does not mean that the approach gives short shrift to exogenous influences (see Chapter 7); nor, certainly, does it preclude – on the contrary, it warmly embraces – the application to Chinese realities of theoretical insights and methodological strategies of non-Chinese provenance (often developed in disciplines other than history), so long as these insights and strategies are sensitive to the perils of parochial (typically, Western-centric) bias.

I would not change any part of this formulation today. There are countless issues in Chinese history for the probing of which a China-centered approach remains, in my view, both appropriate and desirable.[12] There are other issues, however, where this is less plainly the case. I have in mind a number of areas of recent scholarly interest that, although unquestionably *relating to* Chinese history, are best identified in other ways, either because they pose questions (for instance in addressing world historical issues) that are broadly comparative in nature, or because they examine China as part of an East Asian or Asian regional system, or because even while dealing with the subject matter of Chinese history they are principally concerned with matters that transcend it, or because they focus on the behavior and thinking (including self-perception) of non-Han ethnic groups within the Chinese realm, or because their paramount interest is in the migration of Chinese to other parts of the world. Each of these issues – and doubtless there are others – raises questions about the boundaries of "Chinese history" and, indeed, in some instances the very meaning of the word "China." Inevitably, therefore, each in its own way challenges the adequacy of the China-centered approach.

For historians of China (and surely others as well), the most interesting and deservedly influential exercise in comparative history in recent years has been the work of R. Bin Wong and Kenneth Pomeranz – I refer specifically to the former's *China Transformed* (1997) and the latter's *The Great Divergence* (2000) – grappling with the thorny issue of the West's ascendancy in the world during the past two centuries or so.[13] There are significant differences between Wong and Pomeranz. Pomeranz is more exclusively interested in questions pertaining to economic development, while Wong in addition devotes much space to issues of state formation and popular protest.[14] Pomeranz, moreover, as he himself notes, places greater emphasis on "global conjunctures and reciprocal influences and bring[s] more places besides Europe and China into the discussion,"[15] whereas Wong is more consistently and exclusively concerned with Europe–China comparisons. What the two scholars share is, however, far more important than what separates them. Most noteworthy in this regard is their agreement that in the past Westerners venturing comparisons between Europe and other parts of the world have posed the wrong sorts of questions. Tightly bound by the Eurocentrism of nineteenth-century social theory, they have assumed that the trajectories of change that occurred in Europe were the norm and that if something like the Industrial Revolution took place in Europe but not in, say, China the proper line of inquiry was to ask what went awry in the Chinese case.

Contesting this approach frontally, Wong and Pomeranz insist upon the need to engage in two-way comparison, Wong using the phrase "symmetric perspectives" to describe this process, Pomeranz, "reciprocal comparisons."[16] Freed of Eurocentric presuppositions about normative trajectories of change, both scholars, when they look at the economic situations of Europe and China (or, in Pomeranz's case, parts of Europe, parts of China, and parts of India and Japan) in the latter half of the eighteenth century, find a remarkable degree of parallelism. "In key ways," Wong states, "eighteenth-century Europe shared more with China of the same period than it did with the Europe of the nineteenth and twentieth centuries." And Pomeranz makes a similar point in more nuanced spatial terms, observing that in the middle of the eighteenth century

> various core regions scattered around the Old World – the Yangzi Delta, the Kantō plain, Britain and the Netherlands, Gujarat – shared

some crucial features with each other, which they did not share with the rest of the continent or subcontinent around them (e.g., relatively free markets, extensive handicraft industries, highly commercialized agriculture).[17]

Given the largely common economic circumstances prevailing between parts of Europe and parts of Asia at this time, the key question for both Wong and Pomeranz shifts from what went wrong in Asia to what made possible the radically discontinuous economic change that occurred in Europe after 1800 – first in England and then in other European core areas – and did not occur even in the most highly developed regions of the Asian continent. Although both scholars, in responding to this question, agree that technological innovation along with the shift to new sources of energy (coal) in England were of critical importance, Wong also emphasizes the liberating function of certain structural features of the evolving European political economy (states, for example, that stood in a competitive relationship with one another), while Pomeranz develops an explanation that lays greater stress on factors external to Europe, in particular its involvement in a new kind of trading system and the windfall the New World and its resources provided.[18]

Although Wong asserts at one point that his work "is primarily a book about Chinese history and secondarily a book about European history,"[19] and although when dealing with China he is exquisitely sensitive to the need to approach its history without blinders carried over from the history of Europe, my distinct sense is that "China" is not what the book is principally about. The supreme value of Wong's book, for me, is its careful construction and elaboration of a fresh and more even-handed way of doing comparative history, one that does not privilege the historical path followed in one part of the world over those followed in other parts and therefore frees us to ask questions of any part's history that are not, as it were, preloaded. In Pomeranz's study, the overall approach places less exclusive emphasis on comparison (even though the spatial *field* of comparison is wider than Wong's) and is more single-mindedly focused on the question of the divergent economic trajectories taken by Europe and East Asia after the mid-eighteenth century. Although seriously concerned with showing "how different Chinese development looks once we free it from its role as the presumed opposite of Europe and...how different European history looks once we see the *similarities* between its economy and one with which it has most often been contrasted,"[20] his paramount objective is to shed light on the substantive question of how the modern world economy came into being. Pomeranz too, therefore, like Wong, although devoting much space to China and caring a great deal about getting his China stories right, is ultimately interested in matters that transcend Chinese history.

Application of the designation "China-centered" to scholarship (such as that of Wong and Pomeranz) that so clearly pertains to world history (regardless of whether this scholarship is primarily comparative or also pays serious notice to conjunctures and influences) seems obviously inappropriate. The same, moreover, may be argued with respect to studies that look at China as part of a broader regional system in Asia. Regions, as intermediate categories between individual states and the world, have their own historical dynamic and must therefore (we are told by those who study them) be scrutinized from a region-centered perspective. Takeshi Hamashita,[21] for example, wants us "to understand East Asia as a historically constituted region with its own hegemonic structure" – a region that "entered modern times not because of the coming of European powers but because of the dynamism inherent in the traditional, Sinocentric tributary system."[22] The tributary system, inaugurated by China many centuries ago, formed a loose system of political integration embracing East and Southeast Asia. More than just a relationship between two states, China and the tribute-bearing country, it also at times encompassed satellite tributary relationships – at various points, Vietnam required tribute from Laos, Korea while tributary to China also sent tribute missions to Japan, and the kings of the Liuqiu (Ryūkyū) Islands during the Qing/Tokugawa had tributary relations with both Edo and Beijing – thus forming a complex web of relationships throughout the region.

The other key feature of the Asian regional system, according to Hamashita, was economic. A network of commercial relations (often multilateral in nature), operating symbiotically with the tribute system, developed in East and Southeast Asia, closely intertwined with the commercial penetration of Chinese merchants into Southeast Asia and the emigration there of workers from South China. "The relationship between tribute goods and 'gifts' was substantially one of selling and purchasing." Prices of commodities "were determined, albeit loosely, by market prices in Peking." In fact, from the late Ming on, Hamashita argues,

> it can be shown that the foundation for the whole complex tribute-trade formation was determined by the price structure of China and that the tribute-trade zone formed an integrated "silver zone" in which silver was used as the medium of trade settlement. The key to the functioning of the tribute trade as a system was the huge "demand" for commodities outside China and the difference between prices inside and outside China.[23]

(The importance Hamashita attaches to regional economic integration, it may be noted, is one of the more salient ways in which his analysis departs from earlier accounts of the "tributary system" by Fairbank and others.[24])

Although China is an absolutely fundamental part of Hamashita's region-centered perspective (indeed, he frequently uses the term "Sinocentric" to describe it), it should be evident from the foregoing paragraphs that a China-centered approach would be inadequate for understanding the Asian regional system he elaborates.[25] This becomes even clearer in another part of his analysis, in which he advances the notion that the *sea* was as important a locus and determinant of historical activity as the *land* in Asia. Although we are accustomed to viewing the Asian region as a collection of landed territorial units, it may also be seen as a series of interconnected "maritime regions" stretching from Northeast Asia all the way to Oceania. Once we adopt this sea-centered geographical perspective, Hamashita shrewdly suggests, it is easier to understand why intra-Asian political relationships developed as they did over the centuries:

> The states, regions, and cities located along the periphery of each sea zone ... [were] close enough to influence one another but too far apart to be assimilated into a larger entity. Autonomy in this sense formed a major condition for the establishment of the looser form of political integration known as the tributary system.[26]

The adequacy (or sufficiency) of the "China-centered" approach may also, in certain instances, be called into question in regard to scholarship that is far more directly and extensively concerned with Chinese history. A good illustration would be my most recent book, *History in Three Keys: The Boxers as Event, Experience, and Myth* (1997). Certainly, in large portions of this work I make a sustained effort to get inside the world of the Boxers and other Chinese inhabiting the North China plain in the spring and summer of 1900, and in this respect the approach may be viewed as China-centered. But I'm also interested, albeit to a much lesser degree, in the thoughts, feelings, and behavior of the non-Chinese participants in the events of the time and frequently point out commonalities between the Chinese and foreign sides, suggesting an approach that, at least at certain junctures, is more human-centered than China-centered. (I will return to this point later.)

Finally, and most importantly, as I make clear throughout, my main purpose in the book is to explore a wide range of issues pertaining to the writing of history, "the Boxers functioning as a kind of handmaiden to this larger enterprise."[27] This is rather different from the usual procedure in historical studies. It is not at all uncommon in such studies (not just in the Chinese field but in others as well) for authors to conclude by situating their findings in a broader frame of reference, in the hope of enhancing the significance and importance of their work. In *History in Three Keys*, I start right off with the broader question and never really let go of it. Although I use the Boxers as an extended case study, moreover, I make it clear, especially in the concluding chapter, that there is no necessary or exclusive connection between the Boxers and the larger points I am interested in exploring. Many other episodes of world history could serve equally well. The main object of the book is to say something not about Chinese history, but about the writing of history in general. And there's nothing especially China-centered about that.[28] (For a more detailed discussion of the larger historical issues dealt with in the book, see Chapter 8.)

Research on non-Han ethnic groups[29] points to another arena of historical scholarship that is not especially well served by China-centered analysis. Such research has taken a variety of forms. A small but unusually talented coterie of historians have in recent years injected new life into the question of the Manchuness of the Qing empire, looking at such topics as the evolution over time of Manchu identity (cultural and/or ethnic), the special character of the Qing frontier, the multiform nature of Manchu rulership and its contributions to the functioning of the Qing imperium, important Manchu institutions (most notably the Eight Banners), the contribution of the Manchus to twentieth-century nationalism, and so on.[30] Often supplementing Chinese sources with those in the Manchu language and sharply contesting the old view that the Manchus were largely absorbed or assimilated into a "Chinese world order," these scholars are in broad agreement that, as one of them has phrased it, "the notion of Manchu difference mattered throughout the [Qing] dynasty."[31] Indeed, several of them have used such phrases as "Qing-centered" and "Manchu-centered" to highlight this very difference.[32] The argument is not that the Manchus weren't, in important ways, a part of Chinese history, but, rather, that Chinese history during the final centuries of the imperial era looks very different when seen through Manchu eyes. To view the parts taken by the Manchus in this history from a Han Chinese perspective – the conventional assimilation or sinicization model – is therefore to invite the same kinds of distortions that result when Chinese history is depicted in Eurocentric terms.

If Manchu difference mattered throughout the Qing, a major (although not the only) reason for its mattering was that the Qing was a conquest dynasty that brought China and eventually Inner Asia under the Manchu sway during this period. It was a quite different story in the case of other non-Han groups, such as (to cite one of the more important examples) Muslim Chinese. Muslims in China also raise questions concerning the aptness of the China-centered approach, but because their experience over the centuries has been very different from that of the Manchus the sorts of questions they raise also are different. One difference from the Manchus is that although Muslims at various points in time (above all, the Yuan dynasty) served as high officials they never ruled China as a group, in the sense that the Manchus (and Mongols) did. Another difference is that Muslims were (and continue to be) linked, albeit to varying degrees and in widely different ways, to a religion – Islam – that is of non-Chinese origin and worldwide embrace.

As both Dru Gladney and Jonathan Lipman have insisted,[33] Muslims in different parts of China (even in some instances within a single province) also tend to be very different from each other. Some Muslims, many of the Uyghurs, for example, in present-day Xinjiang (an area that until its subjugation by the Qing in the eighteenth century had been situated outside the Chinese realm), although inhabiting a space that is politically China, do not speak Chinese and tend to identify culturally and religiously more closely with their counterparts in the Central Asian states to the north than with Han Chinese. Other Muslims, scattered in various places throughout the Chinese realm, are descended from families that have lived in China for generations, speak one or another form of Chinese, and are indistinguishable in many aspects of their lives from non-Muslim Chinese. In recent centuries, in short, individuals in China could be both Chinese and Muslim in a vast array of different ways, making it hard to claim (as was done in the People's Republic in the 1950s) a "unified 'ethnic consciousness' " for Sino-Muslims.[34]

Given the heterogeneous character of the Muslim population of China, the argument could be made, at least in theory, that while a China-centered approach would be clearly misguided if applied to the Turkic-speaking Uyghur population of Xinjiang,[35] it ought to be perfectly appropriate in the case of more acculturated Muslim Chinese. A key feature of the approach, after all, is that it seeks to cope with the immense variety and complexity of the Chinese world by breaking it down into smaller, more manageable spatial units, thereby facilitating close scrutiny of the whole range of local variation (including religious, ethnic, and social difference).[36] As it turns out, however, even in the case of Chinese-speaking Muslims, China-centered analysis can present problems. Lipman provides a fascinating illustration of the potential complications in his discussion of Muslims in a subprovincial part of Gansu in the nineteenth and twentieth centuries. The political center of Gansu and the center of Chinese-oriented economic life throughout this period was Lanzhou, the provincial capital. But Lanzhou, situated on the edges of two distinct Muslim spheres – one around Ningxia, the other centering on Hezhou – would from a Muslim perspective be considered a peripheral area. And, conversely, Hezhou, some sixty miles southwest of Lanzhou, although for Muslims (who constituted 50 per cent of its population in the nineteenth century) a major commercial and religious center, "would be the periphery of the periphery in any China-centered mapping." In other words, a China-centered mapping would be insufficiently sensitive to aspects of social, economic, and religious existence that were of vital importance to the Muslims of Gansu. Beyond this, moreover, it would more than likely have the drawback of presenting an undifferentiated picture of the province's Muslim community, flattening out its members' diversity, when, as Lipman clearly demonstrates, Muslims in different parts of the province – and how much more would this be the case nationwide – in fact occupied a wide range of different social and occupational niches (and took different parts *vis-à-vis* the state), sometimes engaged in violence against each other, and were anything but unified in the nature and degree of their religious commitments.[37]

The new work on Manchus and Muslims relates to a much broader scholarly concern in recent years with the whole *minzu* ("nationality" or "ethnic group") question in China. Energized in part by Han-minority tensions on China's peripheries, in part by growing interest in and sensitivity to multicultural and multiethnic issues globally, this concern has been discernible in writing on the Uyghurs, Mongols, Tibetans, Yi, and many other groups.[38] Insofar as it challenges the notion of a transparent, unproblematic "Chineseness," complicating this category and forcing us continually to rethink its meaning, it has understandably not been very hospitable to China-centered analysis.

If a China-centered approach is not especially well equipped to address the distinctive perspectives and experiences of non-Han communities within China, it also poses problems in regard to Han Chinese who have migrated to places outside the country – another phenomenon that has of late attracted growing interest in the scholarly world. Chinese migration abroad is an enormously complicated subject, which scholars are only now beginning to conceptualize anew.[39] Certain of its characteristic features derive from broader (and prior) patterns of migration within China, and insofar as the focus is on the "push" part of the process – the factors that favored decisions to migrate, whether internally or overseas, from a specific part of the country – the sensitivity of China-centered analysis to local particularity and variation is of potential value. But even at this stage we begin to encounter problems. Although local conditions of impoverishment or social unrest were fairly widespread in both North and South China in the nineteenth and early twentieth centuries, migration overseas originated largely from specific locales in the southern provinces of Fujian and Guangdong, rather than from the northern part of the country. A major reason for this had to do with the access these places had to highly developed Chinese networks in a few southern treaty ports and, above all, the British colony of Hong Kong. These "in-between places," to use Elizabeth Sinn's apt phrase, served as points of transit or hubs, enabling people, goods, remittances, and even the bones of the dead to move, in one direction or the other, between villages in South China and destinations all over the globe. Migration, using such networks, became for families in certain parts of the south – and even in some instances for entire villages and lineages – a prime economic strategy.[40] It was manifestly part of the regional and global systems discussed earlier.

At this point in the migration process, the utility of the China-centered approach as an exclusive – or even a primary – avenue to understanding becomes seriously diminished. The most obvious reason, of course, is the fact of important links with locales outside China. Once Chinese settled in Java or California or Lima or Pretoria, whether temporarily or permanently, even if they remained in important ways embedded in Chinese social and historical narratives, they also became integrated into Indonesian, American, Peruvian, and South African histories. Their adaptations to a range of environments that varied not only from place to place but also over time – Philip Kuhn uses the phrase "historical ecology" to characterize the process – can hardly be comprehended in terms of a single national or cultural perspective.[41] But the complication created for China-centered analysis by the need to factor in multiple place-based understandings is only part of the problem. Beyond this, Adam McKeown argues persuasively, if we are to gain a fuller comprehension of Chinese migration, nation-based perspectives as such (China-centered or America-centered or Indonesia-centered or whatever) must be complemented by approaches that put special emphasis on mobility and dispersion, "drawing attention to global connections, networks, activities, and consciousness that bridge these more localized anchors of reference."[42] Migration, in other words, is not just a matter of push factors and pull factors, a sending place and a receiving place. It must also be understood as a *process* – a process that involves constant movement back and forth along well-established, highly articulated corridors and that, for this very reason, is profoundly subversive of conventional national boundaries.[43]

The research themes treated in the preceding pages all raise problems of one sort or another for the China-centered approach, requiring in some instances that it be abandoned, but more often that it be used in nuanced conjunction with a variety of other approaches. When, twenty years ago, I first described the China-centered approach – and I hasten to add that, from my perspective at the time, all I was doing was giving articulation to a set of research strategies that others had already begun to use and that seemed to me an appropriate and salutary direction for American China scholarship to be moving in – I expressly linked it to the study of the *Chinese* past. Indeed, the chapter in *Discovering History in China* in which I introduced the approach bore the title "Toward a China-Centered History of China." As long as the topics historians choose to study are centrally, and more or less unambiguously, situated within a Chinese context (political, social, economic, intellectual, cultural) – and despite the new scholarly developments of recent years this remains true of the preponderance of historical work on China – the China-centered approach remains, in my judgment, eminently useful. The difficulty arises when we move into research areas, such as the ones I've been discussing, that either decenter China by linking it to transnational processes (migration, the emergence of the modern world economy, the evolution of an Asian regional system) or general intellectual issues (multiple ways of addressing the past, the conduct of comparative history) or transform it from a physical space into something else (the currently fashionable word is deterritorialization)[44] or in some other way problematize its meaning (the self-perceptions of non-Han ethnic groups within China and of Han Chinese migrants abroad).[45]

Such research directions, although presenting problems for a narrowly conceived China-centered approach, make vitally important contributions to the study of Chinese history more broadly considered. Among the several ways in which they do this are the following: they remove some of the artificial walls that have been erected around "China" over the centuries (as much by Chinese as by Westerners); they subvert parochial readings of the Chinese past (fostered, again, no less by Chinese than by Western historians); they complicate our understandings of what it has meant in different places and at various points in time to be "Chinese"; they enable more even-handed (less loaded) comparisons between China and other parts of the world; and in general they weaken our (the West's) longstanding perception of China as the quintessential other by breaking down arbitrary and misleading distinctions between "East" and "West" and making it possible to see China – its peoples and their cultures – less as prototypically exotic and more as plausibly human.

Let me elaborate on this last point, as it has become an increasingly important theme in my own work. I refer specifically to my skepticism concerning exaggerated Western claims of Chinese and Western cultural difference – claims frequently (though not invariably) rooted in Western-centric perspectives. I take culture seriously in almost everything that I've written and would not for a moment deny that there are important differences between the cultural traditions of China and the West. But, at the same time, I believe that historical approaches that place excessive emphasis on such differences are apt to generate unfortunate distortions, even caricatures, of one sort or another. One such distortion takes the form of cultural essentialization – the radical reduction of a culture to a particular set of values or traits that other cultures are believed incapable of experiencing. The stereotypes of the authoritarian East and the liberal and tolerant West, for example, do not readily allow for the possibility, brilliantly argued recently by Amartya Sen, that the histories of India or China might include traditions of tolerance or freedom, or that authoritarianism might be a significant strain in the West's own past. Yet the actual historical record flies right in the face of such conventional understandings. Indeed, "when it comes to liberty and tolerance," Sen suggests, it might make more sense, giving priority to the substance of ideas rather than to culture or region, "to classify Aristotle and Ashoka on one side, and, on the other, Plato, Augustine, and Kautilya."[46]

Overemphasis on Chinese–Western cultural contrast also – and this was generally true of American historical scholarship until a few decades ago – has had a tendency to desensitize Western historians to China's capacity for change and to encourage a timeless conception of the Chinese past (see Chapter 2). When I initially advanced the notion of a China-centered approach, I observed that one of the approach's more important concomitants was a gradual shift away from *culture* and toward *history* as the dominant mode of structuring problems of the recent Chinese past (by which I meant chiefly the nineteenth and twentieth centuries). During the 1950s and 1960s, when the impact–response and tradition–modernity paradigms held sway in American scholarship, enormous explanatory power was invested in the *nature* of China's "traditional" society or culture – and, of course, in the ways in which this society–culture differed from that of the West (or Japan). Studies of clash between China and the West – Fairbank's *Trade and Diplomacy on the China Coast*, my own *China and Christianity* – although devoting much space to political, economic, social, institutional, and other factors, tended to view cultural difference and misunderstanding (as expressed, above all, in the realm of attitudes and values) as the ultimate ground of conflict.[47] Similarly, influential treatments of such themes as China's failure to industrialize in the late Qing (Feuerwerker), the ineffectiveness of China's response to the West as compared with Japan's (Fairbank, Reischauer, and Craig), the fruitless efforts of the Confucian state to modernize (Wright), and the inability of Chinese society to develop on its own into a "society with a scientific temper" (Levenson) all attached fundamental importance to the special nature of Chinese society and culture.[48]

This emphasis on the social or cultural factor was a natural by-product of intellectual paradigms that were built around the notion of sociocultural contrast and that sought to explain China principally in terms of its social and cultural differences from the West. The reason, I argued, why the China-centered approach, in contrast to this, lent itself to a structuring of the Chinese past more in historical than in cultural terms was that its locus of comparison was not the differences between one culture and another (China and the West) but the differences between earlier and later points in time within a single culture (China). The former kind of comparison, by drawing attention to the more stable, ongoing properties of a culture – a culture's "intrinsic nature" – encouraged a relatively static sense of the past. The latter, by stressing variation over time within one culture, fostered a more dynamic, more change-oriented sense of the past, one in which culture as an explanatory factor receded into the background and history – or a heightened sensitivity to historical process – moved to the fore.[49]

When historians seek to understand the people of another culture, an exaggerated attention to cultural difference – aside from making it more difficult to apprehend the complex, often contradictory elements in that culture's make-up or (as just argued) to appreciate the changes it has undergone over time – can also conceal from view aspects of the thought and behavior of its people that, reflecting transcultural, inherently human characteristics, overlap or resonate with the thought and behavior of people elsewhere in the world. This universal human dimension, I would argue, must be addressed, along with cultural difference, if we are to gain a fuller, more nuanced, less parochial understanding of the Chinese past.[50] Addressing it is also one of the more effective ways of traversing the boundaries that Western and Chinese historians both, albeit in different ways and for different reasons, have too often inscribed around China and its history.

Although I first touched on the notion of cultural convergence or resonance between China and the West and its possible reflection of basic human psychological proclivities in an essay on Wang Tao published in 1967,[51] I did not pursue the idea extensively until my work on the Boxer uprising. In *History in Three Keys*, in an effort to naturalize or "humanize" the thought and behavior of the Boxers I had frequent recourse to cross-cultural comparison, often in the process enlarging the scope of China's "other" to embrace Africa and other parts of the world, in addition to the West (see, in this volume, Chapter 3). An example is afforded by my discussion of the experience of rumor and mass hysteria in North China at the height of the Boxer crisis in the spring and summer of 1900. By far the most widely circulated rumor at the time was one that charged foreigners and Chinese Christians with contaminating the water supply by placing poison in village wells. The well-poisoning charge, according to a contemporary, was "practically universal" and "accounted for much of the insensate fury" directed by ordinary Chinese against Christians.[52]

An interesting question has to do with the content of the hysteria in this instance. Why mass poisoning? And why, in particular, the poisoning of public water sources? If one accepts the view that rumors convey messages and that rumor epidemics, in particular, supply important symbolic information concerning the collective worries of societies in crisis, one approach to answering such questions is to try to identify the match or fit between a rumor panic and its immediate context. In the case of kidnapping panics, which have a long history not only in China but in many other societies as well, the focus of collective concern is the safety of children, who (as the term *kidnap* seems to imply) are almost always seen as the primary victims. Rumors of mass poisoning, on the other hand, are far more appropriate as a symbolic response to a crisis, such as war or natural disaster or epidemic, in which *all* the members of society are potentially at risk.

A look at the experience of other societies amply confirms this supposition. Charges of well-poisoning and similar crimes were brought against the first Christians in Rome and the Jews in the Middle Ages at the time of the Black Plague (1348). During the cholera epidemic in Paris in 1832 a rumor circulated that poison powder had been scattered in the bread, vegetables, milk, and water of that city. In the early stages of World War I rumors were spread in all belligerent countries that enemy agents were busy poisoning the water supplies.[53] Within hours of the great Tokyo earthquake of September 1, 1923, which was accompanied by raging fires, rumors began to circulate charging ethnic Koreans and socialists not only with having set the fires but also with plotting rebellion and poisoning the wells.[54] Newspaper accounts in 1937, at the onset of the Sino-Japanese War, accused Chinese traitors of poisoning the drinking water of Shanghai.[55] And rumors of mass poisoning proliferated in Biafra during the Nigerian civil conflict of the late 1960s.[56]

In many of these instances the rumors targeted outsiders (or their internal agents), who were accused, symbolically if not literally, of seeking the annihilation of the society in which the rumors circulated. This, it turns out, closely approximates the situation prevailing in China at the time of the Boxer uprising. Like the charge that the Christians, by challenging the authority of China's gods, were the ones ultimately responsible for the drought in North China in the spring and summer of 1900 (see Chapters 3 and 4), rumors accusing foreigners and their native surrogates of poisoning North China's water supplies portrayed outsiders symbolically as depriving Chinese of what was most essential for the sustaining of life. The well-poisoning rumor epidemic thus spoke directly to the collective fear that was uppermost in the minds of ordinary people at the time: the fear of death (see Chapter 3).[57]

Let me conclude this discussion of problems created by excessive emphasis on cultural contrast by paraphrasing an argument I made in a talk on the Boxers in the summer of 2001. The talk had the unlikely (and, for a largely Western audience, somewhat provocative) title "Humanizing the Boxers."[58] The position I took in it was that culture, in addition to forming the prism through which communities express themselves in thought and action, also has the potential to distance one community from another, thereby facilitating processes of stereotyping, caricaturing, essentialization, and mythologization. In light of the unusual degree to which, throughout the twentieth century, the Boxers had been subjected to such processes in both China and the West, I made a special effort in the talk to focus on what the Boxers shared with, rather than what separated them from, human beings in comparable historical and cultural settings. My point was not to deny the Boxers their cultural particularity (nor, certainly, to portray them as angels); it was, rather, to rescue them from the aura of dehumanizing exceptionalism and distortion that had surrounded their history almost from the beginning. My firm conviction, which a number of the chapters in this book attempt to convey, is that the same point writ large is worth making about China, Chinese history, and the people who have made and experienced this history over the centuries.

The present volume embraces a wide spectrum of topics, including – in addition to Wang Tao, American China historiography, the writing of history in general, and the Boxers – nationalism (especially Chapter 6), reform (Chapters 1 and 5), popular religion (Chapters 3 and 4), and continuities across historical divides (Chapters 2, 5, and 6). Although the substantive themes vary, my effort throughout has been to identify and explore fresh approaches to the Chinese past, alternately interrogating Western historians, Chinese historians, and the history itself. My ultimate hope – a hope that I am confident most other Western students of China share – is to demystify Chinese history, to undermine parochial perspectives that continue to cordon it off in a realm by itself, so that it can be rendered intelligible, meaningful, and, yes, even important to people in the West.

Notes

1 My first article was published in 1957 when I was a graduate student at Harvard: "Missionary Approaches: Hudson Taylor and Timothy Richard," *Papers on China* 11 (1957): 29–62.

2 Benjamin I. Schwartz, "Introduction," in his *China and Other Matters* (Cambridge: Harvard University Press, 1996), p. 1.

3 *China and Christianity: The Missionary Movement and the Growth of Chinese Antiforeignism, 1860–1870* (Cambridge: Harvard University Press, 1963), p. vii. See also John K. Fairbank, "Patterns behind the Tientsin Massacre," *Harvard Journal of Asiatic Studies* 20 (1957): 480–511.

4 Cohen, *China and Christianity*, pp. 264–5.

5 It was a very different matter, of course, in the eighteenth century (and in some respects earlier), when China's impact on the thought world, decorative arts, and economy of Europe was substantial, as has been generally recognized.

6 Cohen, "Ch'ing China: Confrontation with the West, 1850–1900," in James B. Crowley, ed., *Modern East Asia: Essays in Interpretation* (New York: Harcourt, Brace, and World, 1970), pp. 29–30; the Schwartz quotation is from Benjamin Schwartz, *In Search of Wealth and Power: Yen Fu and the West* (Cambridge: Harvard University Press, 1964), pp. 1–2.

7 This was clearly seen in some of the more influential writings of Fairbank. See, especially, Ssu-yü Teng and John K. Fairbank, *China's Response to the West: A Documentary Survey, 1839–1923* (Cambridge: Harvard University Press, 1954), and the portions of Fairbank's *The United States and China*, 4th edn. (Cambridge: Harvard University Press, 1979) dealing with the nineteenth century.

8 Cohen, "Ch'ing China," pp. 29–61; and, as revised, in Paul A. Cohen, *Discovering History in China: American Historical Writing on the Recent Chinese Past* (New York: Columbia University Press, 1984), pp. 9–55.

9 There are some, especially those who look at China from a global or regional perspective, who might be inclined to argue that, in an interconnected world, "endogenous" and "exogenous" cease to be viable as concepts. This is, of course, very different from the nineteenth-century Western view that all significant change in the "non-West" had to result from the Western impact and be modeled after Western precedents. Still, it is not, in my judgment, a tenable position. I am firmly convinced that, even as we begin to break down some of the artificial walls separating China from the rest of the world (a process that I applaud and directly address later on in this introduction) and acknowledge that influences from outside have shaped Chinese history from the beginning, it is both possible and desirable to identify certain kinds of changes as, in the main, internally generated. I would make the same claim, moreover, for other histories – that of the United States, for example – that have had (and continue to have) important links to other parts of the world.

10 *Between Tradition and Modernity: Wang T'ao and Reform in Late Ch'ing China* (Cambridge: Harvard University Press, 1974).

11 The resulting tension in the intellectual framework of the book is touched on in the preface to the original edition of *Discovering History in China*, p. xii.

12 Examples of books with a China-centered perspective that appeared in the latter half of the 1980s and the early 1990s (that is, after the publication of *Discovering History in China*) are supplied in Chapter 7.

13 R. Bin Wong, *China Transformed: Historical Change and the Limits of European Experience* (Ithaca: Cornell University Press, 1997); Kenneth Pomeranz, *The Great Divergence: China, Europe, and the Making of the Modern World Economy* (Princeton: Princeton University Press, 2000). The work of Wong and Pomeranz is the focus of a recent forum in the *American*

Historical Review. See Kenneth Pomeranz, "Political Economy and Ecology on the Eve of Industrialization: Europe, China, and the Global Conjuncture," *American Historical Review* 107.2 (April 2002): 425–46; R. Bin Wong, "The Search for European Differences and Domination in the Early Modern World: A View from Asia," *ibid.*, pp. 447–69. For lengthy critiques of Pomeranz's book, see Philip C.C. Huang, "Development or Involution in Eighteenth-Century Britain and China? A Review of Kenneth Pomeranz's *The Great Divergence: China, Europe, and the Making of the Modern World Economy*," *Journal of Asian Studies* 61.2 (May 2002): 501–38; and Robert Brenner and Christopher Isett, "England's Divergence from China's Yangzi Delta: Property Relations, Microeconomics, and Patterns of Development," *ibid.*, pp. 609–62. Pomeranz responds to Huang in "Beyond the East–West Binary: Resituating Development Paths in the Eighteenth-Century World," *ibid.*, pp. 539–90.

14 Although I pass over these issues here, they constitute by far the larger portion of Wong's book and form an important part of the context for his analysis of economic developments in China and Europe over the centuries.

15 *The Great Divergence*, p. 8, n. 13.

16 *China Transformed*, p. 282; *The Great Divergence*, pp. 8–10.

17 *China Transformed*, p. 17; *The Great Divergence*, pp. 7–8 (see also pp. 70, 107, 112–3, 165). Pomeranz and Wong both discuss the resemblances between the economies of Asia and Europe on the eve of the Industrial Revolution mainly in the first two chapters of their studies.

18 This is a radically simplified characterization of the nuanced positions of the two scholars. Although both, for example, emphasize the importance of coal, Pomeranz makes much of the accident of geography that in Europe, in contrast to China, located some of the largest coal deposits – those in Britain – in close proximity to excellent water transport, a commercially vibrant economy, and a high concentration of skilled craftspeople. *The Great Divergence*, pp. 59–68. For an insightful review essay comparing Wong and Pomeranz and placing them in the context of earlier efforts to address similar "macrohistorical" issues – most famously, perhaps, Andre Gunder Frank's *ReOrient: Global Economy in the Asian Age* (Berkeley: University of California Press, 1998) – see Gale Stokes, "The Fates of Human Societies: A Review of Recent Macrohistories," *American Historical Review* 106.2 (April 2001): 508–25; also the same author's "Why the West? The Unsettled Question of Europe's Ascendancy," *Lingua Franca* 11.8 (November 2001): 30–8.

19 *China Transformed*, p. 8.

20 *The Great Divergence*, pp. 25–6.

21 Although I focus here on Hamashita, partly because of his wide-ranging and deeply grounded historical perspective, a number of other scholars, among them Mark Selden and Giovanni Arrighi, have also done (or are doing) work on the Asian region as a system.

22 Hamashita, "The Intra-regional System in East Asia in Modern Times," in Peter J. Katzenstein and Takashi Shiraishi, eds., *Network Power: Japan and Asia* (Ithaca: Cornell University Press, 1997), p. 113.

23 Hamashita, "The Tribute Trade System and Modern Asia," in A. J. H. Latham and Heita Kawakatsu, eds., *Japanese Industrialization and the Asian Economy* (London: Routledge, 1994), pp. 92–7 (the quotations are from pp. 96–7).

24 Fairbank's understanding of the tribute (or tributary) system was developed in many of his writings. See, for example, the early article (jointly authored with S.Y. Teng), "On the Ch'ing Tributary System," *Harvard Journal of Asiatic Studies* 6 (1941): 135–246, and the later edited volume, *The Chinese World Order: Traditional China's Foreign Relations* (Cambridge: Harvard University Press, 1968). For an insightful critique of earlier understandings of the system,

see James L. Hevia, *Cherishing Men from Afar: Qing Guest Ritual and the Macartney Embassy of 1793* (Durham: Duke University Press, 1995), pp. 9–15.

25 As I make explicit in *Discovering History in China* (p. 196), the China-centered approach is to be clearly distinguished from the concept of Sinocentrism, with its connotations of a world (or in Hamashita's case a region) centering on China.

26 Hamashita, "The Intra-regional System in East Asia in Modern Times," p. 115. Hamashita develops other aspects of his sea-centered understanding of the Asian regional system in "Overseas Chinese Networks in the Asian Historical Regional System, 1700–1900," in Zhang Qixiong [Chi-hsiung Chang], ed., *Ershi shiji de Zhongguo yu shijie: Lunwen xuanji* [China and the world in the twentieth century: Selected essays], 2 vols. (Taibei: Institute of Modern History, Academia Sinica, 2001), 1: 143–64.

27 *History in Three Keys: The Boxers as Event, Experience, and Myth* (New York: Columbia University Press, 1997), p. xiv.

28 Given my effort to talk about historical issues without being confined to Chinese history, some of the responses of non-China historians have been especially gratifying. "He wants," one such historian commented, "to find a way in which historians cross the boundaries of their topical histories":

> His constant message is that historians can and should be polyglot. Asianists can talk with medievalists, Americanists with Europeanists. His book is full of examples of how time and culture aren't confining to any historian trying to understand and explain the past.
> Greg Dening, "Enigma Variations on *History in Three Keys*: A Conversational Essay," *History and Theory: Studies in the Philosophy of History* 39.2 (May 2000): 210

> See also the comments of Peter Burke, "History of Events and the Revival of Narrative," in Peter Burke, ed., *New Perspectives on Historical Writing*, 2nd edn. (University Park, Pennsylvania: Pennsylvania State University Press, 2001), p. 295.

29 This is not the place to get into an involved discussion of the problems posed by the term "Han" as an ethnonym. Although "Han," according to one recent effort at clarification, is "the label that was used during the Qing to distinguish the Chinese culturally and ethnically from the non-Han Other," "'Han Chinese' is the modern ethnic label used to describe the majority of people in China, as distinct from the approximately three-score 'minority nationalities' as defined by the present Chinese state." Mark C. Elliott, *The Manchu Way: The Eight Banners and Ethnic Identity in Late Imperial China* (Stanford: Stanford University Press, 2001), pp. 383–4, n. 75.

30 Jonathan Spence, Joseph Fletcher, and Beatrice Bartlett were among the first scholars to show the way to a new understanding of the Manchu experience in China during the Qing. A sampling of the more important studies in English that have been published over the past decade and a half might include: Pamela Kyle Crossley, *Orphan Warriors: Three Manchu Generations and the End of the Qing World* (Princeton: Princeton University Press, 1990), and the same author's *A Translucent Mirror: History and Identity in Qing Imperial Ideology* (Berkeley: University of California Press, 1999); Elliott, *The Manchu Way*; James A. Millward, *Beyond the Pass: Economy, Ethnicity, and Empire in Qing Central Asia, 1759–1864* (Stanford: Stanford University Press, 1998); Evelyn S. Rawski, *The Last Emperors: A Social History of Qing Imperial Institutions* (Berkeley: University of California Press, 1998); Edward J.M. Rhoads,

Manchus and Han: Ethnic Relations and Political Power in Late Qing and Early Republican China, 1861–1928 (Seattle: University of Washington Press, 2000). Two stimulating review essays covering four of the most recent of these studies (those by Elliott, Rawski, and Rhoads, and Crossley's *The Translucent Mirror*) are R. Kent Guy, "Who Were the Manchus? A Review Essay," *Journal of Asian Studies* 61.1 (February 2002): 151–64, and Sudipta Sen, "The New Frontiers of Manchu China and the Historiography of Asian Empires: A Review Essay," *ibid.*, pp. 165–77. See also Evelyn Rawski's reconceptualization of the significance of the Qing dynasty in her "Reenvisioning the Qing: The Significance of the Qing Period in Chinese History," *ibid.*, 55.4 (November 1996): 829–50, and the response of Ping-ti Ho in his "In Defense of Sinicization: A Rebuttal of Evelyn Rawski's 'Reenvisioning the Qing,'" *ibid.*, 57.1 (February 1998): 123–55.

31 Elliott, *The Manchu Way*, p. 34.

32 Rawski, "Reenvisioning the Qing," pp. 832–3; Elliott, *The Manchu Way*, pp. 28, 34; Millward, *Beyond the Pass*, pp. 13–15.

33 Dru C. Gladney, *Muslim Chinese: Ethnic Nationalism in the People's Republic*, 2nd edn. (Cambridge: Council on East Asian Studies, Harvard University, 1996); Jonathan N. Lipman, *Familiar Strangers: A History of Muslims in Northwest China* (Seattle: University of Washington Press, 1997).

34 Jonathan N. Lipman, "Hyphenated Chinese: Sino-Muslim Identity in Modern China," in Gail Hershatter *et al.*, eds., *Remapping China: Fissures in Historical Terrain* (Stanford: Stanford University Press, 1996), p. 109; also p. 100. Lipman uses the term Sino-Muslim in his book (cited above) as well as in this article.

35 The Uyghurs were the second largest Muslim minority in China, as of the 1990 census, numbering at that time some 7.2 million. Unlike the largest Muslim minority, the Hui, who are to be found throughout the country, almost 100 per cent of Uyghurs live in the Uyghur autonomous region of Xinjiang. Gladney, *Muslim Chinese*, pp. 20, 29.

36 Cohen, *Discovering History in China*, pp. 161–72.

37 Lipman, "Hyphenated Chinese," pp. 100–2 (the quotation is from p. 101). The difference that serious attention to ethnic difference makes in core–periphery mapping is also suggested in Millward, *Beyond the Pass*, pp. 10–12. With respect to violence among Muslim communities, Gladney observes that it "continues to be intra-factional and intra-ethnic, rather than along Muslim/non-Muslim religious lines." *Muslim Chinese*, p. viii.

38 From this burgeoning literature, a few examples may be cited: Stevan Harrell, ed., *Perspectives on the Yi of Southwest China* (Berkeley: University of California Press, 2001); Harrell, *Ways of Being Ethnic in Southwest China* (Seattle: University of Washington Press, 2001); Uradyn E. Bulag, *Nationalism and Hybridity in Mongolia* (Oxford: Clarendon Press, 1998), especially chaps. 6, 8; Bulag, *The Mongols at China's Edge: History and the Politics of National Unity* (Lanham, Md.: Rowman and Littlefield, 2002); Melvyn C. Goldstein, *A History of Modern Tibet, 1913–51: The Demise of the Lamaist State* (Berkeley: University of California Press, 1989); Goldstein, "The Dragon and the Snow Lion: The Tibet Question in the 20th Century," in Anthony J. Kane, ed., *China Briefing 1990* (Boulder: Westview Press, 1990), pp. 129–67; Tsering Shakya, *The Dragon in the Land of Snows: A History of Modern Tibet Since 1947* (London: Pimlico, 1999); Gardner Bovingdon, "The History of the History of Xinjiang," *Twentieth-Century China* 26.2 (April 2001): 95–139.

39 There is a very large literature, which I make no pretense to having mastered. For my discussion here, I have drawn much stimulation from Adam McKeown, "Conceptualizing Chinese Diasporas, 1842–1949," *Journal of Asian Studies* 58.2 (May 1999): 306–37; Philip Kuhn, "Toward an Historical Ecology of

Chinese Migration," unpublished conference paper (2001); and the work of, and ongoing conversation with, Elizabeth Sinn, especially in regard to the key role of Hong Kong in the Chinese diaspora.

40 Sinn, "In-Between Places: The Key Role of Localities of Transit in Chinese Migration," paper presented at the Association for Asian Studies annual meeting, Washington D.C., April 6, 2002; see also McKeown, "Conceptualizing Chinese Diasporas," pp. 314–15, 319–21.

41 Kuhn, "Toward an Historical Ecology of Chinese Migration." For an interesting discussion of the variety of pasts available to people of Chinese descent in Southeast Asia for the fashioning of new identities, see Wang Gungwu, "Ethnic Chinese: The Past in Their Future," paper presented at conference on "International Relations and Cultural Transformation of Ethnic Chinese," Manila, November 26–28, 1998.

42 McKeown, "Conceptualizing Chinese Diasporas," p. 307; see also *ibid.*, p. 331.

43 The Chinese diaspora is, of course, only one of several such large-scale migratory movements of recent centuries; others include the Indian, African, and Armenian diasporas.

44 The Chinese diaspora involves various forms of deterritorialization. A specific instance is the notion of "cultural China," as advanced by Wei-ming Tu. Substantively, cultural China refers to a cluster of values, behavior patterns, ideas, and traditions that people agree to define as in some objective sense "Chinese," and to which, speaking more subjectively, those who identify themselves as "Chinese" feel themselves to belong. Strategically, the idea of cultural China affords Chinese living in the diaspora a way of talking about, shaping the meaning of, and even defining China and Chineseness without inhabiting the geographical or political space known as Zhongguo. See Wei-ming Tu, "Cultural China: The Periphery as the Center," *Daedalus: Journal of the American Academy of Arts and Sciences* 120.2 (Spring 1991): 1–32; Paul A. Cohen, "Cultural China: Some Definitional Issues," *Philosophy East and West* 43.3 (July 1993): 557–63.

45 A Uyghur in Xinjiang or a Tibetan in Qinghai, while incontestably (although not necessarily uncontestedly) part of political China, might well object to being considered Chinese culturally. Conversely, a recent Chinese migrant to California, while no longer inhabiting a political space called China, would more than likely continue to view him/herself as part of China culturally.

46 Sen, although not using the phrase "cultural essentialization," contests the claims of cultural boundary, cultural disharmony, and cultural specificity in his "East and West: The Reach of Reason," *The New York Review of Books* 47 (July 20, 2000): 33–8 (the quotation is from p. 36).

47 Fairbank begins his book by placing China's response to the West in the context of prior Chinese experience with and attitudes toward barbarians. *Trade and Diplomacy on the China Coast: The Opening of the Treaty Ports, 1842–1854* (Cambridge: Harvard University Press, 1953), chap. 1. In my book I explicitly characterize the political problem created for Chinese officials by missionaries as "derivative in nature. Underlying it was the much larger issue of Sino-Western cultural conflict." *China and Christianity*, p. 264.

48 Albert Feuerwerker, *China's Early Industrialization: Sheng Hsuan-huai (1844–1916) and Mandarin Enterprise* (Cambridge: Harvard University Press, 1958); John K. Fairbank, Edwin O. Reischauer, and Albert Craig, *East Asia: The Modern Transformation* (Boston: Houghton-Mifflin, 1965); Mary C. Wright, *The Last Stand of Chinese Conservatism: The T'ung-chih Restoration, 1862–1874*, rev. edn. (New York: Atheneum, 1965); Joseph R. Levenson, *Confucian China and Its Modern Fate*: Vol. 1, *The Problem of Intellectual Continuity* (Berkeley: University of California Press, 1958), 1: 3.

49 Cohen, *Discovering History in China*, pp. 189–90.
50 I should note here that not all historians accept the view of a common human condition. Jacques Gernet, in his otherwise excellent book on Sino-Western cultural conflict during the late Ming and early Qing, argues that in China Western missionaries "found themselves in the presence of a different kind of humanity." *China and the Christian Impact: A Conflict of Cultures*, trans. Janet Lloyd (Cambridge: Cambridge University Press, 1985), p. 247. Implicitly throughout his book and explicitly in its concluding pages, Gernet advances a linguistic determinism so powerful, at least in potential, as to place in jeopardy any sort of meaningful cross-cultural inquiry or understanding. See my review in *Harvard Journal of Asiatic Studies* 47.2 (December 1987): 674–83.
51 Paul A. Cohen, "Wang T'ao's Perspective on a Changing World," in Albert Feuerwerker, Rhoads Murphey, and Mary C. Wright, eds., *Approaches to Modern Chinese History* (Berkeley: University of California Press, 1967), pp. 158–62.
52 Arthur H. Smith, *China in Convulsion*, 2 vols. (New York: Fleming H. Revell, 1901), 2: 659–60.
53 These examples are all drawn from Richard D. Loewenberg, "Rumors of Mass Poisoning in Times of Crisis," *Journal of Criminal Psychopathology* 5 (July 1943): 131–42.
54 Andrew Gordon, *Labor and Imperial Democracy in Prewar Japan* (Berkeley: University of California Press, 1991), p. 177.
55 Loewenberg, "Rumors of Mass Poisoning," pp. 133–4. Another report from Shanghai, published in a Japanese newspaper, stated that Chinese dropped bacteria into wells before retreating from the city (*ibid.*, p. 135).
56 Nwokocha K. U. Nkpa, "Rumors of Mass Poisoning in Biafra," *Public Opinion Quarterly* 41.3 (Fall 1977): 332–46.
57 For a fuller discussion of the well-poisoning rumor panic, see Cohen, *History in Three Keys*, pp. 167–72.
58 It was presented at a conference entitled "1900: The Boxers, China, and the World" and held at the School of Oriental and African Studies, London, June 22–24, 2001.

1 Wang Tao in a changing world

The genesis of a new man

Early in 1894 a brash young man set out from his home in the south of China to present a memorandum on reform to Li Hongzhang, the most powerful official in the land. On his way north he stopped off in Shanghai and made the acquaintance of an elderly reformer of some prominence who helped him put his memorandum into acceptable form and agreed to write a letter of introduction to a member of Li's staff. The young man was Sun Yat-sen. The subject of this book is the older man, whose name was Wang Tao (Figure 1.1).[1]

Wang Tao's career prefigured Sun's in significant respects. Through his writings he may even have exerted a direct impact on some of Sun's ideas.[2] But the importance of the crossing of their lives in 1894 is more symbolic than anything else. Sun, full of the future, shortly went on to achieve worldwide fame as a Chinese revolutionary. Wang, after a long and productive career, died in obscurity in May 1897,[3] on the very eve of changes which he, as much as any Chinese of his day, had anticipated.

To "anticipate" change is, in some sense, to help bring it about, to make it possible. Before the kind of dramatic event called a revolution can take place, there must be a period of preparation, a period of incremental change during which increasing numbers of people are brought to the point where, for the first time, they can contemplate radical change as a real possibility. This is what happened in China in the last sixty years of the nineteenth century. Many of the basic patterns of Chinese life during this period remained, doubtless, much the same as before. But in certain realms, above all the intellectual, changes took place that, cumulatively considered, can only be described as revolutionary.

Scholars whose perceptions of nineteenth-century China are defined – one is tempted to say confined – by the comparison with Meiji Japan may balk at such a statement. From the vantage point of Japanese "success," the late Qing epitomizes "failure," and next to the dynamism of the Meiji era, China, during the latter half of the nineteenth century, appears as the very embodiment of stasis. The trouble with this perspective is that it

Figure 1.1 Wang Tao (1828–97).
Source: *Shanghai yanjiu ziliao* (Shanghai: Zhonghua Shuju, 1936).

glosses over a very important fact, namely that China and Japan, in their respective encounters with the West in the nineteenth century, did not start out at the same point. Cross-cultural comparison is an elusive enterprise. It is enormously valuable for the identification of similarities and differences. But as a yardstick for the measurement of change (and speed of change) it presents problems. Modernization, after all, is not a horserace. And two cultures do not share a common "baseline" just because they both happen to be "premodern."

A much more valid way of measuring change in nineteenth-century China is by internal points of reference. It is not until we compare the China of 1900 with that of 1800–40 – the final phase of what Frederic Wakeman calls "High Ch'ing [Qing]"[4] – that we begin to appreciate the scale of the transformation that occurred. In the early years of the nineteenth century, England, France, and America were as remote from China, intellectually and psychologically, as China had been from the West in Roman times. Many Chinese – and I refer to the educated – had never heard of these countries. Few had even a vague notion of where they were located on the map. And if there was anybody in the Qing empire who knew about the French Revolution or had heard "the shot heard round the world," he guarded his secret well. The one point of contact between China and the West in these years was the regulated trade carried on at Canton (Guangzhou). Unlike the Dutch trade at Nagasaki, however, the Canton contact did not serve as a funnel for the transmission of Western intellectual influences. Confucian China, isolated by choice and totally self-absorbed, had no way of knowing what was in store for it.

By the end of the nineteenth century – five foreign wars, five domestic upheavals, and dozens of imposed treaties later – this proud and comfortable world had been shattered. Not, perhaps, in outward physical terms: an imaginary visitor from the pre-Opium War epoch, if he steered clear of the Western-influenced littoral and riveted his gaze upon hinterland China, might not have found too much that was startlingly different. Ruan Yuan could have survived in 1900. The great change was in the mental landscape of China's educated. The invisible bars that two or three generations earlier had locked the minds of Chinese scholars in a closed Confucian world had first been made visible and then, after much painful effort, had been pried apart, letting in a whole new universe of ideas, information, and values. Granted, there were learned Chinese in 1900 who still did not know the precise location of England, just as there are American college graduates today who, given a map of Southeast Asia, are unable to place Vietnam. But England, like Vietnam, meant *something* to everyone. And there were plenty of Chinese – easily numbering by 1900 in the tens of thousands – whose outlooks had been fundamentally transformed by sixty years of Sino-Western interaction. Sun Yat-sen could not have inhabited the Chinese world of 1800.

Nor could Yan Fu or Kang Youwei or Liang Qichao, the point being not that these men all happened to have been influenced by Westerners who lived and wrote after 1800, but that they were in a position – historically – to be influenced by Westerners at all. This circumstance, more than any other, distinguishes 1900 from 1800. Chinese, in 1800, had the sense of being a universe unto themselves, of literally encompassing the world. This sense was still alive in 1840. But by 1900 it had become moribund. During the intervening years an awareness had first been kindled of something very important happening, of change on a scale that it was not given to all generations to experience. Then, one or two people ventured to describe the change as "unprecedented" – something not experienced by *any* previous generation. Like Nietzsche's madman, wandering through the early morning dark with his lantern proclaiming "God is dead," these percipient individuals were unable, initially, to make people listen. In time, however, the number of madmen grew, and by 1900 they had become so numerous that to talk of revolutionary change was no longer considered mad at all. The unthinkable had happened. The civilization whose eternal validity no Chinese of the pre-Opium War period had for a moment doubted stood on the verge of disintegration.

To say that Sun Yat-sen was not a possibility in 1800 is simply to say that there are limits to what can take place in any given generation, limits that no individual, however extraordinary, is capable of transcending. This is the negative aspect of the process of historical change. On the positive side, every generation contributes something new to the world, thereby changing the limits – and the possibilities – for the following generation. According to this "logic of generations,"[5] what Sun Yat-sen thought and did at the turn of the century was built in part on what others had thought and done before him. Sun did not create a revolution (qua event) out of thin air. The China into which he was born (in 1866) was one in which revolution (qua process) was already immanent.

This was not true, however, of the China into which Wang Tao was born (in 1828). Every generation produces its new men. But the *degree* of newness can vary greatly from one generation to the next. It did not take very long for human beings to get from trains to airplanes, but it took them thousands of years to get to trains. In these relative terms, Wang Tao's generation, with one foot in prerevolutionary China, was newer than Sun Yat-sen's. For Wang's generation – and only Wang's – experienced the enormous leap in modern Chinese history from no trains to trains. The same applied, moreover, to Wang Tao and Sun Yat-sen as individuals. Although Sun Yat-sen represented a later stage in the revolutionary process and in that sense was a newer man than Wang Tao, in terms of the amount of cultural change each man encompassed in his lifetime – generational change viewed in relative, rather than cumulative, perspective – it was Wang Tao who was the newer of the two.

Perspective, indeed, is everything. When we look at Wang Tao from the vantage point of Sun Yat-sen, we catch ourselves using words like "limited," "not very advanced," "still quite traditional." But when we view him from the perspective of his origins, the China of his birth, we are impressed by Wang's newness. Both perspectives are legitimate. It depends on the book one is writing. This book is about the *beginnings* of the revolutionary process in modern China, the pioneer phase. It's focus, therefore, is not on why Wang Tao failed to become a revolutionary, but on how he succeeded in becoming a pioneer.

Perspectives on a new world

Wang Tao represented something very new on the Chinese scene. The life crises he faced – failure in the examinations, the abrupt death of a father-provider, the charge of *lèse-majesté* – were such as could have been encountered by Chinese in any age. But the specific means by which he worked his way out of these crises were available only after the mid-nineteenth century.[6] Similarly, although there were Chinese in all ages who were critical of dynastic policy, their capacity to give vent to this criticism was, in general, scrupulously limited. Wang Tao, operating through a new medium, the daily newspaper, and protected (whether in Hong Kong or Shanghai) by a new institution, foreign law, was restricted in his criticisms only by his own cultural presuppositions. Finally, Wang's extensive exposure to the West and to Westerners, while it did not serve to uproot him, did serve to give him perspectives that were not accessible to Chinese of earlier epochs or, for that matter, to most of his contemporaries.

For all his newness, on the other hand, Wang Tao remained in some ways profoundly steeped in the culture and learning of the Chinese past. In fact, it could be argued that it was precisely the security afforded by this immersion in the past that permitted him to entertain certain highly untraditional notions without experiencing the shock of cultural dislocation. As Erik Erikson has said, "it takes a well-established identity to tolerate radical change."[7]

The fragile, often strained, equilibrium maintained by Wang Tao between new perspectives and older habits of thinking that continued to crowd his mind is plainly revealed in his writings on Western history and the contemporary world. These writings are extensive and, spanning the period from the early 1870s to the early 1890s, afford us ample opportunity to reconstruct the world view arrived at by Wang Tao in his mature years. In doing so, however, we shall encounter a number of pitfalls and it is best to make these as explicit as possible beforehand.

First, although Wang Tao had an extremely nimble and wide-ranging mind, he was not a systematic thinker. Asked to dilate on the current world scene or the shape of things to come in Asia or Europe, Wang could – and quite regularly did – give his views at the drop of a hat. But if someone tried to pin him down concerning his "conception of world order" or his "theory of history," it is doubtful whether he would have been able to respond comfortably. In talking about Wang's "world view," then, we have to be especially careful not to overschematize, not to impose rigor and order where in fact there is untidiness, even inconsistency.

The second pitfall – really a syndrome of pitfalls – is much more formidable, involving the relationship between "tradition" and "modernity" and the complex process of transition from the one to the other. It is common to think of tradition and modernity as well-defined sociocultural landmarks, having wholly different, often mutually antagonistic, qualities, and of "transition" as the bridge connecting the two. The trouble is that this is too rigid and mechanical. It overlooks the fact that transition has been a perennial characteristic of the history of mankind. It suggests a simplistic view of tradition as a self-contained organic entity, homogeneous and more or less static. And it excludes from consideration the possibility that certain facets of a traditional culture, not being intrinsically "traditional," may survive quite comfortably the corrosive pressures of modernization.

C.E. Black cautions that "tradition" and "modernity" are at bottom abstractions from the "continuum of variables" that make up reality, "single frames in the motion picture of history that have been enlarged for purposes of study."[8] Like all historical concepts, they thus stand in an ambiguous relationship to the actual record of human experience. Clearly, they are needed in order to make sense out of this record. But, just as clearly, in the process they oversimplify and to varying degrees misrepresent the very thing they are designed to elucidate.

This quandary, characteristic of historical inquiry in general, is additionally complicated in the case of the application of "tradition" to the Chinese past by two special circumstances. First, there is the fact that among modern Chinese, "tradition" (the Chinese equivalent for which is *chuantong*) has of necessity been much more than a simple organizing generalization. In the kaleidoscopic whirl of nineteenth- and twentieth-century Chinese history, it has also been an object of deep emotional involvement – something to believe in, defend, or reject. In a situation where a Mao Zedong can ideologize tradition as an incessant struggle between oppressor (the feudal-autocratic-landlord ruling class) and oppressed (the peasantry), a Lu Xun can curse it as a record of hypocrisy with the words "Eat men!" scrawled over every page, and a Chiang Kai-shek can enshrine it as the Confucian pursuit of virtue, China's gift to the civilization of the world, it becomes immediately apparent that the past is being drafted (consciously or unconsciously) into the service of present needs and purposes. Such angular visions of tradition, from the standpoint of the scholar, can only be viewed as caricatures of the real past.

A second kind of caricaturization (somewhat less severe usually) is contributed by Westerners, who, as beneficiaries of a seductive heritage of romantic exoticism, are easily drawn to those aspects of another culture that least resemble our own and seem "unique." For students of the Sino-Western encounter of the nineteenth century, this hypnotic power of the unfamiliar is reinforced by historical reality. For there is no denying that the civilizations of China and the modern West did indeed contrast sharply at many points. Given this weighted situation, a special effort is required not to overlook those aspects of the Chinese past that, because they parallel facets of modern Western civilization, have less visibility and are harder to single out. Such points of convergence between cultures that in other respects are so far apart may be significant in at least two ways. For one thing, there is always the possibility that in them we have a reflection of basic human responses to inherently *human* – and hence to a degree supracultural – predicaments [see Introduction to this volume]. For another, we are doubtless safe in assuming that, in those areas where the cultures of China and the modern West have tended to overlap, the need of modern Chinese to abandon earlier habits of thinking has been weaker and the predisposition toward continuity or revival stronger.

The real Chinese past, before being dramatized as "Chinese tradition," was fluid and dynamic, rich in variety and permeated with unresolved strains and tensions. Alongside the assumptions and views that, at any given point in time, most Chinese shared were others that were embraced only by select classes or individuals. Even in the minds of single persons, moreover, there were often areas of inconsistency – assumptions and attitudes that, when scrutinized, appear to be logically (though not necessarily psychologically) incompatible.

Some of these phases of Chinese reality were brought into sharp focus by the West's intrusion and their continued viability threatened. Others, however, because they were not inherently "Chinese" or irretrievably "traditional," were less brightly illuminated by the impingement of the West. To a degree, these muted, less exposed areas of the Chinese past lay outside of the conflicts between "traditional" and "modern," "Chinese" and "Western" – as normally depicted – and injected an added dimension of complexity into the whole process of intellectual transition in nineteenth-century China. In my consideration of Wang Tao's mature perceptions of the world, a special effort is made to capture this extra dimension.

Prescriptions for a new China

When the *Clermont* steamed up the Hudson River in August 1807, throngs of excited Americans lined the banks to cheer it on its way. The mood was festive; the onlookers felt good. It was a far cry from the atmosphere of suspicion and fear that greeted the first appearance of steamboats in Chinese waters. And yet, each response was intelligible in its own terms. "In our new land," John Fairbank wrote, "we helped invent the modern world; the Chinese had it thrust upon them and rammed down their throats."[9] As the West closed in on China in the nineteenth century, it caught the Chinese off-balance, so off-balance that it took decades before they began to comprehend, even dimly, the nature and depth of the challenge facing them. In these circumstances, it was far from self-evident how the challenge was to be met, and it was not uncommon to encounter approaches such as the following:

> According to Daoism, softness can overcome hardness and the way to advance is by retreating. Therefore, if one uses one's weakness with skill, it can be turned to strength. When something becomes too hard it must snap; when one advances too hastily one must stumble. Therefore, if one uses one's strength imprudently it will invariably turn to weakness. A glance at history shows that no dynasty ruled longer than the Zhou, despite the fact that after the shift [of its capital] eastward under King Ping [r. 770–719 B.C.E.], the [Zhou] was weakened to the point of being virtually powerless...[Similarly], the Song was the

feeblest of houses, yet it was able to contend successively with the Liao, Jin, and Yuan, and to prolong its rule for over three hundred years. Through weakness, it was able to survive.[10]

This passage appeared in a Hong Kong newspaper article in the late 1860s. The intent of the article was to show that Chinese were fooling themselves if they believed that the way to meet the Western challenge was to exchange the time-honored usages of China for those of the West. China's best defense consisted not in training armies, manufacturing weapons, and constructing fortifications, but in the exercise of Daoist passivity and such hallowed Confucian virtues as righteousness, loyalty, and trust.

The editor of the newspaper sent the article to Wang Tao in Scotland (where he was staying at the time with his employer, the great missionary-translator James Legge) and Wang wrote a lengthy rebuttal, spelling out his position on the need for change and articulating an intellectual frame-work for coping with the Western menace.[11]

Wang began by boldly proclaiming that the world was undergoing changes of such magnitude that the customs and institutions that had been preserved by Chinese for three thousand years were in real danger of being destroyed. He then drew a comparison between the northwestern portion of the globe (the West) and the southeastern portion (China):

> The southeast is soft and quiescent, the northwest, hard and active. Quiescent [civilizations] are adept at conserving; active ones are adept at changing.... Soft [civilizations] are able to maintain themselves; hard ones are able to control others. Therefore, the [countries] of the northwest have always been able to visit harm upon those of the southeast, but the [countries] of the southeast have never been able to hurt those of the northwest.[12]

Wang was prepared to grant that sometimes change could be countered by nonchange (conserving) and hardness overcome by softness. But this was at best a slow and uncertain process, and the West, in the meantime, could be counted on to seize every opportunity to make trouble for China. China's only sensible course of action, therefore, was to beat the West at its own game by mastering its strengths (*shi qi suo chang*). This would, of course, mean change. But it was change necessitated by circumstance, and such change, according to Wang, had always been sanctioned:

> When the course of Heaven changes above, the actions of men must change below. The *Yijing* [Classic of changes] states: "When the possibilities inhering in a situation have been exhausted, change must take place; when there has been a change, things will run smoothly again."[13]

If China had to change before she could stand firm as a nation, did this mean that she must abandon her traditional customs, government, and culture and undergo a process of all-out Westernization? "No," Wang answered emphatically,

> when I speak of change, I mean changing the outer, not the inner, changing what it is proper to change, not what cannot be changed. The change I have in mind, [moreover], must proceed from us.... If they make us change, the advantage will be reaped by them; only if we change of our own volition will we retain control over our affairs.

Wang went on to note that, just as China had started out as a small country and gradually expanded, reaching its greatest extent under the Qing, a parallel development had now taken place in European history. Like a great tidal bore, the Europeans, in a century's time, had spread from India to Southeast Asia and from Southeast Asia to South China, their knowledge advancing all the while.

A change of so fundamental a character could not have been programmed by man; it had to have been designed by Heaven. And since it was Heaven's will at work, it could not but be for China's good, one of the deepest strains in Wang Tao's "belief system" being the assumption that Heaven (or destiny) was on China's side:

> Heaven's motive in bringing several dozen Western countries together in the single country of China is not to weaken China but to strengthen it, not to harm China but to benefit it. Consequently, if we make good use of [this opportunity], we can convert harm into benefit and change weakness into strength. I do not fear the daily arrival of the Westerners; what I fear is that we Chinese will place limits upon ourselves. We have only one alternative, and that is to undergo complete change (*yibian*).

Earlier Wang Tao had specified that what he meant by "change" was change of the outer (*wai*), not change of the inner (*nei*). Now he called for "complete change." How was this inconsistency to be resolved? Actually, I think the inconsistency is more apparent than real. Wang, if I understand him correctly, used *yibian* to signify not change of *everything*, but change of everything that was *capable* of being changed. *Yibian* did not embrace the realm of *nei*, the inner, the essence, for *nei*, which was comparable in value to *dao*, was not subject to change. It did, on the other hand, encompass *wai*, the outer realm, the realm of the changeable, and since *wai* included everything that was not *nei*, the potential scope for change was considerable. So considerable that, without impinging on the security of *nei*, Wang was able to envisage a fairly sweeping transformation of the Chinese landscape:

in the military sphere we should make a complete conversion (*yibian*) from swords and spears to firearms; in the field of navigation we should make a complete conversion from [old-style] boats to steamboats; in the sphere of overland travel we should make a complete conversion from carriages and horses to trains; and in the realm of work we should make a complete conversion from [traditional] tools to machines. Although...[the old and the new means in these several areas] are alike in regard to their end results, they cannot be compared in respect to speed, precision, relative difficulty, and amount of labor required.

[The Westerners] have all four of these things; we do not have a single one. If the situation were one in which we lacked them and they had them and there were no relations between us, our lack of them would not be a shortcoming and their possession of them would give them nothing to brag about. We could carry on in our accustomed fashion and it would be perfectly all right. But when they insult us in an overbearing manner and on comparison we are found to be inferior, when they constantly insist upon contending and competing with us so that there is mutual wrangling and recrimination, can we afford for a single day to be without these things?...We may be certain that before a hundred years are out, all four will be in China's possession, functioning as if they had always been with us and viewed [by everyone] as commonplace contrivances. It is not that I *want* this prediction to come true; it cannot help but come true. Circumstances and the times make it so. It is Heaven's wish that the eastern and western halves of the globe be joined in one.

The significance we attach to these paragraphs will depend on the framework of assumptions with which we approach them. It has been common among students of nineteenth-century China to assume that Confucianism and "modernity" were incompatibles;[14] that the traditional order had to be torn down before a new modern order could be built up; and that any commitment to reform that stopped short of a fundamental critique of Confucian values and institutions was, by implication at least, inadequate [see Chapter 2 in this volume]. Those who accept this sequence of assumptions have tended to deprecate the mere advocacy of technological change: technological change is tinkering; only through value-change can a major systemic overhaul be effected.

I find this line of reasoning defective on a number of counts. First, there is a growing body of scholarly opinion which, in defining the relationship between "modern" and "traditional," rejects the implication that they are necessarily antithetical, mutually repellent conditions. As Michael Gasster has summarized it:

Most societies, Western as well as non-Western, are dualistic, in the sense that they are *mixtures* of the modern and the traditional, not *either* modern *or* traditional. They are "systems in which culture change is taking place," and they are distinguished from each other in terms of the type of relationship between the "modern" and the "traditional" components that exists in each.... From this point of view, modernization is best understood as a process *leading toward* a condition of modernity but never quite reaching it; indeed, there is no final condition of modernity but only a continuing process of adjustment among many modernizing and traditional forces.[15]

To this, I would only add that I see no reason why we must limit ourselves to the two categories, "modern" and "traditional." Presumably, there are elements in the make-up of every society that do not fall neatly under either rubric.

If it is accepted that modernity is a relative concept and that all societies, however modern, still retain certain traditional features, two questions arise: How much of the Confucian order, *objectively* considered, had to be abandoned before substantive change could take place in nineteenth-century China, and was it necessary, as a prelude to such change, for this order to be *openly* challenged? These questions uncover a hornet's nest of further questions: Granting that Confucianism and the traditional order were not coterminous, where do we draw the line between the two? Did the conscious rejection of the Confucian order (however defined) necessarily immunize against continued contamination by it? Conversely, did refusal to take open issue with Confucianism have the ineluctable effect of protecting it against attrition? What, to put it more succinctly, is the relationship between real change and perceived change? Between perceived change and desired change?

My object, in posing these questions, is to warn against overhasty acceptance of the answers that have already been given them. These are fiendishly difficult questions. Some of them may be ultimately unanswerable. None of them, certainly, can ever be answered with finality, and therefore it is essential to keep asking them.

The tendency to deprecate the "ships-and-guns" stage of Chinese reform thought also reflects the widely held assumption that Chinese reform efforts prior to 1895 were a "failure." This assumption was fed initially by treaty port opinion, which was consistently impatient with Chinese "bungling." In more recent times it has been reinforced by scholarly misinterpretation of the meaning of the Japanese example. Comparison of Chinese and Japanese modernization efforts can, as suggested earlier, be invaluable. But it must be done with extreme caution. If, from the fact that Japan defeated China in 1895 and went on to become a world power while China continued to flounder in weakness, we conclude that Japan's "response to the West" was rapid and successful, China's slow and unsuccessful, we ignore a fundamental fact about modern Japanese history, namely that Japanese modernization had begun long before the arrival of the Westerners.[16] It is useful, as a corrective to such reasoning, to broaden our comparative perspective and measure the modernizing experiences of China and Japan not merely against each other but against those of the rest of the world's nations, the impact of the West being taken as only one variable among many. When we do this, we find that both China *and* Japan come off relatively well.[17] China is still way behind Japan, but it started much later.

Words like "failure" and "success," "rapid" and "slow," have a relative value only, and it is essential to keep this in mind when making comparisons. Perhaps the key question to ask, in comparing the modernizing experiences of China and Japan, is not why the two countries responded to the West with such differing rates of speed and degrees of success, but why China's modernization began in earnest only *after* the intrusion of a substantial outside stimulus while Japan's began long before.[18]

Partly as a result of the pervasive influence of assumptions such as those discussed in the foregoing paragraphs, there has been a general reluctance to bear down on the technological aspects of reform in nineteenth-century China. In the upshot, some of the most elementary distinctions have been obscured. Technological change, as an objective fact, has been confused with *commitment* to technological change, which is subjective and indicates a value preference. Also, there has been relatively little effort to distinguish different *kinds* of commitment to technological change. People may advocate limited changes in technology or they may favor what amounts to a technological revolution. They may have warm, positive feelings toward technological change, viewing it as a natural concomitant of the "forward march of civilization," or they may see it as an unavoidable misfortune, something required by the pressure of circumstances but not desirable in itself. Finally, the commitment to technological change may be entered into for a variety of specific reasons (not all mutually exclusive): to improve living conditions, to compete more effectively with other countries, to increase state power, to preserve existing values and institutions, and so forth.

Assuming it to be true that the nature of a person's commitment to technological change reflects, to a greater or lesser extent, his orientation toward change in general, where did Wang Tao stand as of the late 1860s? Relative to what other Chinese were proposing at the time, how radical was his reform program? His proposals for the future? While it is impossible to say *exactly* how far Wang was prepared to go at this juncture – he probably did not know himself – it was certainly a lot farther than his contemporaries. Other reformers agreed on the necessity of introducing Western firearms and steamships. But leading Chinese officials were unanimous in their opposition to the building of railways,[19] and, with the exception of a few highly Westernized treaty port types, no one in the late 1860s, as far as I know, was ready to advocate extensive mechanization of the Chinese economy.

Equally important were the specific reasons Wang gave for advocating technological change. Many late nineteenth-century reformers, identifying the West with "matter" and China with "spirit," argued that only by the adoption of Western material civilization could China's spiritual civilization be saved from extinction. This was the *ti-yong* approach, immortalized in the 1890s by Zhang Zhidong in the famous phrase, "Chinese learning for the essential principles (*ti*), Western learning for the practical applications (*yong*)."

While it would be incorrect to say that Wang Tao was wholly invulnerable to the *ti-yong* approach – here as elsewhere he was capable of inconsistency – the central thrust of his thinking pointed in a quite different direction. Wang assumed that the essence of Chinese civilization – the core values, China's *dao* – was indestructible. Therefore he was in theory free to take any position he wished in regard to technological change. He could reject even token technological change as being unnecessary. Or, with equal logic, he could espouse massive technological change on the grounds that it could do not harm. If he chose the latter course, however, it would necessarily be for reasons other than the preservation of Chinese essence. And in fact this is precisely what we find to have been the case. In the above-summarized article, Wang gave two justifications for technological revolution: first, that this was the only way in which China could compete with Western countries that had already undergone such a revolution, and, second, that Heaven demanded it as the means to future world unification. In either instance, the preservation of Chinese values was viewed less as the justification of technological change than as its limiting condition.

In proposing sweeping technological change, was Wang, then, merely advocating the inevitable or was he to some extent using the argument of inevitability to buttress his advocacy? In other words, did he view such change as desirable because it was going to happen anyway or did he simply say it was going to happen anyway because he felt it to be desirable? On the face of it, it would appear that Wang regarded technological revolution as a necessary evil. It was not, he insisted, that he *wanted* his predictions to come true; they *had* to come true, as a result of "circumstances and the times." In a context like this, however, we must be very wary of accepting Wang's words at face value. This was not, after all, a letter to a friend or a private diary; it was a newspaper article. Wang's object was to persuade the newspaper's readership. And since it had to be assumed that this readership was opposed to massive technological change, it only made sense, tactically speaking, to portray such change as inevitable. Wang's personal feelings about the advent of the "machine age" were probably more accurately reflected in the travel diary he kept during his visit to Europe (1868–70), in which his response was one of unqualified admiration and awe.[20]

The radical quality of Wang Tao's commitment to technological change brought him, quite early, to the recognition that other kinds of change would also be necessary. Wang became one of the first proponents, in the 1870s, of institutional change (*bianfa*) and it was not long before his commitment to innovation widened still further to embrace basic social, economic, educational, and political reforms. Inevitably, as this happened, the old sanctions for change proved increasingly inadequate and Wang was obliged to seek new ones.[21]

One such, historical in character, reflected the developmental, noncyclical side of Wang's view of history:

> Westerners who have perused the annals of Chinese history think that for five thousand years there has been no change. When, on the contrary, has China not experienced change? First, Youchao, Suiren, Fuxi, and the Yellow Emperor cleared the wilderness and gave China governmental institutions. Then, Yao and Shun, following in their footsteps, styled China the center of the firmament and provided it with the attributes of civilization. From the Three Dynasties to the Qin there was another complete change and from the Han and Tang to the present yet another complete change.[22]

Wang's defensiveness, in the face of Western criticism of Chinese stasis, is interesting. He could, after all, have turned the criticism into a back-handed compliment – a glorification of China eternal. The fact that, instead, he chose to respond with an insistent "We too have had change" implied an emotional identification with the idea of change that was not commonly encountered in the traditional Chinese setting.

The same positiveness of spirit may be seen in another of Wang's sanctions for reform, his assertion that it had always been the Way of the Sages (that is, the Confucian Way) to make proper accommodations to the times and that if Confucius were living in the nineteenth century he would certainly have lent his support to the introduction of Western technology and the general cause of reform.[23] The view of Confucius as a would-be reformer – here Wang clearly anticipated Kang Youwei – was potentially revolutionary. For it not only provided a powerful justification for particular changes but also introduced into Confucianism a more affirmative attitude toward change in general.

Just as revolutionary, though much less obvious, were the implications of Wang's universalistic conception of *dao*. The prevailing tendency among his contemporaries was to equate China with *dao* and the West with *qi* (technology). Wang's conviction that *dao* was an attribute of *human* civilization, and therefore the property of the West as well as of China, injected something very new into the picture. It brought the West into a Chinese world of discourse and, willy-nilly, in the process it furnished China with a rationale for borrowing more than mere *qi* from the West.

Did Wang Tao's dynamization of Confucius and his universalization of *dao* modify the Confucian tradition to the point where it could no longer be called Confucian? In his efforts to find a basis of legitimacy for China's modernization, did Wang reinterpret Confucianism to death? It is easy, when faced with such questions, to lapse into a kind of retrospective determinism that, starting from the conscious rejection of Confucianism in the May Fourth period, sees all modifications of Confucianism in the immediately preceding decades as leading inexorably to this conclusion. One antidote to such reasoning is to remind ourselves that radical changes in Confucian doctrine had taken place before in Chinese history without bringing an end to the tradition. It is very possible that neither Han nor Song Confucianism would have been recognizable to Confucius, but this did not keep their adherents from seeing themselves as authentic followers of the Sage. Similarly, in the case before us, there is probably no way of determining whether the liberties Wang Tao took with Confucianism were fatal to it in any objective sense. All we can say for sure is that Wang continued to regard himself as a Confucian.

Littoral and hinterland in modern Chinese history

The decision to study the life and thinking of a man like Wang Tao deserves explicit justification. Some would maintain that a life – any life – is significant just because it happened. Human existence justifies itself. In a rigorously individual-centered historical approach, I suppose this would be true. But where we are principally concerned with the history of a country, something else is necessary. My main interest is less in Wang Tao than in what Wang Tao tells me about modern China. If Wang is not instructive in this larger-than-Wang sense, his life, for my purposes, is reduced in importance.

One of the ways in which a life may acquire larger meaning is through influence on other lives. The range of variation here is of course great, stretching from the individual who influences events only incrementally all the way to the man – a Jesus or a Mao – whose life (presumably) changes the course of history. The case for the latter has to be built with extreme caution, as it involves the sticky methodological problem – ultimately intractable – of determining what would have been different had the "great man" never lived. We may *presume* that modern Chinese history would have run a different course had Mao Zedong not been a part of it. But we cannot prove this. Nor can we determine how different it would have been.

A difficulty of another sort arises in the case of the individual whose influence on history is incremental. Here the problem is one of visibility. It is perfectly plausible to argue that, within limits set by the physical environment (biological, geographical, and so forth), history is neither more nor less than the sum total of individual influences. Social classes do not have positions on issues. Political parties do not formulate decisions. Institutions do not act. It is the individuals who comprise these larger groupings who are the ultimate makers of events. The individual role, however, is not always accessible to the public eye, and even when it is, it is often so imperceptible that it cannot be "tracked." Historical change takes place. We know that influence has been exerted. But we are unable to follow the process.

We are unable, that is, to reconstruct the process by which one life influences another and the sum total of individual lives translates into collective historical experience. Faced with this difficulty, many historians still find it profitable, in their quest for insight into the aggregate experience, to study the life of a single individual. This individual need not be a person of great influence. Indeed, his influence – whatever its extent – may have been quite invisible. The only requirement, really, is that his biographical development focus on problems or embody patterns that, in some fashion, are discernible in other individuals as well. In this way, even though his role as a *maker* of history may have been small, his value as an *experiencer* of history becomes potentially great.

Wang Tao is a case in point. Scholars judge Wang to have been a probable influence upon the thinking of Sun Yat-sen, Kang Youwei, Zheng Guanying, Wu Tingfang, and others. Yet, I have not taken pains to trace this influence, because I am convinced that, if (like laboratory scientists) we could isolate Wang out from modern Chinese history, not very much would be changed. It is not, in other words, for his actual shaping of the larger picture that Wang Tao is important to the historian. His importance lies in his capacity, as an individual human being with thoughts and feelings, to throw light on this picture, to articulate what it was like to be part of it.

Building on this premise, my point of departure in the first three sections of *Between Tradition and Modernity* is essentially biographical. That is, I seek, through detailed exploration of Wang Tao's life and mind, to illuminate processes of change that many Chinese (albeit each in his own way) experienced in the nineteenth century. In the book's final part I try a somewhat different approach, known more and more commonly among historians as prosopography or collective biography.[24] As just suggested, Wang Tao, for all his individuality, was not unique. There were other people in the China of his day who were, in important respects, like him. And if, by studying these people as a group, we can define the characteristics they held in common, insights that Wang Tao's life alone might offer only in a very tentative way may be placed on a more solid footing.

One of the great, unworked themes in modern Chinese history has been the polarity between littoral and hinterland. This polarity can probably be traced to the sixteenth century, if not earlier (which is one reason why I use the term "littoral" instead of "treaty port"; another is that Hong Kong, while becoming an important part of the littoral culture, was not a treaty port). The historic event that lay behind the creation of the littoral–hinterland polarity was the emergence, from about 1500 on, of a maritime civilization of global embrace. As inhabitants of the southeastern littoral of China became more and more deeply involved in this new civilization, their identification with the culture of the Chinese hinterland progressively weakened.[25]

The contrast between littoral and hinterland became increasingly pronounced after 1842, as Western beachheads were established, first, on the China coast, and, later, along the Yangzi. In and around these beachheads, a culture grew up that was more commercial than agricultural in its economic foundations, more modern than traditional in its administrative and social arrangements,[26] more Western (Christian) than Chinese (Confucian) in its intellectual bearing, and more outward- than inward-looking in its general global orientation and involvement. The center of gravity of Chinese civilization remained firmly planted in the hinterland. But, with the passage of time, the littoral became increasingly important as a stimulus to hinterland change – a "starter" in the bacteriological sense – and some of the foremost actors in modern Chinese history were products of the new coastal-riverine culture.

In probing the significance of these individuals and their interaction with representatives of the hinterland culture, I find it helpful to postulate a general framework for the analysis of cultural change. Sweeping cultural change, as a rule, takes place in two phases. The first phase belongs to the pioneers. These are the individuals who, through their writings and their activities, transform what was once totally strange into something a little less strange, gradually desensitizing people to the newness of the new, making it less conspicuous, more palatable. At some point, the culture then moves into a second phase, in which broad acceptance is given to changes that a short time before would have been acceptable only on the acculturated fringes. This stage is dominated by the legitimizers – people who have been converted to the need for deep-seated change but who insist, all the while, that such change be accompanied by some form of indigenous validation.

In the context of modern Chinese history, this two-phase process assumes the form of a succession of littoral assaults upon the hinterland, followed in each instance by hinterland attempts to legitimize the assaults through sinicization. The first assault was the Taiping Rebellion (1850–64). In the course of being sinicized,[27] however, the Taipings lost their original innovating spirit. They began to look less like Christian revolutionaries and more like traditional Chinese rebels. It was different in the case of the second assault, that of the pioneer reformers (defined here as those reformers, or reform-minded modernizers, who were active or first achieved prominence prior to 1890). The legitimation of this assault was carried out, initially, by the self-strengthening officials and, later on, by the hinterland reformers of the 1890s, reaching a peak in the Reform Movement of 1898. The leader of that movement, Kang Youwei, was successful insofar as he preserved the reform impetus of the littoral while justifying it in hinterland (Confucian) terms. Where Kang failed was in the realm of execution. The final assault from the littoral was Sun Yat-sen's revolutionary movement. Its legitimizing phase, successful both in conception and in execution, was dominated by the figure of Mao Zedong.

So formulated, this sequence of assaults and legitimations is overly schematic and probably misleading. I would not want to suggest, for example, that all pioneer reformers and revolutionaries were products of the littoral or that the hinterland was the only possible source of legitimation. Nor do I wish to convey an idea of innovation and legitimation as totally severable processes or of Kang Youwei and Mao Zedong as mere legitimizers of change, unimportant as innovators.[28]

The qualifications one can think of are endless. And yet the broad picture still stands. We have, in modern Chinese history, two largely separate and distinct cultural environments evolving side by side. Although to a high degree self-contained, these two environments interacted in strategic ways, each performing essential functions over time. In the nineteenth century, and for a while in the twentieth, the littoral assumed primary responsibility for the pioneering of change, the hinterland for its validation. Moreover, as long as neither could do what the other did (or at least not as well), this symbiotic relationship between the two cultures persisted. But once the hinterland, in addition to legitimizing change, also became the principal locus of innovation, the littoral atrophied. Shanghai and Canton, in the second half of the twentieth century, are still there, and they will always be "littoral" in a geographical and economic sense. Culturally, however, they have been absorbed into a new Chinese hinterland.[*]

Revisiting *Between Tradition and Modernity* (1987)

When the idea of a paperback edition of *Between Tradition and Modernity* was first suggested, my initial response was one of hesitation. Almost fifteen years had elapsed since my completion of the original typescript, and I felt quite removed from the subject matter. Besides, I had already confessed in print my worries about the book's intellectual design, above all certain of the more problematic assumptions underlying the tradition–modernity polarity that serves as an important part of its conceptual framework [see Introduction to this volume]. On the other hand, I still felt that Wang Tao, the subject of eight of the book's nine chapters, was a remarkable historical figure, and I remained no less convinced of his importance both as a promoter of change in the last decades of the nine-

---

[*]   These last lines, written (as was most of the original book) while China was in the throes of the Cultural Revolution, are clearly in need of amendment. The changes I would make are discussed in the following section, which consists of the preface to the paperback edition of *Between Tradition and Modernity*.

teenth century and as a negotiator between civilizations. Although articles on Wang in Chinese and Japanese have appeared from time to time, in some cases adding details to the story,[29] and although Wang has a secure spot in the vast Chinese scholarly literature on the *yangwu* (Westernization) and reform movements of the late Qing,[30] no one has ventured to do another book on him in any language.[31] This alone, I felt, was sufficient justification for keeping him in print.

Beyond this, I tried in the final chapter of the book to address some broader issues having to do with change in nineteenth- and twentieth-century China. And, although if I were writing that chapter today I would frame it somewhat differently, the issues themselves seem to me every bit as important now as they were a decade and a half ago. Indeed, it is arguable that, with the end of the Cultural Revolution and the accelerated opening of China to external influences, as part of the Four Modernizations policy of the post-Mao leadership, these issues have become more salient than ever.

Let me briefly summarize the main themes of the book's last chapter and then suggest some of the modifications I would be inclined to make if I were to rework it. The framework of interpretation that I advanced embodied three propositions: first, that sweeping culture change generally takes place in two phases, the first dominated by pioneers (or innovators), the second by legitimizers (or validators); second, that Chinese history since the Opium War may be viewed as a product of the interaction between two largely distinct and self-contained cultural environments, the littoral or coast (Hong Kong, Shanghai, and so on) and the hinterland or interior; and, third, that, in the nineteenth century and for a while in the twentieth, the primary responsibility for the initation of change rested with the subculture of the coast, the interior functioning mainly as a vehicle of legitimation. In an effort to clarify the ways in which the littoral served as an initiator of change in the late Qing period, I shifted in this concluding chapter from individual to collective biography and probed the careers of a dozen pioneer reformers, eight of them (including Wang Tao) closely affiliated with the culture of the littoral, four products of the Chinese hinterland.

I openly acknowledged this framework at the time to be tentative and exploratory in nature and hedged it with a fair number of qualifications.[32] It wasn't, however, until I was able to put some distance between myself and the book that I gained a clearer sense of where the soft areas were and how I might go about firming them up. The most critical of these soft areas, I would say, was a tendency, visible not only in the final chapter but elsewhere as well, to imply that the key measure of change in late Qing China was the extent of the West's impact on Chinese institutions and on the world view of China's educated strata. Change, in other words, was overidentified with Western influence upon Chinese life, with the triple consequence that endogenous patterns of change were either overlooked or trivialized; that the process of institutionalizing change, referred to in the book as "legitimation," was too readily reduced to simple sinicization (or de-Westernization); and, finally, that attention was diverted from social, economic, and political barriers to change to focus almost exclusively upon intellectual and cultural barriers.

If I were reconceiving this chapter today, I would retain the polarity between coast and interior and continue to insist upon the importance of distinguishing between the pioneering and legitimizing phases of culture change (using "culture" in a broadly anthropological sense). However, I would devote much more attention to patterns of internally powered change emerging in China in the latter half of the nineteenth century – commercial development,[33] growing politicization of local elites, and so on – and, even more crucially, I would say something about the special problems involved in validating such change and how these problems differed from those involved in the legitimation of foreign-influenced changes. To illustrate, Feng Guifen's far-reaching proposals for the reform of Chinese local government, which were largely (if not entirely) endogenous in inspiration, encountered barriers to incorporation into the Chinese world of the 1860s, 1870s, and 1880s that were arguably no less formidable than those confronting the reform efforts of a man like Wang Tao. In Wang Tao's case, however, because so many of his reform proposals reflected the influence of the West, the obstacles to legitimation tended to be more cultural and social in nature, whereas in Feng's case they were apt to be more political and economic.

Greater recognition of the importance of internal *processes* of change in the late Qing (as distinct from the indigenous "impulse to change" now stressed in the last chapter) would serve as a natural corrective to overstatement of the role of the West; it would also make it more difficult to misstate this role. In rereading the book, I note, for example, a tendency in places to assume, almost in spite of myself, that the more radical forms of change in the latter half of the nineteenth century were generally (if not invariably) those stemming from the "Western challenge." Apart from the fact that, from my present perspective, I would be inclined to steer clear of the "challenge" terminology altogether, I would here make the more basic point that Chinese promotion of Western-inspired change (initially in the area of technology, but eventually in many other sectors as well) was often justified, especially when the promoters were members of the government or the social elite, as a defensive strategy to block far more fundamental – and hence more threatening – changes of partially or wholly indigenous origin. Western-related change, in other words, could in certain circumstances be allied with forces of a relatively conservative nature in Chinese society. There was no guarantee that, just because it was Western in inspiration, it would necessarily be more "radical" or "fundamental" or "system-threatening" in character.

Finally – and somewhat paradoxically in light of the points I have just been making – if I were redoing the final part of the book today, I would be less hasty in writing off the littoral as a major source of innovation in China in the latter decades of the twentieth century. One of the main features of the post-Mao era has been an opening to the outside world far exceeding anything even remotely imaginable in the early 1970s when the original edition of *Between Tradition and Modernity* was completed. Although not all of the foreign influences that have flowed into China in recent years have been channeled through the littoral, a great preponderance of them have, and the contrast, in respect to accessibility and receptivity to foreign-inspired innovation, between such coastal urban entrepots as Shanghai, Tianjin, and Canton (Guangzhou) and the more remote cities of the Chinese hinterland is still immense.

By the same token, the post-Mao years have also underscored the persistence of the distinctive problems of incorporation and acceptance presented by foreign-patented (especially Western-patented) changes. The suppression of the "democracy movement" in 1979, the campaign against "spiritual pollution" in 1983, and the sharp attack on "bourgeois liberalization" that began in the winter of 1986–7 all bespeak an ongoing resistance to the legitimation of certain kinds of foreign-linked ideas in the Chinese world. The sources of this resistance, however, are complicated and differ in important respects from those that operated in Wang Tao's day. Now, after all, it is the perception that the purity not of native cultural traditions but of a *foreign*-derived ideological system, Marxism–Leninism, is being threatened that provides a major justification for clampdowns on other foreign-derived ideological influences (such as capitalism or democratic liberalism). Moreover, where resistance is shown to such Western-grounded political demands as the right to demonstrate or greater freedom of expression or an independent judiciary, it seems clear that the basis for the resistance is only partly the Westernness of the demands; far more important is their challenge to a tradition of political authoritarianism that is at least as intractable today as it was under the emperors.

Proprietary feelings about China's cultural distinctiveness and self-sufficiency, on the other hand, are still a force to be reckoned with. In spite – and partly because – of all the foreign influences that have buffeted China over the past century and a half, a deep reservoir of ethnocentrism remains to be tapped, especially in the vast Chinese hinterland areas and sectors of the bureaucracy, and especially in situations of crisis. This ethnocentrism establishes an unstable standard of Chineseness that foreign ideas can negotiate with but cannot easily meet; also, it places individuals who have been profoundly influenced by such ideas (including maverick or unorthodox forms of Marxism) in a uniquely marginal, tenuous, and potentially illegitimate position in the larger Chinese world. Although the substantive ideas of these Western-influenced individuals are very different from those of the pioneer reformers of a century ago, the problems they encounter with respect to their own legitimacy in Chinese society and the legitimacy of certain of their intellectual orientations resonate palpably with the problems faced by Wang Tao and his generation. In this sense, the themes explored, however preliminarily, in the final section of my book may speak not only to the late Qing but also to the more recent situation in China.

Notes

This chapter consists of the prologues to the four parts of *Between Tradition and Modernity: Wang T'ao and Reform in Late Ch'ing China* (Cambridge: Harvard University Press, 1974), plus the preface to the paperback edition, published in 1987.

1 All references to the meeting between Wang Tao and Sun Yat-sen ultimately derive from Chen Shaobai's oral account, *Xing Zhong hui geming shiyao* (Outline of the revolutionary history of the Revive China Society), in Chai Degeng *et al.*, eds., *Xinhai geming* (The 1911 revolution), 8 vols. (Shanghai: Shanghai renmin chubanshe, 1957), 1: 28. Chen says that the two met at the home of Zheng Guanying, who was from the same county in Guangdong as Sun and was a long-time friend of Wang Tao. I am grateful to Harold Schiffrin for elaborating on the circumstances of this meeting in a letter of November 20, 1964, to the author. See also his book *Sun Yat-sen and the Origins of the Chinese Revolution* (Berkeley: University of California Press, 1968), p. 38.
2 *Ibid.*, p. 27.
3 Some sources give a much earlier date for Wang's death. But the evidence supporting the 1897 date is overwhelming. A number of works (including an edition of Wang's *Taoyuan wenlu waibian* [Additional essays of Wang Tao] and several books by other reformers) were printed under Wang Tao's name in 1897. A postface by Wang is found in two 1897 editions of Feng Guifen's *Jiaobinlu kangyi* (Straightforward words from the Jiaobin studio), one of them published by Wang himself. John Fryer, one of Wang's foreign colleagues, in a report on the activities of the Chinese Polytechnic Institution from February 11, 1896, to July 1, 1897, states: "The prize-essay scheme has not been carried on with the same energy as formerly through the illness and death of Mr. Wang T'ao" (*North-China Herald and Supreme Court and Consular Gazette*, July 16, 1897, p. 128). Cai Erkang, a Chinese friend and associate, in his *Zhutiean dushu yingshi suibi*, says that Wang died in the fourth month of the 23rd year of Guangxu (May 2–30, 1897). Although I have not seen Cai's work (it may exist in manuscript form only), it is cited in two independent studies of Wang Tao: Wu Jingshan, "Wang Tao shiji kaolüe" (A brief inquiry into the life of Wang Tao), in *Shanghai yanjiu ziliao* (Materials for the study of Shanghai) (Shanghai: Zhonghua shuju, 1936), p. 686; Xie Wuliang, "Wang Tao: Qingmo bianfalun zhi shouchuangzhe ji Zhongguo baodao wenxue zhi xianquzhe" (Wang Tao: Originator of the concept of *bianfa* in the late Qing and pioneer in Chinese journalistic writing), *Jiaoxue yu yanjiu* (Teaching and research), March 1958, p. 39. See also Tan Zhengbi, comp., *Zhongguo wenxuejia da cidian* (A dictionary of Chinese writers) (Shanghai: Guangming shuju, 1934), pp. 1713–14.
4 Frederic Wakeman, Jr., " 'High Ch'ing' 1683–1839," in James B. Crowley, ed., *Modern East Asia: Essays in Interpretation* (New York: Harcourt, Brace, and World, 1970), pp. 1–27.
5 The phrase is Albert Craig's. See his "Introduction: Perspectives on Personality in Japanese History," in Albert M. Craig and Donald H. Shively, eds.,

Personality in Japanese History (Berkeley: University of California Press, 1970), p. 10.

6 This career pattern became increasingly common in the late Qing. See Benjamin Schwartz, *In Search of Wealth and Power: Yen Fu and the West* (Cambridge: Harvard University Press, 1964), pp. 25–6, 32.

7 Erik H. Erikson, *Insight and Responsibility: Lectures on the Ethical Implications of Psychoanalytic Insight* (New York: W.W. Norton, 1964), p. 96.

8 Cyril E. Black, *The Dynamics of Modernization: A Study in Comparative History* (New York: Harper and Row, 1966), p. 54.

9 John K. Fairbank, *China: The People's Middle Kingdom and the U.S.A.* (Cambridge: Harvard University Press, 1967), p. 104.

10 Wang Tao, *Taoyuan wenlu waibian* (Hong Kong, 1883), 7: 19a–b.

11 It appears in *ibid.*, 7: 15b–19.

12 A similar theme is pursued in *ibid.*, 5: 16b.

13 The *Yijing* formula was widely quoted by nineteenth-century protagonists of reform. Its meaning, according to Yang Lien-sheng, was similar to Kroeber's "exhaustion of possibilities." "Chaodai jian de bisai" (Dynastic comparison and dynastic competition), in *Qingzhu Li Ji xiansheng qishi sui lunwen ji* (Symposium in honor of Dr. Li Chi on his seventieth birthday), vol. 1 (Taibei: Qinghua xuebao she, 1965), p. 146.

14 Two influential books that advance this hypothesis, either explicitly or implicitly, are Mary C. Wright, *The Last Stand of Chinese Conservatism: The T'ung-chih Restoration, 1862–1874* (Stanford: Stanford University Press, 1957), and Joseph R. Levenson, *Confucian China and Its Modern Fate*, 3 vols. (Berkeley: University of California Press, 1958–65).

15 Gasster, "Reform and Revolution in China's Political Modernization," in Mary C. Wright, ed., *China in Revolution: The First Phase, 1900–1913* (New Haven: Yale University Press, 1968), p. 83 (italics in original).

16 Referring to Japanese political modernization, Robert E. Ward says:

> While the complete modern political synthesis may date only from the 1860s and 1870s, basic elements of that synthesis...have histories that go back from one and a half to five or six centuries beyond that. This substantially alters the traditional time perspective on the political modernization of Japan. It is seen in these terms not as a process that has taken place in the single century that has intervened since the Restoration but as a cumulative product of two and a half to six or seven centuries of gradual preparation, the last century of which was characterized by a greatly increased pace and scope of political change.
>
> See the "Epilogue" in Robert E. Ward, ed., *Political Development in Modern Japan* (Princeton: Princeton University Press, 1968), p. 580

See also Gasster, "Reform and Revolution," p. 84.

17 See Paul A. Cohen, "Ch'ing China: Confrontation with the West, 1850–1900," in Crowley, ed., *Modern East Asia*, pp. 48–9. In his stimulating essay *The Dynamics of Modernization: A Study in Comparative History*, Cyril E. Black, adopting a worldwide perspective, argues for the existence of seven distinct patterns of political modernization. Significantly, he views China and Japan as belonging to the same pattern (along with Russia, Iran, Turkey, Afghanistan, Ethiopia, and Thailand).

18 Patriotic twentieth-century Chinese, in an effort to emancipate modern Chinese history from the grip of the Western impact, have argued that the seeds of capitalism and modern science were planted in China from the late Ming on – prior to the full onslaught of the West. Even if this is granted, however, it pales in

significance compared to developments in Tokugawa Japan. For a critique of the view that modern scientific thought emerged independently in the early Qing, see Levenson, *Confucian China and Its Modern Fate*, 1: 3–14.

19 Wright, *The Last Stand of Chinese Conservatism*, p. 274.

20 See Cohen, *Between Tradition and Modernity*, pp. 67–73.

21 The evolution of Wang's justifications for change is discussed in Leong Sow-theng, "Wang T'ao and the Movement for Self-strengthening and Reform in the Late Ch'ing Period," *Papers on China* 17 (1963): 118ff.

22 *Taoyuan wenlu waibian*, 1: 10; see also *ibid.*, 1: 12b, 5: 17.

23 *Ibid.*, 1: 10, 13, 11: 13b.

24 The approach is defined, and its advantages and limitations discussed, in Lawrence Stone, "Prosopography," *Daedalus: Journal of the American Academy of Arts and Sciences*, Winter 1971, pp. 46–79.

25 For suggestive remarks on this development, see Frederic Wakeman, Jr., "The Opening of China," in Joseph R. Levenson, ed., *Modern China: An Interpretive Anthology* (New York: The Macmillan Company, 1971), pp. 147–54.

26 From my vantage point today (2003), I would be less inclined to use the term "modern" to characterize the distinctive administrative and social arrangements that evolved in places like Shanghai and Hong Kong.

27 The sinicization of the Taipings is discussed in So Kwan-wai and Eugene P. Boardman (with the assistance of Ch'iu P'ing), "Hung Jen-kan, Taiping Prime Minister, 1859–1864," *Harvard Journal of Asiatic Studies* 20.1–2 (June 1957): 292–4.

28 The whole question of radicalism in this context is intriguing. Who was the more radical: Kang Youwei or Yung Wing (Rong Hong)? Mao Zedong or Sun Yat-sen? My choices, unhesitatingly, are Kang and Mao, not because they were "newer" than Yung and Sun (see my discussion of the ambiguity of the label "new" in the first section of this chapter), but because they spearheaded important attempts to integrate change with tradition (the primary mechanism for doing this, in each instance, being the identification and reinterpretation of traditions that, although authentically Chinese, had strongly unorthodox affiliations). Perhaps one can generalize that the more acculturated one became in modern China, the less chance one had to generate radical change. For acculturation, in making a person newer, also made him or her more remote from the native scene.

29 See, for example, Nishizato Yoshiyuki, "Ō Tō to *Junkan nippō* ni tsuite" (On Wang Tao and the *Xunhuan ribao*), *Tōyōshi kenkyū* 43.3 (December 1984): 508–47; Liu Shilong, "Qing mo Shanghai Gezhi shuyuan yu zaoqi gailiang sichao" (The Shanghai Polytechnic Institute and Reading Room of the late Qing and the early wave of reform thought), *Huadong shifan daxue xuebao* 4 (1983): 45–52, 84; Yang Qimin, "Wang Tao shangshu Taipingjun kaobian – jian yu Luo Ergang xiansheng shangque" (An inquiry into Wang Tao's letter to the Taiping army – and a challenge to the view of Mr. Luo Ergang), *Jindaishi yanjiu* 4 (July 1985): 241–61. For more recent scholarship on Wang, which appeared after the publication of this preface, the reader is referred to Lin Guohui and Huang Wenjiang, "Wang Tao yanjiu shuping" (A review of scholarship on Wang Tao), *Xianggang Zhongguo jindaishi xuehui huikan* (Modern Chinese history society of Hong Kong bulletin) 6 (July 1993): 67–85; and Elizabeth Sinn, "Fugitive in Paradise: Wang Tao and Cultural Transformation in Late Nineteenth-Century Hong Kong," *Late Imperial China* 19.1 (June 1998): 79–81.

30 See, for example, Chen Jiang, "Lun zaoqi gailiangpai renwu dui yangwupai cong yifu dao pipan de fazhan" (The evolution of the early reformers from

dependence upon to criticism of the *yangwu* group), in Cai Shangsi *et al.*, *Lun Qing mo min chu Zhongguo shehui* (Chinese society in the late Qing and early republican eras) (Shanghai: Fudan daxue chubanshe, 1983), pp. 197–221.

31 Since writing this preface a number of books on Wang Tao have appeared in Chinese. Among those that I have seen are Xin Ping, *Wang Tao pingzhuan* (A critical biography of Wang Tao) (Shanghai: Huadong shifan daxue chubanshe, 1990); Zhang Hailin, *Wang Tao pingzhuan* (A critical biography of Wang Tao) (Nanjing: Nanjing daxue chubanshe, 1993); Zhang Zhichun, comp., *Wang Tao nianpu* (A chronological biography of Wang Tao) (Shijiazhuang: Hebei jiaoyu chubanshe, 1994); and Lin Qiyan and Huang Wenjiang, eds., *Wang Tao yu jindai shijie* (Wang Tao and the modern world) (Xianggang: Xianggang jiaoyu tushu gongsi, 2000).

32 So many, in fact, that one frustrated reviewer charged me with "stretching the foot to fit the sock." See C.A. Curwen, *Bulletin of the School of Oriental and African Studies* 39.3 (1976): 683–4. Another reviewer who found fault with the last chapter was W.S. Atwell, *China Quarterly* 67 (September 1976): 640–3. The reactions of most people, on the other hand, were on balance quite favorable. See, for example, Jerome B. Grieder, *Intellectuals and the State in Modern China: A Narrative History* (New York: The Free Press, 1981), pp. 130–1, 379.

33 Two important recent books that make a persuasive case for much higher levels of hinterland commercialization during the late Qing than had previously been acknowledged are William T. Rowe, *Hankow: Commerce and Society in a Chinese City, 1796–1889* (Stanford: Stanford University Press, 1984), and Susan Mann, *Local Merchants and the Chinese Bureaucracy, 1750–1950* (Stanford: Stanford University Press, 1987). Mann, on the basis of her findings explicitly questions (*ibid.*, p. 27) the validity of my suggested division of late imperial China into two distinct cultural environments. This part of her argument I find less persuasive for two reasons. First, no matter how commercialized one judges the economy of the hinterland to have become by late Qing times, it still rested on an economic base that was massively agrarian; these emphases are exactly reversed in the case of the littoral culture, which, I remain convinced, "was more commercial than agricultural in its economic foundations." Second, even if it should be proved that the economic contrast between littoral and hinterland was very much less pronounced than I had once supposed, this still leaves the noneconomic terms of the contrast – degree of exposure to Western influence, elite value orientations, administrative and legal arrangements, and the like – basically intact.

2 Moving beyond "Tradition and Modernity"

For some years now a major change has been in progress in American writing on the recent Chinese past. The old picture of a stagnant, slumbering, unchanging China, waiting to be delivered from its unfortunate condition of historylessness by a dynamic, restlessly changing, historyful West, has at last begun to recede. China is, indeed, being liberated. It is being liberated, however, not from itself but from us, not from an *actual* state of changelessness but from an externally imposed perception of changelessness derived from a particular – and heavily parochial – definition of what change is and what kinds of change are important.

This basic shift in American scholarship has been closely allied with another shift that has begun to take place in the conceptual realm. I refer to the increasing disenchantment that has emerged with respect to modernization theory as a framework for approaching recent Chinese history. The literature on modernization theory is enormous, and I make no pretense here to a comprehensive treatment of it. What I am particularly interested in is that aspect of the theory that divides societies into "traditional" and "modern" phases of evolution. It is this tradition–modernity dyad, rather than modernization theory in its more elaborated form, that has cast the greatest spell over American historians of China.[1] Virtually all such historians in the 1950s and 1960s used the terms *traditional* and *modern* to subdivide China's long history (*modern* usually referring to the period of significant contact with the modern West), and even now, although the way in which these terms are used has changed substantially, they are still very much in evidence in scholarly writing. Few individuals have become so sensitive to their capacity for historical mischief as to call for their complete abandonment.[2]

Modernization theory, as a corpus of societal analysis, first assumed explicit shape in the years following World War II. Against the backdrop of the Cold War, it served the ideological need of Western – primarily American – social scientists to counter the Marxist–Leninist explanation of "backwardness" or "underdevelopment." It also provided a coherent intellectual explanation of the processes whereby "traditional" societies became "modern" – or, as the editors of a series on the "modernization of traditional societies" phrased it, "the way quiet places have come alive."[3]

Although the proximate origins of modernization theory were the conditions of the postwar world, in its most fundamental assumptions about non-Western cultures and the nature of change in such "quiet places," it drew heavily on a cluster of ideas that were widely current among Western intellectuals of the nineteenth century. This nineteenth-century connection has occasionally been noted in general discussions of modernization theory.[4] It has been largely overlooked, however, by American students of China, who have been more prone to emphasize and take pride in the ways in which postwar historical scholarship has moved beyond the assumptions of the Victorian era.

The nineteenth-century Western view of China

Although these assumptions were held with reference to the non-West in general, I will discuss them here mainly as they were reflected in commentary on China. One almost invariable ingredient in such commentary was the image of China as a static, unchanging society, a society in a state of perpetual repose. Just prior to the beginning of the nineteenth century, the French mathematician-philosopher Condorcet wrote of the "human mind...condemned to shameful stagnation in those vast empires whose uninterrupted existence has dishonoured Asia for so long." Johann Gottfried von Herder, around the same time, pronounced that in Europe alone was human life genuinely historical, whereas in China, India, and among the natives of America there was no true historical progress but only a static unchanging civilization. Playing a variation on the same theme, Hegel, some years later, entered the judgment, "We have before us the oldest state and yet no past...a state which exists today as we know it to have been in ancient times. To that extent China has no history." The historian Ranke described China as being in a state of "eternal standstill," and John Stuart Mill referred in his writings to what he called "Chinese stationariness."[5]

A particularly nasty example of this kind of thinking, on the American side, was supplied by Ralph Waldo Emerson in a notebook entry of 1824:

> The closer contemplation we condescend to bestow, the more disgustful is that booby nation. The Chinese Empire enjoys precisely a Mummy's reputation, that of having preserved to a hair for 3 or 4,000 years the ugliest features in the world.... Even miserable Africa can say I have hewn the wood and drawn the water to promote the civilization of other lands. But China, reverend dullness! hoary ideot!, all she can say at the convocation of nations must be – "I made the tea."[6]

The view of China as unchanging was nothing new. It had enjoyed wide currency prior to the nineteenth century also. What was new was the negative judgment placed upon China's alleged immobility. For numbers of writers prior to the French Revolution, the stable, changeless quality of Chinese society had been regarded as a definite mark in its favor, a condition worthy of Western admiration and respect. (Oliver Goldsmith, in *The Citizen of the World*, for example, described "an Empire which has thus continued invariably the same for such a long succession of ages" as "something so peculiarly great that I am naturally led to despise all other nations on the comparison."[7]) However, from the late eighteenth century, the Industrial Revolution brought what appeared to be a widening gap between European and Chinese material standards, and as Europeans began to identify "civilization" with a high level of material culture, China, whose technical skill and material abundance had once been the envy of the West, came to be identified as a backward society.

This new picture of China was reinforced by important intellectual shifts that were taking place in Europe. In the economic sphere there was a strong reaction against mercantilist constraints and an increased tendency to espouse the principles of free trade and laissez faire; the political arena saw a growing revulsion (at least in some quarters) for despotism, enlightened or any other kind; more generally, Europeans became wedded to the values of progress, dynamic movement, and change in all spheres of life. As this new world view came more and more to be equated with being "enlightened," China, with its annoying restrictions on trade, its autocratic government, and its apparent resistance to change of any sort, took on the aspect, for many Westerners, of an obsolescent society doomed to languish in the stagnant waters of barbarism until energized and transformed by a dynamic, cosmopolitan, and cosmopolitanizing West.

In the *Communist Manifesto* (1848), Marx and Engels expressed the prevailing vision of the nineteenth-century West with admirable succinctness:

> The bourgeoisie, by the rapid improvement of all instruments of production, by the immensely facilitated means of communication, draws all, even the most barbarian, nations into civilization. The cheap prices of its commodities are the heavy artillery with which it batters down all Chinese walls, with which it forces the barbarians' intensely obstinate hatred of foreigners to capitulate. It compels all nations, on pain of extinction, to adopt the bourgeois mode of production; it compels them to introduce what it calls civilization into their midst, *i.e.*, to become bourgeois themselves. In a word, it creates a world after its own image.[8]

If Marx and Engels displayed a touch (and it was only a touch) of ambivalence with respect to the credentials of the Western bourgeoisie to be considered civilized, there was little hesitation in their judgment of the Chinese as barbarians or in their assumption that China, like the rest of the "underdeveloped" world, would be made over in the image of the modern West. "The oldest and most unshattered Empire on this earth," Marx wrote in 1850,

> has been pushed, in eight years, by the cotton ball of the English bour-geois toward the brink of a social upheaval that must have most profound consequences for civilisation. When our European reac-tionaries, on their next flight through Asia, will have finally reached the Chinese Wall, the gates that lead to the seat of primeval reaction and conservatism – who knows, perhaps they will read the following inscription on the Wall:
>
> *République Chinoise*
> *Liberté, Égalité, Fraternité!*[9]

Joseph Levenson and the historiography of the 1950s and 1960s

The assumptions underlying the nineteenth-century Western perception of China exerted a powerful shaping influence on American historiography in the period from World War II through the late 1960s. This nineteenth-century drag effect is nowhere more dramatically evidenced than in the writings of Joseph R. Levenson, a man who addressed the issues of modernization and cultural change more persistently, imaginatively, and, for many of his readers, persuasively than perhaps any other American historian of China in the immediate postwar decades. Today, the younger generation of China historians pays little heed to Levenson,* but in the 1950s and 1960s he was a compelling presence – someone with whom one felt one had to come to terms.

When Levenson's major works began to come out, in the early 1950s,[10] the Chinese Communists had only recently come to power, the dust of revolution had not yet settled, and Cold War attitudes and assumptions cast a heavy pall over American scholarly thinking. Levenson's mind, however, was far too complex to be framed by the battles of the Cold War, and although he was much concerned with "placing" Chinese communism historically, this concern was subsidiary to the larger aim of elucidating the process by which, in his view, one of the great civilizations of world history had, in the face of the modern Western invasion, disintegrated, passing (as he would have phrased it) into history, to be replaced by a new and fully modern Chinese culture. His analysis of this momentous process was filled with insights that will be of lasting value, if not in terms of the answers he supplied or the data he gathered, at least in terms of the issues

---

* Although this was certainly true in the early 1980s, when *Discovering History in China* was written, there has in recent years been a revived interest in Levenson's writings in the West and a growing interest in China itself.

he posed and the ways in which he posed them. No historian, however, can entirely elude the prevailing assumptions of his time, and it is both ironic and telling that Levenson, for all his originality as a thinker and despite persistent and strenuous efforts to counter the parochialism of American Sinology, [11] approached Chinese history from a perspective that, in its understanding of the imperatives of modernization, bore the clear stamp of the nineteenth century and epitomized the parochial core of the thinking of an entire generation of American historians.

Where this nineteenth-century parochialism was least apparent was in respect to the proposition that the West embodied civilization and China barbarism.[12] The inroads of cultural relativism in twentieth-century America have been substantial. And even though, at the level of deepest feeling, it has still been possible in adversarial situations for Americans to slip back into an exaggerated we–they dichotomization in which "we" stands for civilization and "they" for the opposite (World War II affords one example, the more recent Iranian hostage crisis another[13]), it has also been possible, as Vietnam showed, for such feelings to become inverted and for self-hatred – "we are the barbarians, not they" – to take the place of self-love. Moreover, ranged against those incorrigible spirits who, even after Vietnam, still believe that a high level of technological development is the sine qua non of civilization, there are increasing numbers of Americans who, newly sensitized to the destructive potential of modern technology (in industry as well as war), have begun to wonder whether technological capacity per se is as important a characteristic of the civilized condition as what a culture does with this capacity.

American historians of China did not, in any case, need Vietnam – we already had the Opium War – to develop empathic feelings with regard to China's cultural heritage. Chinese iconoclasts of the May Fourth genera-tion, in the years after World War I, might, with the writer Lu Xun (1881–1936), revile their own heritage as one of extreme barbarism, but no serious American student of this heritage in the twentieth century would think in such terms, much less employ such language. Certainly Levenson, for his part, displayed feelings of profound admiration for Chinese civiliza-tion. It was not this civilization itself, but the refusal of modern Chinese conservatives to acknowledge its death, that aroused his impatience.

With respect to the nineteenth-century notion that Chinese culture was unchanging, that it existed in a kind of steady state or equilibrium, on the other hand, Levenson and other American historians of the 1950s and 1960s were far more equivocal in their thinking. To be sure, there was a strong predisposition to believe that China's culture, like that of the West, was dynamic and changing in nature, and the contrary judgment of our forebears was repudiated as offensive and hopelessly ethnocentric. Yet this generalized profession of faith frequently did not square with concrete statements about "traditional China," which tended still to be framed in terms of unchanging or insignificantly changing categories, structures, and patterns. Students of the pre-Western impact phase of Chinese history did, it is true, make a strenuous and increasingly successful effort to get inside China and began to depict a culture pulsating with energy and change. By and large, however, historians of the period of Sino-Western confrontation, because they had one eye trained on the West, tended to approach China with a more parochial picture of the shape of change, judging it to be relatively unchanging when measured against the enormous transformations experienced in the West (and Japan) in modern times.

To speak of change as having "shape" is, of course, to speak in metaphorical language. The point, which is an important one, is that change is not just something that happens "out there." It is not just "past events." It is also, and perhaps predominantly, something that historians determine or "shape," on the basis of what they happen to be looking for in the events of the past. The "facts," E.H. Carr reminds us,

> are like fish swimming about in a vast and sometimes inaccessible ocean;...what the historian catches will depend...mainly on what part of the ocean he chooses to fish in and what tackle he chooses to use – these two factors being, of course, determined by the kind of fish he wants to catch.[14]

If, to put it more prosaically, the historian is looking for A, he is not likely to find B or C, for even though he may encounter B or C, he won't recognize them as significant.

That the Chinese past, when seen from the vantage point of the Sino-Western encounter, still tended in the 1950s and 1960s to be perceived as *relatively* unchanging, is clearly documented in the two volumes of *A History of East Asian Civilization* (1960, 1965), the most sophisticated and deservedly the most influential postwar American textbooks on East Asian history. Significantly, in the first volume of this textbook, covering the period of Chinese history in which the Western intrusion had not yet become a factor, there is a great deal of emphasis on linear change.[15] It is only in the second volume, where the encounter with the West looms large, that the perception of the East Asian past as stable and minimally changing comes to the fore. The authors of this volume, John K. Fairbank, Edwin O. Reischauer, and Albert M. Craig, discuss in the opening pages the major interpretive concepts that they found helpful in organizing their data. One such concept is "change within tradition," which they describe in the following terms:

> [In each East Asian country] the major traditional forms of thought and action, once established, had an inertial momentum, a tendency to continue in accepted ways. As long as their environment remained without direct Western contact, they underwent only "change within tradition," not transformation.[16]

The trouble with the concept "change within tradition" is that it reflects certain subjective preferences as to what kinds of change are more and less significant. There is an implicit circularity in the lines just quoted. "Transformation," it would appear, is what the West itself went through in modern times or what happens to a non-Western society when it encounters modern Western culture. To say, therefore, that "without direct Western contact, [the countries of East Asia] underwent only 'change within tradition,' not transformation," is a little like saying that these countries did not become Westernized until they underwent Westernization.[17] Fairbank, Reischauer, and Craig have obviously gone far beyond the cruder formulations of the nineteenth century, but they are still working, I would argue, within a framework that virtually compels them to lay particular stress on the more stable and abiding features of Chinese culture.[18]

Another widely used text that takes essentially the same approach is Immanuel C.Y. Hsü's *The Rise of Modern China* (1970). In the period from 1600 to 1800, Hsü tells us, "China's political system, social structure, economic institutions, and intellectual atmosphere remained substantially what they had been during the previous 2,000 years."[19]

Still another example, though from a sharply different intellectual and ideological perspective, is provided by Karl A. Wittfogel in his imposing theoretical analysis *Oriental Despotism* (1957). Wittfogel, who although bitterly anticommunist proudly traces his intellectual lineage to Marx and Engels and beyond them to the classical economists, sees "hydraulic society" (of which China is a prime example) as "the outstanding case of societal stagnation." Although originating in several ways and under favorable circumstances developing complex patterns of property and social stratification, hydraulic society, he argues, "did not abandon its basic structures except under the impact of *external* forces."[20]

Joseph Levenson, too, shared this perspective. For all his emphasis in volume 2 of *Confucian China and Its Modern Fate* on the tensions pervading Chinese culture – tensions between monarchy and bureaucracy, between Confucianism and the monarchy, and even within Confucianism itself – Levenson's vision of the Chinese past, from the establishment of the imperial-bureaucratic state in the third century B.C.E. until the nineteenth century, was an essentially harmonic vision in which everything (including the tensions) meshed with everything else and "a whole pattern of cultural preferences hung together, all appropriate to one another and to a specific social order."[21] So stable and harmoniously balanced was this social order that it not only could not (it would appear) generate significant change from within itself but was even proof against modification on any scale from without. Foreign influences might bring about cultural enrichment (an infusion of new "vocabulary"), but they had never, prior to modern times, been the source of fundamental transformation (a change in "language").[22]

Levenson's understanding of the impact of Buddhism, in terms of this distinction, is clear and unambiguous:

> The Indian homeland of Buddhism had not impinged on China socially; the contact was only intellectual, and while Chinese society had some throes of its own in Buddhism's early Chinese centuries, from the end of the Han to mid-T'ang [Tang], and the foreign creed seemed a serious menace then to the Confucianism appropriate to *a normally operating Chinese bureaucratic society, the revival of this normal operation confirmed Chinese Confucianism as the master of an originally Indian Buddhism, which settled into a modified but invincibly Chinese background.*[23]

In the very next sentence Levenson, his attention now riveted to the quantum changes generated in twentieth-century China by communist ideas, insists that "the old saw about China's absorbing everything...be buried once and for all."[24] There is more than a little irony in this insistence, given Levenson's minimal assessment of the earlier impact of Buddhism, by common judgment the most powerful foreign influence on Chinese cultural development prior to the nineteenth century. The irony, however, is less important than the strong implication in Levenson's phrasing that there was a "normal way" in which Chinese society operated and that the pivotal presence in this normal way was a highly stable entity called Confucianism. Levenson obviously knew better.[25] He knew that Confucianism's revival in the late Tang and Song, its reconfirmation as China's cultural overlord, was achieved at a steep price, the form of payment of which was its own very substantial transformation under Buddhist influence. Levenson's vantage point for viewing this transformation, however, prevented him from appreciating it in its full measure and prompted him, instead, to emphasize out of all proportion the regularities of past Chinese culture.[26] The reference to Buddhism's settling, finally, into "a modified but invincibly Chinese background" was but a rephrasing of the "change within tradition" concept earlier discussed.

The final component of the nineteenth-century perception of China broke down into a number of related propositions: first, that China could be jolted from its somnolent condition only by means of a major external shock;[27] second, that the modern West, and only the modern West, was capable of administering such a shock; and third, that this process, already in motion, would end in the making over of Chinese culture in the Western image.

American historians of the 1950s and 1960s would certainly not have subscribed to this characterization in all of its details. For "somnolent" (a favorite image of the nineteenth century) they would insist on substituting some less pejorative modifying phrase like "slow-motion" or "stable" or "gradually changing." Also, they would have been uncomfortable with the implicitly deterministic structure of the first proposition and would have greatly preferred to see it recast in descriptive terms (as, for example, in the assertion about the countries of East Asia already quoted from the Fairbank, Reischauer, and Craig text: "As long as their environment remained without direct Western contact, they underwent only 'change within tradition,' not transformation"). Prior to the middle or late 1960s, on the other hand, most American historians would have gone along with the unidirectional view of convergence embodied in the third proposition, and few would have seriously questioned the assumption that the sole or primary factor forcing the transformation of Chinese culture and society during the last century and a half has been the Western intrusion. There is a direct line of descent from Marx's prediction of 1853 that, its "isolation having come to a violent end by the medium of England," China's "dissolution must follow as surely as that of any mummy carefully preserved in a hermetically sealed coffin, whenever it is brought into contact with the open air,"[28] to the declaration by Fairbank, Reischauer, and Craig that "increased contact with the technologically more advanced Occident gave the major initial impetus to the great changes in East Asia that started in the nineteenth century," when, in the face of the Western onslaught, the countries of this region "suddenly found their defenses crumbling, their economies disrupted, their governments threatened, and even their social systems undermined."[29]

Philip Kuhn's landmark study *Rebellion and Its Enemies in Late Imperial China* (1970) begins to modify this overall line of interpretation. In an introductory discussion of the "boundaries of modern history," Kuhn notes that the prevailing view of China's transformation in modern times defines "modern" at least by implication as "that period in which the motion of history is governed primarily by forces exogenous to Chinese society and Chinese tradition." Uncomfortable with this definition, Kuhn recognizes that, before we can dispense with it, we must free ourselves from the old picture of a cyclically changing China. The central question to which he addresses himself in his introduction is, therefore, that of the nature of the changes taking place in Chinese society *prior* to the full Western onslaught. After noting the "phenomenal population rise (from 150 to 300 million during the eighteenth century); the inflation in prices (perhaps as much as 300 percent over the same period); the increasing monetization of the economy and the aggravation of economic competition in rural society," Kuhn expresses doubt as to whether changes of such character and magnitude can be viewed as cyclical and suggests as an alternative to the prevailing view the partly counterfactual hypothesis that "the West was impinging, not just upon a dynasty in decline, but upon a civilization in decline: a civilization that would soon have had to generate fresh forms of social and political organization from within itself."[30]

Joseph Levenson, too, was interested in the nature of the changes taking place in China on the eve of the nineteenth century. But Levenson's interest was less disinterested than Kuhn's, and the question he posed was more parochial. Kuhn's question, neutral and open-ended, is: What was happening in eighteenth-century China? He asks this question because he senses that the answer to it is going to be essential to a fuller understanding of how China became a modern society. Levenson's question, opening the first volume of *Confucian China and Its Modern Fate*, is: Is there any indication, in the existence of a group of materialist thinkers in seventeenth- and eighteenth-century China, "that the seemingly stable, traditionalistic Chinese society had the capacity to develop under its own power, without a catalytic intrusion of Western industrialism, into a society with a scientific temper?"[31]

The reason why Levenson's question is parochial is that, like Max Weber's inquiry into the origins of the spirit of capitalism or Levenson's own question, addressed on another occasion, concerning the roots of expansionism,[32] it is based on the assumption that the only kind of "development" that is important – and therefore worth looking for in the Chinese past – is development leading toward modernity, as defined by the Western historical experience. Of even greater moment than the parochial tone of Levenson's question is its lack of neutrality and open-endedness. The fact is, the only possible answers to his question are yes or no. And if the answer turns out to be yes, if "modern values" can indeed be located in early and mid-Qing China, the whole edifice of Levenson's analysis of modern Chinese intellectual history collapses. Levenson recognized this clearly and made it very explicit in his introduction to the trilogy:

> Before one may suggest...that the great problem for Chinese thinkers in the last century has been the problem of reconciliation of their general intellectual avowals and their special Chinese sentiments, he must reflect on the history of early-modern, "pre-western" Chinese thought. For if that history was a history of burgeoning modern values (a growing spirit of science, for example – such a major strain in modern thought), then a later nagging doubt about Chinese continuity was unnecessary; if, on the other hand, the modern values cannot be traced to pre-western roots in Chinese history, such a doubt was unavoidable.[33]

The analogue of Levenson's question, equally loaded, and analyzed with great perceptiveness by Levenson himself, is the question posed by Chinese Communist historians: Are there indications of the emergence of embryonic capitalism in China prior to the arrival in force of the Westerner? If the answer to this question is no (which appears to have been the preference of Marx himself), patriotic Chinese historians are hard-pressed to demonstrate the autonomy of their own modern history. If the answer is yes, on the other hand, they can argue (1) that Chinese history ran a course paralleling that of the West (thus making it not derivative in character but part of a universal historical pattern), and (2) that Western imperialism, far from *introducing* capitalism (or, by extension, modern history) into China, actually impeded or distorted capitalism's normal development (a position of Leninist, not Marxist, inspiration). The Chinese Communist answer to their own question, to no one's particular surprise, has been a fairly consistent, if somewhat labored, yes.[34]

Joseph Levenson's answer to *his* question, equally predictable, is that, prior to the introduction of modern values by the West, such values were nowhere to be found in Chinese thought. When, on the other hand, the West, in the nineteenth century, finally came to China for real – not just with mechanical clocks and Euclid, but with powerful ships and guns – Chinese history, in Levenson's view, was derailed. Total transformation now ensued. The old order, like Marx's mummy upon exposure to the open air, rapidly disintegrated, and out of the rubble and decay a new and wholly modern China emerged.

Levenson's account of this process varied, depending on whether he happened to be dealing (as was generally the case) with intellectual history or whether he was addressing himself (usually only in passing) to total societal change. In the former instance he tended to operate within the impact–response framework; in the latter his views reflected the influence and assumptions of American modernization theorists (in particular, it would appear, Marion Levy). But in either case, the part assigned to the West was staggering. The West, for Levenson, was the author of China's modern transformation; it also was responsible for defining the entire *problematic* of modern Chinese history.

As an intellectual historian, Levenson was principally concerned not with the "exterior" realm of economic, political, and social change in modern China, but with the "interior" realm of what Chinese thought and how they felt about the changing world in which they lived. The key theme he pursued throughout his work on intellectual history, including apparently the new trilogy on provincialism and cosmopolitanism left unfinished at his death,[35] was the distinction between value and history, between those aspects of a culture to which people give their allegiance because they believe them to be generally valid (good for all people for all time) and those aspects to which they commit themselves for reasons of a more subjective and proprietary nature. Under the influence of Morris Raphael Cohen's *Reason and Nature*, Levenson assumed that a stable society would be "one whose members would choose, on universal principles, the particular culture they inherited."[36] Such, he believed, was precisely the situation that prevailed "in the great ages of the Chinese Empire," a time when "conflict between history and value had been impossible," when "Chinese loved their civilization not only because they had inherited it from their fathers but because they were convinced that it was good."[37]

This harmonic condition was, in Levenson's view, totally shattered by the arrival of the West in the nineteenth century. Levenson characterized modern Chinese intellectual history, "the period of western influence,...as two reciprocal processes, the progressive abandonment of tradition by iconoclasts and the petrifaction of tradition by traditionalists." Both of these processes, he maintained, showed "a Chinese concern to establish the equivalence of China and the West." This quest for equivalence, for a new formula that would bring history ("mine") and value ("true") back into harmony and restore the psychological peace, formed "the common ground of all the new currents of Chinese thought since the Opium War."

> Petty distinctions and conflicts between Chinese schools paled into insignificance before the glaring contrast of western culture to everything Chinese. Grounds for discrimination between Chinese schools were blurred when a new western alternative existed for them all, a more genuine alternative than they afforded one another.

When "the West was a serious rival, Chinese rivals closed their ranks." The field of Chinese intellectual history became preempted by Sino-Western syncretisms.[38]

That the impact of the West on nineteenth- and twentieth-century Chinese intellectual history was of critical importance is undeniable. How we establish this importance is, however, a difficult methodological problem. Every conceptual approach carries with it its own logic. But where mathematicians only have to worry about whether their logic is internally consistent, the historian, in addition, has to worry about whether the logic of his approach is congruent with what actually took place in the past. When a historian fails to submit his logic to this test of congruence and instead imposes it upon the data, he substitutes reasonableness for reality and historical understanding suffers. Levenson's heavy reliance on the concept of equivalence enabled him to open up and explore areas of intellectual and psychological change, centering above all on alienation and identity, that previously had been sidestepped by students of the recent Chinese past. The profusion of insights that this approach generated was one of the great strengths of his writing. But the approach itself was flawed in a number of ways, and the flaws highlight some of the major shortcomings of the impact–response framework.

One such shortcoming is the assumption that when there is a Western impact there will necessarily be a Chinese response of corresponding magnitude. Sometimes, in Chinese history, this was indeed the case. But there were many occasions when it was not, when Western impacts that seemed (at least retrospectively) to be of major consequence evoked minimal Chinese responses or, conversely, when a small amount of impact set off a very substantial response. Where Levenson erred most egregiously was in his insistence that, starting with the Opium War, "the glaring contrast of Western culture to everything Chinese" transformed the central *problematic* of the Chinese intellectual world virtually overnight. Whether the culture of the West presented as stark a contrast to everything Chinese as Levenson thought is a debatable proposition in its own right. (See the discussion of this issue in Chapter 1 of this volume.) But the question I would pose, at this juncture, is whether, even if there were such a contrast, the contrast was apparent to any but a tiny handful of Chinese intellectuals at this early date. Awareness, moreover, even where it existed, did not necessarily translate into concern. Lin Zexu (1785–1850), the imperial commissioner directed by the Manchu court in the late 1830s to solve the opium trade crisis, had plenty of contact with Westerners during his sojourn in Canton, and we know from his diary accounts that he perceived the West as being radically different from China. To my knowledge, however, there is no evidence that Lin's interior world was even mildly shaken by this awareness.[39]

The case of the mid-nineteenth-century scholar-official Zeng Guofan is more complex and, for our purposes, more revealing. Levenson discusses at some length Zeng's intellectual eclecticism (which Zeng himself described as *lixue* or the "philosophy of social usage"), arguing that "as a loyal Chinese, but a Chinese among westerners, he [Zeng] seemed to lose the will to dwell on intramural distinctions," that "when western conceptions were seen as alternative, the Chinese creed for a man like Tseng [Zeng] had to be close to all-inclusive."[40] This effort to establish a causal linkage between Zeng's syncretism and a Western challenge is perfectly plausible, and the force of Levenson's logic is overpowering. The linkage, however, has no empirical basis. Syncretism was a phenomenon with a very substantial history in Chinese intellectual life. The particular syncretic formulation that Zeng arrived at was much influenced, it appears, by earlier eclectic thinkers (such as his close friend, Liu Chuanying, who died in 1848). Moreover, there is ample evidence that the basis of Zeng's *lixue* had been pretty well laid during the Beijing phase of his career (1840–52), a good part of which was spent in the Hanlin Academy, well insulated from contact with Chinese foreign affairs. During these years, as one might expect, Zeng's writings betray virtually no awareness of the impact of the West.[41]

Hao Chang goes further than this still, arguing that, prior to the 1890s, the impact of the West on Chinese intellectual life in general remained superficial. Far from becoming the dominant concern of many intellectuals, as in Japan, Western learning initially aroused little response. For such major intellectual figures of the nineteenth century as Chen Li (1810–82), Zhu Ciqi (1807–82), Zhu Yixin (1846–94), and Wang Kaiyun (1833–1916), as for the majority of the scholar-gentry in the fifty-year period after 1840, the central intellectual preoccupations remained the classical problems of the Confucian tradition. Chang further maintains – and Guy Alitto's study of the twentieth-century Confucian rural reconstructionist Liang Shuming (b. 1893) amply bears him out – that, even after the Western impact became a major concern of Chinese intellectuals, it not only did not supplant older philosophical concerns but actually was shaped by these concerns in subtle and complex ways.[42]

Here again the contrast to Levenson is sharp. The enormous potency that Levenson invested in the Western impact caused him not only to date prematurely the point in time at which Western ideas penetrated from the periphery to the center of Chinese concern but also to exaggerate the degree to which, once such penetration occurred, earlier Chinese concerns became moribund. "Confucianism," Levenson maintained, "after so many centuries, had at last been drained of any relevance to Chinese reality...the Chinese tradition was disintegrating, and its heirs, to save the fragments, had to interpret them in the spirit of the Western intrusion." Levenson granted that "China in the nineties still had its many live thinkers of tradi-tional ideas." But the ideas themselves, he insisted, were now "dead." For an idea, in order to be alive, had to have "real reference to an objective situation, and the history of China in the nineteenth century had been the story of the retreat of its ideology from objective significance to a purely subjective one."[43]

Levenson's entire sense of "problem" in recent Chinese intellectual history, in short, revolved around the shattering impact of the West, the problems of equivalence it posed, and the succession of Chinese responses it evoked. It was from this perspective that he wrote his book on the late Qing reformer and publicist Liang Qichao (1873–1929). Consequently, although there is some discussion in the book of the New Text influence on Liang and of his use of Mencius, Confucius, and Buddhism to buttress his intellectual claims, at no point does Levenson attempt to anchor Liang in the Chinese intellectual world of his day. The fact is, with the arrival of the West, Levenson no longer took the inner dynamics of this world seri-ously. It was therefore impossible for him to conceive of an iconoclast like Liang continuing to be intellectually (as opposed to emotionally) attached to any part of it. It was equally impossible for him to imagine Liang (or any other Chinese intellectual) utilizing Western thought to help resolve problems that predated the impact of the West.

Although Levenson's overriding concern was with the "interior" realm of intellectual change, the part taken by the West in effecting such change was, in his view, essentially a subset of the larger role of the West in the "exterior" realm of China's political, economic, and social transformation in modern times. Indeed, as Levenson made clear on a number of occa-sions, it was precisely the fact that the Western impact was a total societal impact, not just an intellectual one, that made it possible for the intellectual dimension of this impact to have the transformative consequences it had:

> The effect of ideas in diffusion, the degree of their disarrangement of their fresh intellectual environment, depends, it seems, not on their disembodied character as abstract ideas but on how much of their mother societies they drag with them to the alien land. As long as one

society is not being conclusively shaken up by another, foreign ideas may be exploited, as additional vocabulary, in a domestic intellectual situation. But when foreign-impelled social subversion is fairly under way (and that has been so in China, not in the West, and in China only in the nineteenth century and after), then foreign ideas begin to displace domestic. This change of language in a society may be described objectively as new choices made under conditions of total invasion, not of purely intellectual insinuation.[44]

In his periodic allusions to total societal change in China, Levenson assigned two roles to the West. One was as the precipitator of such change, the force ultimately responsible for the undermining of the old order. "The breakdown of traditional Chinese society," he asserted, "is the result of the western impact, the same western incursion that ruffled and finally ruined Chinese confidence in China's intellectual self-sufficiency." Again, in insisting that the continuity of Chinese history could be affirmed without explaining the Communist phase as the Confucian eternal return, Levenson wrote:

> Revulsion against the landlord system, the family system, the Confucian education has been building up for a long time in China, certainly not just since yesterday in doctrinaire directives. Though communists in power have helped such ideas along, *their sources are deep in a century and a half of unplanned western action on the earlier social structure that was offered up to the contact.*[45]

The flaw in Levenson's reasoning here is the same flaw that we have already encountered on several other occasions. The question is not whether Chinese society was in fact breaking down in the nineteenth century. Nor is it whether the intrusion of the West was one important factor in the acceleration of this breakdown. The argument is over Levenson's ready assumption that the West *alone* initiated the breakdown and remained its principal (if not exclusive) causal agent. The gathering evidence of recent years suggests that major social and economic changes were already under way in China in the eighteenth century, prior to the Western onslaught. Some of this evidence, above all the demographic, has been around for a long time and was known to Levenson. Yet Levenson (along with most other scholars of the 1950s and 1960s) was still operating in a mental world, inherited from the nineteenth century, in which it was assumed that Chinese society was immune to fundamental change from within and could therefore be transformed only as a result of a "fatal infection...from a foreign body."[46] Operating in this world it was difficult, if not impossible, to develop a more complex causal explanation of the transformation of Chinese society in the nineteenth and twentieth centuries.

In addition to initiating the breakdown of the old order, the West, in Levenson's view, also served as the primary shaping influence on the new Chinese order. His most explicit assertions in this regard were made in the 1950s, when the impact of modernization theory on American scholarship was in the ascendant and some of its more questionable premises had yet to be seriously challenged. Although modernization theory had originally developed, in part, as an alternative to the Marxist explanation of societal change, it perpetuated, ironically, the claim of Marx and other nineteenth-century thinkers that the industrialized West would create "a world after its own image." As S.N. Eisenstadt has written:

> Most of the studies of modernization in general and of convergence of industrial societies in particular, which developed in the fifties up to the mid-sixties,…stressed that the more modern or developed different societies [became], the more similar…they [would] become in their basic, central, institutional aspects, and the less the importance of traditional elements within them.[47]

Levenson, too, at least in his early writings, accepted the assumption of convergence, arguing that "as China industrialize[d], any distinction between its own culture and the West's…must become more and more blurred," that under the transforming agency of industrialization, Chinese society would become "an approximation of modern western society."[48] While it is possible that by the time of his death in 1969 he may have retreated somewhat from this stark picture of convergence – certainly he referred again and again to the distinctiveness of China's modern quest and was deeply sensitive to the Chinese need to own their own history – the whole structure of Levenson's analysis of recent Chinese history, above all the massive role that he ascribed to the West, made significant retreat contingent upon a basic rethinking of the analysis itself.

To sum up, in Levenson's perspective, modern society, as embodied in the culture of the West, acted upon Chinese culture in two ways concurrently: first, as a solvent, against which the old culture stood defenseless; and, second, as a model on which a new Chinese culture was increasingly patterned. The picture of the Chinese revolution that emerged from this perspective was one that was shaped, from beginning to end, by problems posed for China by the modern West. It was, to use Levenson's own language, a revolution against the West to join the West. There was little room in this picture for a conception of the revolution as a response, in significant measure, to indigenous problems of long standing – problems that might be aggravated by the West but were not its exclusive, or even in all instances its primary, creations. Even less was there room in Levenson's picture for the possibility that past Chinese culture might contain significant features that, far from acting as barriers to China's modern transformation, might actually assist in this transformation and take an important part in directing it.

Redefining the tradition–modernity polarity

In his assumption that Confucianism and modernity were fundamentally incompatible and that the traditional order had to be torn down before a new modern order could be built up, Levenson was joined by many other scholars of the fifties and sixties. Among the most prominent and influential of these was Mary C. Wright, whose study *The Last Stand of Chinese Conservatism* first appeared in 1957. Wright's book, which deals with the Tongzhi Restoration of 1862–74, is a model of exacting and thorough scholarship and offers valuable insights into virtually every aspect of the Confucian state on the eve of its disintegration and final collapse. The central thesis of the book, however, has borne up less well. This thesis, which Wright returns to again and again, is that "the obstacles to [China's] successful adaptation to the modern world were not imperialist aggression, Manchu rule, mandarin stupidity, or the accidents of history, but nothing less than the constituent elements of the Confucian system itself."[49]

Albert Feuerwerker's pathbreaking study of China's early industrialization, published in 1958, makes essentially the same point. Feuerwerker is less explicit than Wright and far less inclined to ringing historical pronouncements. Throughout his account, nonetheless, traditional Chinese values and institutions are treated almost exclusively as obstacles, as "barriers" to be overcome or broken through, rather than as potential sources of support for China's economic modernization.[50]

The reasoning behind this pattern of thinking (which, it should be noted in passing, was given a powerful boost by the Chinese themselves in the early decades of the twentieth century) has been challenged in recent years by a growing body of scholarly opinion, which, in defining the relationship between "modern" and "traditional," rejects the implication that they are dichotomous, mutually antithetical conditions. With reference to Chinese history in particular, Benjamin Schwartz, in his critique of Levenson's organic or holistic view of culture, insists that "areas of experience of the past may, for good or ill, continue to have an ongoing existence in the present," that " 'Chinese past' and 'modernity' may not confront each other as impenetrable wholes."[51]

The assumption of radical discontinuity between tradition and modernity is attacked in a somewhat different fashion by Lloyd and Susanne Rudolph in their illuminating study of Indian political development, *The Modernity of Tradition* (1967). The Rudolphs see the problem as being rooted in the angle of vision of the investigator. They note that when modern societies alone are the subject of investigation, there has been an increasing tendency to stress traditional survivals, whereas when modern societies are compared with traditional societies, the traditional features of the former either disappear from view or "are pictured as residual categories that have failed to yield, because of some inefficiency in the historical process, to the imperatives of modernization." This "misunderstanding of modern society that excludes its traditional features is paralleled," in the Rudolphs' view,

> by a misdiagnosis of traditional society that underestimates its modern potentialities. Those who study new nations comparatively often find only manifest and dominant values, configurations, and structures that fit a model of tradition and miss latent, deviant, or minority ones that may fit a model of modernity.

The cumulative effect of all this, the Rudolphs conclude, "has been to produce an analytic gap between tradition and modernity." The two systems are seen as "mutually exclusive," "fundamentally different and incompatible." For the one to be superseded by the other, "social engineers working with new blueprints and new materials are required. Change takes on a systemic rather than adaptive character."[52]

The attack leveled by Schwartz, the Rudolphs, and many other scholars[53] against the picture of "tradition" and "modernity" as mutually exclusive, wholly incompatible systems bears enormous potential consequences for Western understanding of the recent Chinese past. The entire structure of assumptions inherited from the nineteenth century – the perception of China as barbarian and the West as civilized; of China as static and the West as dynamic; of China as incapable of self-generated change and therefore requiring for its transformation the impact of a "force from without"; the assumption that the West alone could serve as the carrier of this force; and, finally, the assumption that, in the wake of the Western intrusion, "traditional" Chinese society would give way to a new and "modern" China, fashioned in the image of the West – this whole structure of assumptions is thoroughly shaken and a new and more complex model suggested for the relationship between past and present in a modernizing context.

It is surely no coincidence that precisely when the new understanding of the relationship between "tradition" and "modernity" was taking shape (it can be dated to the mid- to late 1960s) studies began to appear that, reflecting this new understanding, painted a sharply altered picture of the role of the past in recent Chinese history. In this picture, certain features of the past continue to be portrayed as antithetical to revolutionary change. Other features, however, not only are not seen as standing in the way of such change, but are viewed as contributing to and even shaping it. Moreover, as a direct corollary to this, the Chinese revolution itself is seen as a response not just to new problems created by the Western intrusion but also to older problems of more internal origin. The upshot has been that the past century and a half of Chinese history has regained some of its lost autonomy, and the way has been paved for a less inflated, more cautious portrayal of the part played by the West in this history.

In some of these studies the focus, either explicitly or implicitly, has been on what the Rudolphs call the "modern potentialities" of traditional society. This is a persistent theme, for example, in the collaborative volume *The Modernization of China* (1981), the contributors to which feel that, alongside a range of factors hindering China's modernization in the nineteenth and early twentieth centuries, there were also important features of the Chinese political, economic, social, and intellectual heritage that were ultimately conducive to modernization (though certain of them, having been in a state of decline since the mid-Qing, slowed China's initial response to the foreign challenge in the nineteenth century). A similar motif is found in the work of Stuart Schram, who, even while acknowledging that China's tradition has been rocked to its foundations as a result of its encounter with the modern West, insists that two features of this tradition – a sense of history and a concern for politics as one of the principal domains of life – have prepared the Chinese "exceptionally well" for survival in the modern world. Along much the same lines, though with reference to a very different realm of human activity, Dwight Perkins argues forcefully that

> traditional Chinese society appears to have nurtured within itself certain values and traits more compatible with modern economic growth than those of many other less-developed states. That is, far from being negative barriers, several principal features of Chinese society were a vital positive force once other real barriers to economic development were removed.

Similar arguments are advanced by Thomas Kennedy with reference to Chinese self-strengthening efforts in the nineteenth century and by Evelyn Sakakida Rawski in connection with late Qing literacy levels.[54]

In practically all of the new studies much attention is paid to problem areas in Chinese society, as defined by the Chinese themselves, to which modernization or revolution has held out some hope of solution. A notable example is Edward Friedman's book *Backward Toward Revolution* (1974). Although ostensibly an examination of the Chinese Revolutionary Party (Zhonghua geming dang), Friedman's study has important things to say about the fundamentally different ways in which the Chinese revolution was defined and experienced by radical intellectuals in urban China and by poor peasants in the vast Chinese hinterland.

For the former, straitjacketed by an uncompromisingly linear understanding of historical process, the past existed only to be overcome, destroyed, left behind. With Marx, Engels, and Lenin, Chinese intellectuals (liberals as much as Marxists) held to the modernizing faith "that change, the bigger the better, [was] the essence of revolution."[55] But for hundreds of millions of Chinese village-dwellers, Friedman argues, it was different. Operating within a frame of reference that was basically cyclical, they did not see their present misery as an inevitable consequence of the structure of the old society; on the contrary, they saw it as resulting from the breakdown of this society. Change in the abstract, in these circumstances, was the last thing Chinese peasants wanted. What they wanted from a revolution was not more disruption but less, not change toward some new and unknown future but the renewal and strengthening of older familial, religious, and communitarian bonds, a restored sense of the wholeness of life. "The point," Friedman stresses at the beginning of his book, "is not that there is nothing new under the sun, but rather that the force of living energy absorbed from the past helps create the power to transcend in a revolutionary fashion massive obstacles to a better future." Revolutions are complex mixtures of return and advance, of old and new. No mere restorations, they offer "another opportunity for the renewed community to come to grips with and try to solve the most basic problems of life."[56]

This ambiguous relationship between "tradition" and "revolution," in which tradition appears not merely as a barrier to revolution but also as a repository of assets for its facilitation, energizing, and legitimation, has also characterized some interpretations of Mao Zedong himself. This is particularly evident in the writings of Schram. Viewing the Sinification of Marxism as Mao's greatest theoretical and practical achievement, Schram maintains in his biography of the Chinese revolutionary that it was Mao's roots in tradition and sensitivity to "the real needs and aspirations of Chinese society in the 1920s and 1930s" that enabled him "to play the role he did."[57] Indeed, Mao eventually became persuaded – and here Schram's understanding sounds even more like Friedman's – that "in the last analysis...only iconoclasm from *within* the Chinese tradition, in a form immediately accessible to the Chinese people, would make it possible to dissolve and transcend the Confucian heritage." The Cultural Revolution, from this vantage point, "could be defined as one vast attempt...to overcome the evils inherited from the past, but to do so in original and specifically Chinese terms."[58]

Although Friedman's account of the problems to which rural revolution was addressed in twentieth-century China gives much weight to foreign imperialism, there is nothing in his analysis to suggest that the breakdown of Chinese village life was not also a result of endogenous forces – population explosion, intensifying class conflict, massive bureaucratic corruption – that predated significant foreign contact.[59] Philip Kuhn, in an article on local government in the late imperial and republican periods, is more explicit in sorting out the endogenous and exogenous aspects of change.[60] Kuhn analyzes the problems of local government in terms of three factors: control, autonomy, and mobilization. The last of these factors, insofar as it reflects the need to enlist local energies in new ways in order to promote economic growth and national power, does not appear on the scene until the late Qing. However, the need to strike an appropriate balance between control and autonomy in local government is a problem that, Kuhn tells us, has plagued Chinese rulers from the Ming dynasty right through to the Communist era. The historical context within which this problem has been manifested has, of course, changed. But the problem itself has endured for centuries and, in important respects, mocks conventionally drawn distinctions between "traditional" and "modern."

These distinctions are also blurred by some of the ideas Chinese thinkers applied to the autonomy–control problem. I have in mind, in particular, the whole complex of political theory known as *fengjian* (commonly, though inadequately, translated by the term *feudal*), which sought in one way or another to foster greater community of interest between the formal bureaucracy and the local population. Kuhn discusses the *fengjian* tradition at length and shows how it was drawn upon by a long line of political reformers stretching from Gu Yanwu in the early Qing to Feng Guifen, Kang Youwei, and finally Sun Yat-sen and other Guomindang ideologues of the twentieth century. Although by the time of Kang and Sun clear conceptual links had been forged between the *fengjian* tradition and Western ideas of representative government, Kuhn is at pains to point out that the reform measures proposed by a Feng Guifen in the 1860s, however "modern"-seeming, were entirely capable of being generated out of Feng's own intellectual inheritance.[61] Thus, both the problems of local government in twentieth-century China and the measures proposed for remedying these problems, although affected and complicated by the Western presence, were deeply rooted in the indigenous setting.

The intricate connection between "traditional" and "modern" elements posited in Kuhn's analysis of local government[62] finds rich support in recent American interpretations of the May Fourth era. Yü-sheng Lin, in his work on the radical intellectuals of this era, has maintained that, in the priority such men as Hu Shi, Chen Duxiu, and Lu Xun gave to cultural and intellectual change over social, political, and economic change and in the totalistic character of their assault on Confucianism, they were influenced unconsciously by deep-seated modes of thinking in the very tradition they were bringing under attack.[63] Jerome Grieder strikes a similar note in the distinction he draws between the liberal and radical conceptions of "politics" in the May Fourth period:

> The radicals, those who sooner or later gravitated toward the revolutionary program of Marxist–Leninist doctrine, found there a restatement…of the traditional idea that human behavior is conditioned by environment…. Though they redefined the meaning of "environment," stripping it of its Confucian moral connotations and substituting a materialist theory of social and cultural determinism, by treating culture as a derivative of political power they echoed a traditional perception.[64]

Even fiction writers of May Fourth, for all their much-vaunted iconoclasm, could not entirely escape the heritage against which they rebelled so hard. Like their literati forebears, Merle Goldman reminds us, they assumed that the essence of society was to be found in its culture and literature and that, as writers, they had a special responsibility to lead and guide their fellow countrymen.[65]

Recent work in the field of intellectual history has followed much the same pattern. In his book on Liang Qichao, Hao Chang formulates the general proposition that "it is mainly in terms of a particular set of concerns and problems inherited from Confucian tradition that Chinese intellectuals responded to the Western impact in the late Ch'ing [Qing]."[66] In the same work Chang carries this theme a step further, arguing, with later support from Don Price's book on the intelligentsia of the late Qing and I-fan Ch'eng's essay on the Hunanese thinker Wang Xianqian (1842–1918), that certain traditional value orientations – Liang's collectivism, the universalist yearnings of late Qing reformers and revolutionaries, and the concept of *gong* or "public good" in the thought of Wang – came to serve (in Ch'eng's language) "not [as] obstacles to, but driving forces behind, China's modernization."[67]

One of the most articulate spokesmen for this overall point of view has been Wm. Theodore de Bary. Taking direct issue with the perception of Neo-Confucianism as "a relentless canonization of tradition" (Max Weber) and "strait-jacket on the Chinese mind" (John Fairbank), a "dead set of values," incapable of modernizing China, de Bary insists that Neo-Confucianism does not "unfailingly serve the status quo," that it "can also stand as a critique of the existing order." Looking to the future, de Bary confidently predicts that "the new experience of the Chinese people will eventually be seen in significant part as a growth emerging from within and not simply as revolution inspired from without."[68]

Some of de Bary's key themes are developed by Thomas A. Metzger in his provocative essay *Escape from Predicament* (1977). Metzger observes that, as long as scholars were mainly intent upon explaining China's failures in modern times, the old perceptions of traditional Chinese society – among them, that it was stagnant – persisted. As China's failures have come to be overshadowed by its successes, however, a new explanation, based on a quite different reading of Chinese tradition, has come to be required.[69] It is to this ambitious task that Metzger addresses himself.

Central to Metzger's thesis is the claim that Neo-Confucians were burdened by an intense, agonizing sense of predicament. This sense of predicament had an "inner" dimension, focusing on psychological, moral, and metaphysical quandaries; it also had an "outer" side, embracing economic and political problems. The Neo-Confucian goal was to escape from this complex of predicaments by transforming self and society. This transformative impulse was, however, continually frustrated, and as the solutions put forward by one thinker after another proved inefficacious, life for Neo-Confucians took on the dismal character of a Sisyphean struggle.

The entry of the West into this situation did not, as Fairbank, Levenson, and a host of other scholars have so often told us, herald disaster; instead, it brought release. Modernization – even revolution – represented not the destruction of traditional Chinese society but its fulfillment. For turn-of-the-century Chinese modernizers, the enormous appeal of Western methods, Metzger argues, was not just the instrumentalist promise that they would make China wealthy and strong; their appeal lay even more centrally in the fact that "they seemed useful for solving agonizing problems and realizing social ideals with which Confucians had long been preoccupied."[70] For what the West brought was

> not the concept of social and economic transformation per se but the belief that with modern technology, new techniques of political participation (whether liberal or Communist), and new forms of knowledge, the "outer" realm of economic and political problems, regarded as largely intractable since the euphoria of Wang An-shih's [Anshi's] "new policies," could in fact be reformed.... As transformative action in the "outer" realm appeared ever more feasible to modern Chinese, the search for transformative power within the mind was relaxed. The "inner" predicament...became less acute and central, and a kind of Panglossian optimism spread over much Chinese thought.[71]

Max Weber, in his search for the source of a society's capacity to transform itself, hit upon the idea of "tension with the world" – the product of a society's recognition of the seemingly unbridgeable distance between its ideals and its actualities. China's failure to develop modern capitalism on its own was, in Weber's view, directly linked to what he perceived as the complete absence in the Confucian ethic of "any tension...between ethical demand and human shortcoming," resulting in a reduction of tension with the world "to an absolute minimum."[72] Weber's thesis not only provided an explanation for China's failure to generate modern capitalism; it also supplied theoretical buttressing for the popular Western image of traditional Chinese society as stagnant, as incapable of even conceiving of its own transformation, must less wishing it.[73]

Metzger, in his argument, appears to accept without hesitation the general Weberian assumption with respect to the link between psychological tension and societal change. However, in his view that Neo-Confucians, far from being oblivious to transformative impulses, literally yearned for the remaking of self and society, he departs from Weber's picture in a radical way. Equally radical is his reversal of the Levensonian picture of Confucian China and its modern fate. Where Levenson saw Confucian China as, at bottom, problem-free and judged its growing sense of problem in modern times to be the direct consequence of an overwhelming shock from without, Metzger sees a Confucian China writhing in problems – problems from which it cannot escape – until, with the coming of the West, solutions are presented that, almost magically, still the sense of problem and transform excruciating anxiety into unbounded optimism.

Weber and Levenson were, in my view, almost certainly wrong. But is Metzger right? A great deal of research will have to be done before this question can be answered. For now, I would simply like to identify two parts of his argument that strike me as being vulnerable. One is the key assumption that there was a massive sense of predicament in late imperial Confucianism. Metzger freely acknowledges, at one point, that "in saying that Neo-Confucians had a sense of predicament, we are saying something about them that they would not have said." He further maintains that the "awareness of this predicament has been filtered out of the leading modern interpretations of Neo-Confucianism."[74] Now the fact that late imperial Confucians did not make their sense of predicament explicit and that modern interpreters of Confucianism, like Tang Junyi (who is an important building block in Metzger's analysis), gloss over it does not in and of itself invalidate Metzger's claim that such a sense of predicament both existed and was pervasive.[75] It may well be, as he himself suggests, that the Neo-Confucian predicament was not made explicit just because it was taken for granted. Nevertheless, the possibility of distortion or exaggeration on Metzger's part does present itself, especially when we consider that, as a Weberian turned inside out, intent upon locating in the Chinese past the secret of China's modern success (much as Weber probed for the secret of its modern failure), Metzger would naturally be inclined to look for precisely what he claims to have found.[76]

The second part of Metzger's analysis that seems to me to be open to question is the mammoth role he ascribes to the West in recent Chinese history. In his insistence that the complex transformative movements of the late Qing cannot be reduced to a simple contrast "between imported, transformative orientations and indigenous, stagnative ones,"[77] Metzger breaks decisively with the earlier view, bequeathed by the nineteenth century, that Chinese society was fundamentally lacking in any impulse to change. However, the notion that China was in a profound bind, a predicament, from which it could escape only with help from the West, has a faintly familiar ring. It parallels Mark Elvin's contention, in *The Pattern of the Chinese Past* (1973), that the late traditional Chinese economy was caught in a "high-level equilibrium trap" ("almost incapable of change through internally generated forces"), which it was "the historic contribution of the modern West to ease and then break" by opening "the country to the world market in the middle of the nineteenth century."[78]

What is troublesome in both of these instances is less the evidence Metzger and Elvin have marshaled in support of their interpretations (though in Metzger's case it is perilously thin and in Elvin's it has been seriously questioned)[79] than the language framing the interpretations and the assumptions underlying this language. In using words like *predicament* and *trap* to characterize Chinese society on the eve of the West's appearance, a picture is conveyed of that society as being "locked into" an intolerable situation, a situation that Metzger's and Elvin's nineteenth-century forebears would, with less squeamishness, have defined as "bad." The role of the West, in this situation, is for both Metzger and Elvin implicitly "good." By presenting China with a golden key, a means of exit equally from moral-psychological predicament and economic-technological entrapment, the West has earned the undying gratitude of all Chinese. It has made it possible for the Chinese economy to renew a pattern of growth that was arrested centuries ago, and it has provided Chinese society, for the first time, with the means of transforming itself in accordance with its own ancient goals.

The interpretations advanced by Metzger and Elvin raise Chinese historical studies in the West to a level of sophistication that was unattainable a generation ago. To the extent that they cast the West in the role of China's redeemer, however, both interpretations arouse a degree of uneasiness. The reason for this is not that either interpretation is necessarily incorrect, but that both are fully consistent with a mindset based on the imperative of Western primacy. In such circumstances, a stronger empirical case than either scholar at present makes is required to allay the suspicion that Chinese history is being pressed into the service of deeply rooted subjective value preferences.

The residual grip of the nineteenth century

The hold of the nineteenth century over American scholarship on recent Chinese history has been much weakened and in some cases substantially broken. But it still persists, at least in a vestigial way. The initial assault on this hold came with the scholarship of the 1950s and 1960s, which, reacting against the "treaty port" historiography of the prewar years, worked assiduously to get "inside" Chinese culture and present the Chinese side of the story. Insofar as this approach was guided by real (if qualified) respect for a non-Western civilization, it represented an important departure from the pejorative view of China that held sway over so much of earlier scholarship. The departure, however, was incomplete. Although much attention was now paid to what was taking place within China and for the first time a serious effort was made to understand Chinese attitudes and values, using archival sources and newly published Chinese documentary collections, this understanding was achieved in terms of a framework of assumptions that granted to Chinese society little potential for self-generated change and assigned to the West almost exclusive responsibility for China's modern transformation. Mary Wright's view of the Chinese revolution as, in the broad sense, a "revolution from without," not in any significant way the product of Chinese history,[80] was typical.

This picture was sharply modified by scholarly studies that began to appear in the 1970s (other examples of which are discussed in the final chapter of *Discovering History in China*). Although these studies point in a number of different directions, they agree for the most part in seeing China's indigenous society not as an inert body acted upon by an all-transforming West but as a changing thing in itself, with its own capacity for movement and powerful inner sense of direction. To this extent, the new studies critically undermine the grip of the nineteenth century on our understanding of recent Chinese history. But insofar as they continue to be influenced by some form of the tradition–modernity contrast,[81] with its deep roots in nineteenth-century thought, they fall short of becoming fully emancipated from the world view of earlier generations.

To understand why this is so, it may be helpful in concluding this chapter to point up a number of problems that seem to be inherent in the tradition–modernity pairing, even in its most sophisticated formulations. One such problem is that the pairing's implied exclusivity forces upon us a rigidly bipolar view of reality. Even where, as in the case of the Rudolphs, tradition and modernity are seen as fluid, mutually interpenetrable states, with traditional societies containing modern potentialities and modern societies embodying traditional features, the assumption persists that all of the characteristics of a culture will arrange themselves someplace along a tradition–modernity continuum. There is no room for the possibility, occasionally alluded to by Schwartz in his writings, that there may be vitally important areas of human experience that, transcending time and space, are not readily identifiable as either "traditional" or "modern."[82]

The assumption of exclusivity is directly related to a second assumption, equally lethal, which J.H. Hexter describes as the

> assumption of the conservation of historical energy,…the idea…that in a given society the energy expended on a single pair of polar elements is fixed, so that any flow of social energy in the direction of one such pole can only take place by way of subtraction from the flow of energy to the opposite pole.

The corollary to this assumption, suggested by Hexter, is that, in any polar pair, an increase in the direction of one of the poles is *in itself* sufficient evidence of a decrease in the direction of the other pole. Hexter refutes the assumption of the conservation of historical energy by reference to the example of secular and religious activity in sixteenth-century Britain. The evidence unmistakably indicates an increase in both sorts of activity. For a long time, however, historians tacitly assumed that, because secular activity had clearly increased, there had to be a decrease in religious activity. Only when it was realized that the religious and the secular, although polar to one another, *could*, both at once, rise to higher levels of intensity, did it become possible to recognize "that they both *did* so rise in the sixteenth century."[83]

Hexter's insight may be applied, with equal profit, to the tradition–modernity polarity.[84] As Dean Tipps has noted,

> Piecemeal "modernization" need not lead to "modernity."...Indeed, the introduction of modern medicine may only compound poverty by increasing population pressures, the transistor radio may be employed merely to reinforce traditional values, and a technologically sophisticated military may be placed in the service of the most reactionary of regimes. Thus, such selective modernization may only strengthen traditional institutions and values, and rapid social change in one sphere may serve only to inhibit change in others.[85]

A particularly apposite illustration from recent history is supplied by the religious leaders of post-Shah Iran who, according to a *New York Times* analysis, used "the technology of the electronic age literally to amplify their message of a return to centuries-old ways."[86]

A modified application of this very point is found in Friedman and Metzger, both of whom (though in quite different ways) argue that a net increase in revolutionary change may go hand in hand with an intensified commitment to older values. By challenging an assumption that has been virtually ubiquitous in Chinese historical studies – the assumption that, in seesaw fashion, China will automatically become less traditional as it becomes more modern – Metzger and Friedman open the door to a whole new world of possibilities in our understanding of the recent Chinese past.

A third problem with the tradition–modernity pairing is that it employs concepts that are neatly symmetrical to describe and explain realities that are fundamentally asymmetrical. "Modernity" may indeed denote a condition with enough uniform characteristics and cross-cultural regularities to enable people who inhabit modern societies to feel themselves, in some sense, part of the same universe. "Tradition," however, refers to no correspondingly uniform condition, in either a subjective or an objective sense. Subjectively, it is inconceivable that the inhabitants of cultures as different, say, as fourteenth-century France and tenth-century China would perceive themselves as living in the same *kind* of society. Objectively, the most we can say concerning the likeness of two such cultures is that neither is "modern." This, however, is a little like saying that fish and birds are alike in not being monkeys. Defining something in terms of what it is not – the word "non-Western" is another unfortunate example – may have a kind of low-grade descriptive utility. Analytically it is a dead end.

If "tradition" fails the test of conceptual congruity, in that it does not fit the reality it purports to describe,[87] "modernity" poses problems of a quite different sort. Two such problems are of paramount concern here. One is that "modernity" is a fundamentally closed concept, with a built-in picture of historical process that is tightly unilinear and highly teleological in nature. "The very words 'modern' and 'modernity,'" Joseph LaPalombara writes,

> imply a social Darwinian model of political development. They suggest that change is inevitable, that it proceeds in clearly identifiable stages, that subsequent evolutionary stages are necessarily more complex than those which preceded them, and that later stages are better than their antecedents.[88]

LaPalombara's strictures, although made with special reference to political development, are just as pertinent to historical change in general. Closed models of change force us, often without realizing it, to shape the data of the past to fit preformed conceptual frameworks. Only with open models of change, accompanied by open-ended questions, will historians be able to form a more empirically sensitive picture of the recent Chinese past.

A second problem with "modernity" stems from what Tipps calls "the fundamental ethnocentrism of modernization theory."[89] This is a special problem for Westerners because, as moderns ourselves, we are part of the very thing we are studying. Since we got there first, we think we have the inside track on the modern condition, and our natural tendency is to universalize from our own experience. In fact, however, our taste of the modern world has been highly distinctive, so much so that John Schrecker has seen fit to characterize the West as "the most provincial of all great contemporary civilizations."

Schrecker's point is that the West alone "has had no outside view of itself" in modern times.[90] Never have Westerners had to take other peoples' views of us really seriously. Nor, like the representatives of all other great cultures, have we been compelled to take fundamental stock of our own culture, deliberately dismantle large portions of it, and put it back together again in order to survive. This circumstance has engendered what may be the ultimate paradox, namely that Westerners, who have done more than any other people to create the modern world, are in certain respects the least capable of comprehending it.[91]

This problem is particularly crippling for Western historians who, imprisoned in the parochial experience of their own modernity, seek to understand and explain processes of modernization in non-Western societies. Certainly there are degrees of sin here. And some historians will fall into traps that others will be clever enough to avoid. None of us, however, can escape entirely the cultural skins within which we live, which suggests that there may be merit in abandoning altogether the nomenclature of modernization theory – above all, the concepts "tradition" and "modernity" – and searching for alternative, less Western-centered modes of describing the large-scale processes that have overtaken the world during the past century.

Notes

This chapter is a reprint of the second chapter of *Discovering History in China: American Historical Writing on the Recent Chinese Past* (New York: Columbia University Press, 1984).

1 A notable exception is the recent volume edited by Gilbert Rozman, *The Modernization of China* (New York: Free Press, 1981). The authors of this book, several of them historians, attempt a systematic application of modernization theory to post-1700 China.

2 One critic of modernization theory, Dean C. Tipps, has argued compellingly that "modernization" is an illusion and that the entire idea should be discarded in favor of some alternative approach. See his "Modernization Theory and the Comparative Study of Societies: A Critical Perspective," *Comparative Studies in Society and History* 15 (March 1973): 199–226. Far more typical is the attitude of Raymond Grew, who, while acknowledging all of the criticisms that can be leveled at modernization theory, still feels that it can be used without harmful consequences and should be retained. See his "Modernization and Its Discontents," *American Behavioral Scientist* 21.2 (November–December 1977): 289–312.

3 Wilbert E. Moore and Neil J. Smelser, foreword, in S.N. Eisenstadt, *Modernization: Protest and Change* (Englewood Cliffs, N.J.: Prentice-Hall, 1966), p. iii.

4 See, for example, Tipps, "Modernization Theory," pp. 200–1 and passim.

5 The quotations are from Raymond Dawson, "Western Conceptions of Chinese Civilization," in Raymond Dawson, ed., *The Legacy of China* (Oxford: Clarendon Press, 1964), pp. 14–15; Herder's views are summarized in R.G. Collingwood, *The Idea of History* (Oxford: Oxford University Press, 1961), p. 90.

6 Quoted in Stuart Creighton Miller, *The Unwelcome Immigrant: The American Image of the Chinese, 1785–1882* (Berkeley: University of California Press, 1969), p. 16. An explanation of Chinese stagnation was offered by the American clergyman Josiah Strong (1893): "In Asia there have been vast organizations of society, but the development of the individual was early arrested, hence the stagnation of everything. Oriental civilization manifests unity with but little diversity, hence the dead uniformity of many centuries." Cited in Alexander Saxton, *The Indispensable Enemy: Labor and the Anti-Chinese Movement in California* (Berkeley: University of California Press, 1971), p. 279.

7 Quoted in Dawson, "Western Conceptions of Chinese Civilization," p. 14.

8 In Karl Marx, *Capital and Other Writings*, Max Eastman, ed. (New York: Modern Library, 1932), p. 325.

9 Cited in Shlomo Avineri, ed., *Karl Marx on Colonialism and Modernization* (Garden City, N.Y.: Doubleday, 1968), p. 45.

10 Levenson's major completed works were *Liang Ch'i-ch'ao and the Mind of Modern China* (Cambridge: Harvard University Press, 1953); and the individually published volumes of the trilogy, *Confucian China and Its Modern Fate*: vol. 1, *The Problem of Intellectual Continuity* (Berkeley: University of California Press, 1958); vol. 2, *The Problem of Monarchical Decay* (Berkeley: University of California Press, 1964); vol. 3, *The Problem of Historical Significance* (Berkeley: University of California Press, 1965). For a full bibliography of Levenson's writings, see Maurice Meisner and Rhoads Murphey, eds., *The Mozartian Historian: Essays on the Works of Joseph R. Levenson* (Berkeley: University of California Press, 1976), pp. 197–203.

11 See Vera Schwarcz's long review of *The Mozartian Historian*, in *History and Theory: Studies in the Philosophy of History* 17.3 (1978): 349–67.
12 Tipps, in "Modernization Theory," would take issue with this, arguing that

> though the terminology of contemporary modernization theory has been cleaned up some to give a more neutral impression – it speaks of "modernity" rather than "civilization," "tradition" rather than "barbarism" – it continues to evaluate the progress of nations, like its nineteenth-century forebears, by their proximity to the institutions and values of Western, and particularly Anglo-Saxon societies.
>
> (p. 206)

13 The reader is referred to two interesting pieces that appeared in the *New York Times* shortly after the release of the American hostages. One, by Bayly Winder, discusses the intensification of cultural stereotyping in conflict situations; the other, a confidential cable sent on August 13, 1979 (just before the hostage crisis began), from L. Bruce Laingen, the American chargé d'affaires in Teheran, to Secretary of State Vance, is a perfect example of such stereotyping (*New York Times*, January 27, 1981, p. A19; January 30, 1981, p. A27).
14 Carr, *What is History?* (New York: Vintage Books, 1961), p. 26.
15 Edwin O. Reischauer and John K. Fairbank, *East Asia: The Great Tradition* (Boston: Houghton Mifflin, 1960).
16 Fairbank, Reischauer, and Craig, *East Asia: The Great Transformation* (Boston: Houghton Mifflin, 1965), p. 5. The "change within tradition" formula was, I believe, first used by E.A. Kracke in "Sung Society: Change Within Tradition," *Far Eastern Quarterly* 14.4 (August 1955): 479–88. It is reiterated by Fairbank in the introductory chapter of John K. Fairbank, ed., *The Cambridge History of China*, vol. 10, *Late Ch'ing, 1800–1911, Part 1* (Cambridge: Cambridge University Press, 1978), pp. 6–8. It also finds support in Albert Feuerwerker, *State and Society in Eighteenth-Century China: The Ch'ing Empire in Its Glory* (Ann Arbor: Center for Chinese Studies, University of Michigan, 1976), p. 113; and in Richard Smith, "An Approach to the Study of Traditional Chinese Culture," *Chinese Culture* 19.2 (June 1978): 75.
17 Or, as Tipps puts it: "'Traditional societies' appeared changeless only because they were defined in a manner that…recognized no significant change save that in the direction of the Western experience" ("Modernization Theory," p. 213). See also Lloyd I. Rudolph and Susanne Hoeber Rudolph, *The Modernity of Tradition: Political Development in India* (Chicago: University of Chicago Press, 1972), p. 5.
18 As confirmation of this, Fairbank's account of Chinese society in the nineteenth century (mainly in chaps. 2 and 5) is liberally peppered with such words as "inertia," "equilibrium," "stability." Fairbank's early views concerning the Chinese economy on the eve of the Western intrusion reflect much the same sort of thinking. In a well-known article, written in collaboration with Alexander Eckstein and Lien-sheng Yang, he portrayed the Chinese economy in the early nineteenth century as being in a stage of "traditional equilibrium," a stage in which "minor growth, innovation and technological change may occur but…not sufficient to break the rigid and inhibiting bonds of the traditional framework of social and economic institutions." "Economic Change in Early Modern China: An Analytic Framework," *Economic Development and Cultural Change* 9.1 (October 1960): 1.
19 Immanuel C.Y. Hsü, *The Rise of Modern China* (New York: Oxford University Press, 1970), p. 6; the same passage appears in the 2nd edn. (1975), p. 6, and 3rd edn. (1983), p. 6, of Hsü's text.

20 Wittfogel, *Oriental Despotism: A Comparative Study of Total Power* (New Haven: Yale University Press, 1957), p. 420 (emphasis in original).
21 Levenson, *Confucian China and Its Modern Fate*, 1: 14.
22 For further discussion of the difference between vocabulary change and language change, see *ibid.*, 1: 156–63, also 3: 113. It is dealt with again later on in this chapter.
23 *Ibid.*, 1: 161 (emphasis supplied).
24 *Ibid.*
25 See, for example, Levenson, "The Genesis of *Confucian China and Its Modern Fate,*" in L.P. Curtis, Jr., ed., *The Historian's Workshop* (New York: Knopf, 1970), p. 282, where Levenson alludes to the variability of Confucianism over the centuries.
26 Or, as Benjamin Schwartz put it in his analysis of Levenson:

> We have something like the vital wholeness of a total culture which is able to maintain itself for centuries as a kind of durable entity. Chinese culture was not outside of history, but it was powerful enough to freeze its flow.
>   See his "History and Culture in the Thought of Joseph Levenson," in
>   Meisner and Murphey, *The Mozartian Historian*, p. 105.

27 As Arthur H. Smith, a major missionary publicist of the late nineteenth century, put it: "To attempt to reform China without 'some force from without' is like trying to build a ship in the sea; all the laws of air and water conspire to make it impossible." *Chinese Characteristics*, reprint edn. (Port Washington, N.Y.: Kennikat Press, 1970), p. 324. For comparable statements, see Jerry Israel, *Progressivism and the Open Door: America and China, 1905–1921* (Pittsburgh: University of Pittsburgh Press, 1971), p. 16; Robert McClellan, *The Heathen Chinee: A Study of American Attitudes Toward China, 1890–1905* (Columbus: Ohio State University Press, 1971), pp. 180–1.
28 Dona Torr, ed., *Marx on China, 1853–1860: Articles from the New York Daily Tribune* (London: Lawrence and Wishart, 1951), p. 4.
29 Fairbank, Reishauer, and Craig, *East Asia: The Modern Transformation*, pp. 6–7.
30 Kuhn, *Rebellion and Its Enemies in Late Imperial China: Militarization and Social Structure, 1796–1864* (Cambridge: Harvard University Press, 1970), pp. 1–2, 5–6. While the monetization of the Chinese economy was to a considerable extent due to the inflow of foreign silver and was thus of partly exogenous origin, Kuhn suggests that population explosion alone might have spelled "disaster of a new sort for traditional Chinese society" (*ibid.*, p. 51).
31 Levenson, *Confucian China and Its Modern Fate*, 1: 3.
32 See Joseph R. Levenson, ed., *European Expansion and the Counter-Example of Asia, 1300–1600* (Englewood Cliffs, N.J.: Prentice-Hall, 1967). The same sort of question underlies Levenson's discussion of the amateur–specialist dichotomy in *Confucian China and Its Modern Fate*, 1: 15–43.
33 Levenson, *Confucian China and Its Modern Fate*, 1: xix.
34 *Ibid.*, 3: 48ff. A report on a conference on the sprouts of capitalism question, convened in 1980 at Shandong University, observed that Chinese historians have been virtually unanimous in their belief that capitalist sprouts emerged in China *prior* to the Opium War (*Renmin ribao* [People's daily], February 25, 1980, p. 5). For a recent assertion of this point of view, see Liu Yao, "Cong Changjiang zhongxiayou diqu nongcun jingji de bianhua kan Taiping tianguo geming de lishi zuoyong" (The historical role of the Taiping revolution seen from the perspective of changes in the rural economy in the middle and lower reaches of the Yangzi River), *Lishi yanjiu* (Historical research) 6

(June 1979): 47–8. The authority on which discussions of this topic have centered is Mao's assertion in 1939: "As China's feudal society had developed a commodity economy, and so carried within itself the seeds of capitalism, China would, of herself, have developed slowly into a capitalist society even without the impact of foreign capitalism." *The Chinese Revolution and the Chinese Communist Party,* in *Selected Works of Mao Tse-tung,* vol. 2 (Peking: Foreign Languages Press, 1965), p. 309. See also Albert Feuerwerker, "From 'Feudalism' to 'Capitalism' in Recent Historical Writing from Mainland China," *Journal of Asian Studies* 18.1 (November 1958): 107–15; the same author's "China's History in Marxian Dress," *American Historical Review* 66.2 (January 1961): 327–30; and, more recently, Arif Dirlik, "Chinese Historians and the Marxist Concept of Capitalism: A Critical Examination," *Modern China* 8.1 (January 1982): 105–32, especially p. 106. The whole "sprouts" question is considerably complicated by the impact of the importation of foreign silver on the monetization of the Chinese economy beginning in the late Ming. See William S. Atwell, "Notes on Silver, Foreign Trade, and the Late Ming Economy," *Ch'ing-shih wen-t'i* 3.8 (December 1977): 1–33.

35 The parameters of the unfinished trilogy are outlined by Frederic Wakeman in his foreword to Joseph R. Levenson, *Revolution and Cosmopolitanism: The Western Stage and the Chinese Stages* (Berkeley: University of California Press, 1971).

36 Levenson, "The Genesis of *Confucian China and Its Modern Fate,*" p. 280.

37 Levenson, *Liang Ch'i-ch'ao,* p. 198.

38 Levenson, *Confucian China and Its Modern Fate,* 1: xvi, xix, 50, 58.

39 See Arthur Waley, *The Opium War Through Chinese Eyes* (London: Allen and Unwin, 1958).

40 Levenson, *Confucian China and Its Modern Fate,* 1: 54, 57.

41 See the careful study by Han-yin Chen Shen, "Tseng Kuo-fan in Peking, 1840–1852: His Ideas on Statecraft and Reform," *Journal of Asian Studies* 27.1 (November 1967): 61–80, especially pp. 62–4, 69.

42 Hao Chang, *Liang Ch'i-ch'ao and Intellectual Transition in China, 1890–1907* (Cambridge: Harvard University Press, 1971), pp. 3–5; Guy S. Alitto, *The Last Confucian: Liang Shu-ming and the Chinese Dilemma of Modernity* (Berkeley: University of California Press, 1979).

43 Levenson, *Liang Ch'i-ch'ao,* pp. 84–5.

44 Levenson, *Confucian China and Its Modern Fate,* 1: 158–9. See also *ibid.,* 3: 113:

> Europe and pre-modern China, reaching each other only through intellectual diffusion, had only broadened each other's cultural vocabulary...the Chinese cultural language changed in the nineteenth and twentieth centuries, when social subversion, not just intellectual diffusion, was set off by the West.

45 *Ibid.,* 1: 145, 162–3 (emphasis supplied).

46 To use Levenson's own metaphor (*ibid.,* 3: 104). For a late nineteenth-century formulation of the same idea, see n. 27. In the same vein, see James T.C. Liu's remark:

> It seems that no force – social, political, or economic – could possibly emerge from within that society itself to cause radical changes, let alone to tear apart the integration...formed over many centuries. The only force capable of causing a disintegration had to come from the outside: an overpowering assault that brought drastic changes in the economy and

economic geography, an intellectual revolution, and an institutional break-down.
"Integrative Factors Through Chinese History: Their Interaction," in James T.C. Liu and Wei-ming Tu, eds., *Traditional China* (Englewood Cliffs, N.J.: Prentice-Hall, 1970), pp. 22–3.

47 Eisenstadt, "Convergence and Divergence of Modern and Modernizing Societies: Indications from the Analysis of the Structuring of Social Hierarchies in Middle Eastern Societies," *International Journal of Middle East Studies* 8.1 (January 1977): 1; also pp. 3–4.

48 Levenson, *Liang Ch'i-ch'ao*, p. 8. Here, as well as in *Confucian China and Its Modern Fate*, 1: 187 n. 12, Levenson cited Marion Levy's *The Family Revolution in Modern China* (Cambridge: Harvard University Press, 1949) in support of his views on convergence.

49 Wright, *The Last Stand of Chinese Conservatism: The T'ung-chih Restoration, 1862–1874*, rev. edn. (New York: Atheneum, 1965), pp. 9–10; see also p. 300, where the author states: "The failure of the T'ung-chih [Tongzhi] Restoration demonstrated with a rare clarity that even in the most favorable circumstances there is no way in which an effective modern state can be grafted onto a Confucian society."

50 Feuerwerker, *China's Early Industrialization: Sheng Hsuan-huai (1844–1916) and Mandarin Enterprise* (Cambridge: Harvard University Press, 1958).

51 Schwartz, "History and Culture in the Thought of Joseph Levenson," pp. 108–9. Schwartz raises further questions concerning the tradition–modernity contrast in "The Limits of 'Tradition Versus Modernity' as Categories of Explanation: The Case of the Chinese Intellectuals," *Daedalus* 101.2 (Spring 1972): 71–88; see also his "Notes on Conservatism in General and in China in Particular," in Charlotte Furth, ed., *The Limits of Change: Essays on Conservative Alternatives in Republican China* (Cambridge: Harvard University Press, 1976), pp. 18–21.

52 Rudolph and Rudolph, *The Modernity of Tradition*, pp. 4–6.

53 See, for example, Tipps, "Modernization Theory," passim; Reinhard Bendix, "Tradition and Modernity Reconsidered," *Comparative Studies in Society and History* 9 (April 1967): 326, 345–6; Joseph R. Gusfield, "Tradition and Modernity: Misplaced Polarities in the Study of Social Change," *American Journal of Sociology* 72 (January 1967): 351–62; C.S. Whitaker, Jr., "A Dysrhythmic Process of Political Change," *World Politics* 19.2 (1967): 190–217.

54 Rozman, *The Modernization of China*, passim; Stuart Schram, *Mao Tse-tung* (New York: Simon and Schuster, 1966), p. 14; Dwight H. Perkins, ed., *China's Modern Economy in Historical Perspective* (Stanford: Stanford University Press, 1975), p. 3; Thomas L. Kennedy, "Self-Strengthening: An Analysis Based on Some Recent Writings," *Ch'ing-shih wen-t'i* 3.1 (November 1974); 9–10; Evelyn Sakakida Rawski, *Education and Popular Literacy in Ch'ing China* (Ann Arbor: University of Michigan Press, 1979), pp. 140, 149–54.

55 Friedman, *Backward Toward Revolution: The Chinese Revolutionary Party* (Berkeley: University of California Press, 1974), p. 224.

56 *Ibid.*, pp. 4, 120–1; see also pp. 118, 130–1, 136–7, 146–7, 158–9, 220–2.

57 Schram, *Mao Tse-tung*, pp. 60, 322.

58 Stuart Schram, "Introduction: The Cultural Revolution in Historical Perspective," in Stuart Schram, ed., *Authority, Participation, and Cultural Change in China* (Cambridge: Cambridge University Press, 1973), pp. 6–7.

59 To the extent that it resulted from the introduction of new food crops from the Americas, the tripling of the Chinese population between 1600 and 1850 was,

of course, only partly endogenous. Overall, however, the role of new foods was probably less crucial than other, basically internal factors. See Dwight H. Perkins, *Agricultural Development in China, 1368–1968* (Chicago: Aldine, 1969), pp. 13, 47–51, 184–5, and passim; Albert Feuerwerker, *Rebellion in Nineteenth-Century China* (Ann Arbor: Center for Chinese Studies, University of Michigan, 1975), pp. 47–8.

60 Kuhn, "Local Self-Government Under the Republic: Problems of Control, Autonomy, and Mobilization," in Frederick Wakeman, Jr., and Carolyn Grant, eds., *Conflict and Control in Late Imperial China* (Berkeley: University of California Press, 1975), pp. 257–98.

61 Feng spent time in Shanghai in the 1860s and seems to have learned something about the tradition and practice of representative government in the West. While Kuhn acknowledged that this information might have "excited resonances with [Feng's] own *feng-chien* [*fengjian*] inheritance," he did not at the time of writing (1975) feel that there was sufficient evidence to warrant the conclusion that Western ideas in this area exerted a shaping influence on Feng's thought (see *ibid.*, p. 265). In a later reassessment, partly based on new archival finds, he shifted his view on this, arguing for more substantial Western influence on some of Feng's ideas. See Kuhn, "Ideas behind China's Modern State," *Harvard Journal of Asiatic Studies* 55.2 (December 1995): 317–37. Although, on the basis of this, I would slightly adjust the phrasing of my reference to Feng Guifen's ideas in the text, I would still hold to the larger point of these pages (as, clearly, Kuhn would also), to wit, that the changes that have taken place in China over the past two centuries have involved a complex interaction between endogenous and exogenous factors, rather than a simple supersession of "tradition" by "modernity."

62 One aspect of this analysis that I have omitted from my summary is Kuhn's discussion of local elites in the late imperial and republican eras. These elites formed a vital part of the contextual framework both for the problems of local government and for the periodic efforts to resolve these problems.

63 Yü-sheng Lin, *The Crisis of Chinese Consciousness: Radical Antitraditionalism in the May Fourth Era* (Madison: University of Wisconsin Press, 1979); see also Lin's earlier essay "Radical Iconoclasm in the May Fourth Period and the Future of Chinese Liberalism," in Benjamin Schwartz, ed., *Reflections on the May Fourth Movement: A Symposium* (Cambridge: East Asian Research Center, Harvard University, 1972), pp. 23–58. The earlier piece, in terms of the argument advanced in this chapter, seems somewhat contradictory in nature. While accepting in general terms the proposition that modernization need not imply the total rejection of tradition and that "the establishment of a viable modern society [may be] greatly helped rather than impaired by some elements from a cultural tradition" (pp. 26–7), with respect to China in particular it appears to embody the spirit at least of the older position:

> The corrosion of the traditional political and cultural order was...a long and complex process that covered the whole history of Western intrusion and was affected by the lack of viable indigenous forces in traditional Chinese society which could cope with the Western challenge.
>
> (p. 28)

64 Jerome B. Grieder, "The Question of 'Politics' in the May Fourth Era," in Schwartz, *Reflections on the May Fourth Movement*, p. 99.

65 Merle Goldman, introduction, in Merle Goldman, ed., *Modern Chinese Literature in the May Fourth Era* (Cambridge: Harvard University Press, 1977), p. 5. Guy Alitto, commenting on the motives underlying Liang

Shuming's behavior in 1917, makes the same point: "Responsibility for the spiritual and material welfare of the people was what he had been born to. It was also natural that he should call on the educated to come forth and fulfill their responsibility to society" (*The Last Confucian*, p. 61).

66 Hao Chang, *Liang Ch'i-ch'ao and Intellectual Transition in China*, p. 3.

67 *Ibid*., passim. I-fan Ch'eng's "*Kung* as an Ethos in Late Nineteenth-Century China: The Case of Wang Hsien-ch'ien (1842–1918)," in Paul A. Cohen and John E. Schrecker, eds., *Reform in Nineteenth-Century China* (Cambridge: East Asian Research Center, Harvard University, 1976), pp. 170–80. Don Price's book is entitled *Russia and the Roots of the Chinese Revolution, 1896–1911* (Cambridge: Harvard University Press, 1974).

68 See de Bary's introduction in Wm. Theodore de Bary *et al.*, eds., *The Unfolding of Neo-Confucianism* (New York: Columbia University Press, 1975), especially pp. 1–2, 32; also the interview with him in Paul M. Evans, "Fairbank: Intellect and Enterprise in American China Scholarship, 1936–1961," Ph.D. dissertation, Dalhousie University, Halifax, Nova Scotia, 1982, p. 381, n. 35.

69 Thomas A. Metzger, *Escape from Predicament: Neo-Confucianism and China's Evolving Political Culture* (New York: Columbia University Press, 1977), p. 197.

70 *Ibid.*, p. 17.

71 *Ibid.*, pp. 214–15.

72 See *ibid.*, pp. 3–4, 200–1; Max Weber, *The Religion of China*, trans. Hans Gerth (Glencoe, Ill.: Free Press, 1951), pp. 226–49.

73 Metzger notes the Weberian influence on S.N. Eisenstadt's picture of Confucian ideology as "stagnative" and "nontransformative" (*Escape from Predicament*, p. 4).

74 *Ibid.*, pp. 49, 160.

75 *Ibid.*, pp. 39–40.

76 Which is, of course, exactly what Weber did also. It is hard to conceive of how *any* ethical system can exist that does not center on the tension between ethical demand and human shortcoming. Two of the basic texts of Neo-Confucianism, the *Book of Mencius* and the *Analects*, develop this tension on virtually every page. (What are Confucius's assertions concerning the difficulty of attaining *ren*, if not a statement of profound human shortcoming?) Yet Weber, because he apparently *assumed* an absence of ethical tension in Confucianism, was unable to "see" what lay before his very eyes. H.D. Harootunian, although using a very different vocabulary in his analysis, arrives at a similar concern over Metzger's emphasis on the centrality of the Neo-Confucian sense of predicament. See his "Metzger's Predicament," *Journal of Asian Studies* 39.2 (February 1980): 251.

77 Metzger, *Escape from Predicament*, p. 211.

78 Elvin, *The Pattern of the Chinese Past: A Social and Economic Interpretation* (Stanford: Stanford University Press, 1973), pp. 312–15. Elvin, although British, has acknowledged his intellectual indebtedness to a number of American scholars. The influence that he, in turn, has exerted on American economists and economic historians is undeniable. See, for example, the discussion of Robert Dernberger's ideas in Cohen, *Discovering History in China*, p. 140.

79 See, for example, Nathan Sivin's review article "Imperial China: Has Its Present Past a Future?" *Harvard Journal of Asiatic Studies* 38.2 (December 1978): 449–80, especially pp. 459–62, 477–80; further reservations are noted in *Discovering History in China*, p. 218, notes 72 and 73.

80 Mary C. Wright, "Revolution from Without?" *Comparative Studies in Society and History* 4 (1962): 247.

81 This has been especially true of studies in the subfield of intellectual history. My own book *Between Tradition and Modernity: Wang T'ao and Reform in Late Ch'ing China* (Cambridge: Harvard University Press, 1974) may be cited as one example. Another is Alitto's *The Last Confucian*. Alitto's subject, Liang Shuming, believed that Confucianism not only was not incompatible with Chinese modernization, but was the only possible basis for such modernization. Alitto himself, clearly unpersuaded by Liang, at times seems to come close to the older view of the absolute incompatibility between tradition (at least Liang's version of it) and modernity; see, for example, pp. 274–8.

82 See, for example, Schwartz, "History and Culture in the Thought of Joseph Levenson," passim; see also Cohen, *Between Tradition and Modernity*, pp. 88–90.

83 J.H. Hexter, *Reappraisals in History* (New York: Harper and Row, 1963), pp. 40–3.

84 See L.E. Shiner, "Tradition/Modernity: An Ideal Type Gone Astray," *Comparative Studies in Society and History* 17 (1975): 252.

85 Tipps, "Modernization Theory," p. 215; see also Bendix, "Tradition and Modernity Reconsidered," pp. 316, 329.

86 *New York Times*, November 9, 1980, p. 1.

87 For an illuminating critique of the notion of "traditional society," see Tipps, "Modernization Theory," pp. 212–13. Shiner argues that, since the tradition–modernity polarity ought properly to be construed as an ideal type, any efforts to make it empirically descriptive are *in principle* wrong. The lack of congruity between the concept of "tradition" and the empirical reality of "traditional societies" is, for him, beside the point ("Tradition/Modernity," passim).

88 Joseph LaPalombara, "Bureaucracy and Political Development: Notes, Queries, and Dilemmas," in Joseph LaPalombara, ed., *Bureaucracy and Political Development* (Princeton: Princeton University Press, 1963), pp. 38–9.

89 Tipps, "Modernization Theory," p. 216. The Western-centric bias of modernization theory has been widely noted. See, for example, Ali A. Mazrui, "From Social Darwinism to Current Theories of Modernization," *World Politics* 21.1 (October 1968): 69–83.

90 Schrecker, "The West in Outside Perspective: An Introduction to the Intercultural-Historical Method" (unpublished paper), p. 2. Compare Schrecker's observation with the following three declarations by Denis de Rougement, in *The Meaning of Europe* (London: Sidgwick and Jackson, 1963), p. 12:

1 Europe discovered the whole of the earth, and nobody ever came and discovered Europe.
2 Europe has held sway on all the continents in succession, and up till now has never been ruled by any foreign power.
3 Europe has produced a civilization which is being imitated by the whole world, while the converse has never happened.

See also Ruth Benedict who, in discussing the psychological consequences of the spread of the white man's culture into every corner of the world, wrote:

This world-wide cultural diffusion has protected us as man had never been protected before from having to take seriously the civilizations of other peoples; it has given to our culture and [sic] massive universality that we have long ceased to account for historically, and which we read off rather as necessary and inevitable.
Patterns of Culture (New York: Mentor Books, 1952), pp. 5–6.

91 This paradox is perfectly illustrated in a statement made by Edward Shils:

> At present [1961] the whole intellectual world outside the West, even the
> most creative parts of that world, is in a state of provinciality. It is preoc-
> cupied with Western achievements, it is fascinated and drawn to the
> intellectual output of the West. Even Japan, the Soviet Union and China,
> which in their different ways have many greatly creative intellectuals, are
> concerned with the West, and not just for reasons of state or for military
> and strategic reasons. They are transfixed by its shining light. They lack
> intellectual self-confidence and intellectual self-esteem.

On one level, Shils is quite correct (and needlessly defensive) in characterizing
the West as the world's intellectual center and everything outside the West as
the provinces. What he fails to see is that on another level it is the West that
exists "in a state of provinciality" by virtue of the fact that of all the cultures of
the modern world it alone has not had the experience of having a center
outside itself by which *it* is, in some sense, "transfixed." See Edward Shils, *The
Intellectual Between Tradition and Modernity: The Indian Situation* (The
Hague: Mouton, 1961), p. 13.

3 New perspectives on the Boxers

The view from anthropology

In *History in Three Keys: The Boxers as Event, Experience, and Myth* (Columbia University Press, 1997), in an effort to present a clearer picture of what exactly historians do when they write history, I examine the distinctive characteristics of the three ways of apprehending or "knowing" the past indicated in the book's subtitle. To ground the theoretical argument I focus on a single – and in many ways highly singular – historical episode, the Boxer movement and uprising of 1898–1900. The theoretical side of the book is discussed in Chapter 8 of this volume. What I would like to dwell on here is how my treatment of the Boxer episode differs from the approaches Chinese historians have tended to follow.[1]

Although the Boxer uprising has in recent years attracted growing attention from Western historians,[2] over the past half century or so it has elicited far more widespread interest among historians in China. Chinese historians have scrutinized the Boxers from many different vantage points. But, despite this variation, it is possible to identify a number of commonly encountered characteristics, resulting in part from Marxist ideology, in part from the influence of centuries-old Chinese historiographical patterns. First, Chinese historians have returned again and again to certain well-defined questions: the nature of the Boxer movement (whether, for example, it was related to the White Lotus sect and had antidynastic pretensions), matters of organization and leadership, the causes of the uprising (with particular stress on the intensification of imperialism in the last years of the nineteenth century), the movement's social composition, its immediate antecedents (the Plum Flower Boxers, the Spirit Boxers, the Big Sword Society), its chronology, and so forth. Second, there has been a great deal of emphasis, especially during the post-Cultural Revolution years, on the collection, editing, compilation, and publication of primary sources relating to the Boxers (including oral history accounts). Third, Chinese historians (including the very best) regularly introduce explicit value judgments into their assessments of the Boxer movement. That is, they regard it as perfectly appropriate to embed in their analyses the language of praise and blame: the Qing court is excoriated as hopelessly reactionary; the foreigners are denounced for their arrogance and brutality;

the Boxer movement is acclaimed for its patriotic resistance to imperialist aggression; Boxer beliefs and behavior are condemned as backward, irrational, and superstitious. Finally (although I want to emphasize that this is by no means a complete inventory of the attributes of Boxer historiography in China), Chinese historians have been quite parochial in their treatment of the Boxers, rarely attempting to compare them with similar phenomena in other societies; cross-cultural comparison in general does not appear to be seen as a valuable exercise for historians to engage in.

Before indicating some of the ways in which my own approach differs from that of Chinese colleagues, let me briefly describe the design of *History in Three Keys*. The book is divided into three parts, each of which is preceded by a prologue in which the broader issues pertaining to that part are introduced. The first part, entitled "The Boxers as Event," contains a single chapter in which the sequence of events comprising the Boxer episode is presented in narrative form. Part 2, "The Boxers as Experience," is divided into five chapters, each of which probes in depth some facet of the experiential context characterizing the North China plain in the spring and summer of 1900. The areas of experience covered are: drought and the foreign presence, mass spirit possession, magic and female pollution, rumor and rumor panic, and death. The third part of the book ("The Boxers as Myth") examines how the Boxers were mythologized in China at three different points in the twentieth century: the period of the New Culture movement (pre-May Fourth), the anti-imperialist 1920s, and the Cultural Revolution. In the book's conclusion I take up several additional issues:

1   the degree to which the Boxers may be viewed as representative in terms of the larger theoretical questions addressed;
2   the comparative validity of event, experience, and myth as ways of knowing the past;
3   my own role as author (the consciousness of the historian) in the book's several parts.

(These issues are treated in depth in Chapter 8 in this volume.)

In the ensuing discussion of divergences between my approach to the Boxers and the approaches of Chinese historians, I will mainly focus on the middle part of *History in Three Keys*, the part that, at least so far, has proved of greatest interest to Western historians of China.[3] This part, which deals with the past as experience, is by far the longest section of the book. In it I borrow heavily from the ideas, strategies, and researches of anthropologists.

Dense description

One of the things I try to do in the second part of *History in Three Keys* is establish the mood or ambience that prevailed in North China during the spring and summer of 1900, not only among the Boxers but also among non-Boxer Chinese, Christians (native and foreign), and nonmissionary foreigners (soldiers, diplomats, engineers, and the like). Since one of my main interests in this part is in capturing, as accurately as possible, what was on people's minds at the time, I make abundant use of contemporary sources, in particular the published notices of the Boxers, the diaries and eyewitness chronicles of elite Chinese (mainly from the Beijing and Tianjin areas and the Taiyuan region in Shanxi), and the letters and journals (many unpublished) of foreign participants and observers. The latter two categories of materials are full of fascinating detail about Boxer beliefs, particularly in regard to magic and female pollution power, but since their authors generally take an anti-Boxer stance, I worried at first about the reliability of this information. My worries were, fortunately, allayed when, upon reading the Boxer oral history materials, I encountered extensive corroboration of the claims made in elite Chinese and foreign sources. According to a former Boxer from the Tianjin area, to cite a single example, the local Boxer leader Cao Futian is said to have announced to his men, as they were advancing toward the Laolongtou Railway Station to attack the Russians: "All of you who are empty-handed, with no weapon, take a stalk of *gaoliang* and continue your forward advance. When you get to the front lines, it will turn into a real gun."[4] (See Figure 3.1.)

Although I knew from the moment I embarked on the research for *History in Three Keys* that one of the things I wanted to explore was the experiential side of the past, I had no idea how to go about it. Initially I thought I would arrange the chapters in this part of the book around such universal characteristics of the experienced past as indeterminacy (or outcome-blindness), cultural construction, biographical (as opposed to historical) consciousness, and multiple motivation. The trouble with this approach was that it was abstract and bloodless, too far removed from the immediacy and concreteness of actual lived experience. I was at a real impasse, therefore, until one summer, early on in my research, I read through several dozen contemporary accounts, contained mainly in *Gengzi jishi* (A record of the events of 1900) (Beijing, 1978) and the four-volume collection *Yihetuan* (The Boxers) (Shanghai, 1951), asking myself: What are the themes the authors of these accounts keep returning to? This question broke the impasse, for it became patently clear as I read that there were indeed certain aspects of the experiential setting of North China in 1900 that attracted the attention of one writer after another. Among them were the social and psychological effects of the prolonged drought, the religious and magical beliefs of the Boxers, the unusual credulousness of the populace as reflected in its eagerness to accept as true the most far-fetched rumors, and the ubiquitous experience of violent and horrific death. I decided that if these were the things people were paying attention to (foreigners, it turned out, as well as Chinese), the best way to retrieve

Figure 3.1 Boxer leader Cao Futian on horseback.

Source: *Jing-Jin quanfei jilüe* (Hong Kong: Xianggang Shuju, 1901).

some sense of what it was like to be alive and conscious in North China at the time was to provide my readers with an in-depth descriptive account of these areas of contemporary experience.

In pursuit of this goal, in the book I delve into certain facets of the experiential setting in far greater detail than is ordinarily the case in Chinese (or Western) writing on the Boxers. The most unusual example perhaps is the chapter on death, a theme that to the best of my knowledge no Boxer historian in China or the West has ever focused on. When the story of the Boxer uprising is told, the high points, depending on one's point of view, are generally the characteristics of the Boxers as a movement (their fearlessness, superstition, backwardness, xenophobia, patriotism), or the place of the uprising in the history of Chinese resistance to imperialist aggression, or the martyrdom endured by the Christian community, or the righteousness and heroism of the foreign military response, or the consequences of the Boxer crisis (and its resolution) for China's subsequent history. We of course hear of the deaths that occurred. But, more often than not, this part of the story is told in the flat, impersonal language of statistics. Death, in such accounts, becomes a collective marker. It stands as a metaphor for the cruelty of the Boxers, or the brutality of the foreign relief forces, or the suffering of the Christians, or the slaying of innocents. But its meaning as an expression of individual experience is largely lost. It is this experiential side of death that I try to reclaim in the book, focusing on the death and destruction that resulted from combat and other acts of violence.

Apart from such actualized death, there was of course the much broader phenomenon of death anxiety, which was pervasive in North China in 1900. Farmers idled by the continued failure of the rains in the spring became progressively more hungry and also progressively more nervous, especially (one imagines) those of them over 30 who retained vivid memories of the catastrophic drought of the late 1870s when close to 10 million people starved to death (Figures 3.2 and 3.3). Young Boxers spent many hours learning and practicing invulnerability rituals designed

Figures 3.2 and 3.3 Images of starvation from the North China famine of the late 1870s. These images originally appeared in a Chinese pamphlet. In *Figure 3.2* the starving stand in pools of blood; in *Figure 3.3* a corpse is being carved up to provide food for the living.

Source: Committee of the China Famine Relief Fund, *The Famine in China* (London: C. Kegan Paul, 1878).

to confer immunity to death, and much of the Boxers' magic was specifically directed either at ensuring the death of their foes or protecting against the death of their supporters among the general population. The anxiety rumors that were rampant throughout the region in the spring and summer – the most widespread was the charge that foreigners and Chinese Christians were poisoning people's wells – typically had as their central content images of death or grave bodily harm; even the wish rumors that also had wide circulation may plausibly be seen as providing emotional release from the fear of death. Finally, as if other sources of death anxiety were not already abundant enough, notices posted all over North China repeatedly concluded with dire warnings of the terrible fate certain to befall those who chose to ignore the Boxers' message (Figure 3.4).

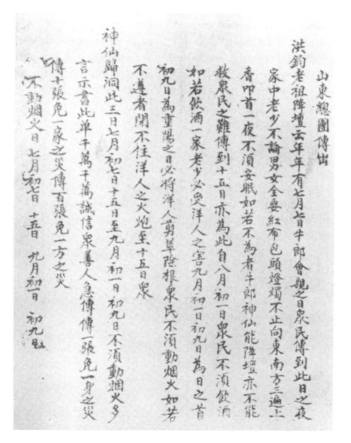

Figure 3.4 Boxer notice. This fairly representative Boxer notice, issued from Shandong, contains a variety of instructions to the populace. Those who disobey the instructions, the notice asserts, will be defenseless against foreign gunfire. By circulating the notice people will safeguard themselves and their families against calamity.

Source: *Yihetuan dang'an shiliao* (Beijing: Zhonghua Shuju, 1959), vol. 1.

Different individuals in 1900 experienced death in different ways. Some were victims, others perpetrators, still others witnesses. Some wrote of the sights and sounds of death – and of death's distinctive smells. Others described the terrors that they personally or people they knew or had observed had gone through in the face of death. And many recounted the fearful choices that had to be made. The experience of death, in short, like the experience of anything, was a highly individual matter. It was also supremely biographical. History, after all, does not die, nor does society. It is the individual who dies. Because of death's unique properties as both the terminator and terminus of life, the fear and apprehension surrounding it are key to the formation of biographical consciousness; they tend to pull people away from history and society, toward an intense concern with their own personal destinies.

Much of the literature on death, I discovered when I first looked, is concerned with the formal and informal rituals people in different cultures have devised to ease the transition across this greatest, and most final, of life's divides. However, as the following eyewitness description from the Tianjin area makes clear, a great deal of the death that people in China experienced in the summer of 1900 was raw death, unmediated by ritual of any kind (Figure 3.5):

> There were many corpses floating in the river. Some were without heads, others were missing limbs. The bodies of women often had their nipples cut off and their genitalia mutilated.... There were also bodies in the shallow areas by the banks, with flocks of crows pecking away at them. The smell was so bad we had to cover our noses the whole day. Still, no one came out to collect the bodies for burial. People said that they were all Christians who had been killed by the Boxers and the populace dared not get involved.[5]

And, so, death, the ultimate object of the anxiety that was so pervasive at the time, also, because of the way in which it was encountered, became an added source of this very anxiety.

Disciplinary pluralism

Although *History in Three Keys* is written from the point of view of a historian and is primarily concerned with addressing issues of importance in the writing of history, it draws, at times heavily, on the insights of other disciplines, including literature, psychology, philosophy, comparative religion, sociology, and above all anthropology. I found the evidence from comparative religion, for example, extraordinarily helpful in elucidating the role played in the Boxer world by drought. In Boxer notices that began circulating throughout North China in the winter of 1899–1900 a clear link was established between the severe drought that had overtaken much

Figure 3.5 Bodies floating in the Baihe in Tianjin. This photograph, taken by James Ricalton, also shows shell-damaged buildings along the French bund.

Source: Courtesy of the Library of Congress.

of the region and the growing presence of foreigners and foreign influences (in particular Christianity). The gods were angry, announced one notice after another, and they would permit the rains to fall again only after all foreigners and foreign influences had been completely eliminated from China. (On this point, see also Chapter 4 in this volume.) A notice pitched directly at Chinese Christians in Taigu, Shanxi, went as follows:

> The gods of happiness and wealth issue these instructions for the information of the members of the Catholic and Protestant religions: You have abandoned the gods and done away with your ancestors, causing the gods to be angry so that the rains do not fall from the sky. Before long heavenly soldiers and heavenly generals will descend to

earth and wage a great battle with the adherents of your two religions. It is a matter of great urgency that you quickly join the Boxers and sincerely mend your ways.[6]

In an ecological setting in which people periodically suffered from severe hunger, owing to actions of nature that were unpredictable and beyond human control, the most natural thing in the world for many of society's members was to predicate a supernatural connection between the immediate cause of the hunger – lack of precipitation – and some form of inappropriate human action – the intrusion, in this case, of a foreign religious rival – that was perceived as upsetting the normal balance of the cosmos. Such thinking had been deeply etched in Chinese cultural behavior for centuries. What was fascinating for me was the discovery that it is a pattern that has also been widely displayed in other cultures (especially agrarian ones) in many different historical eras.

A classic statement of the logic informing this construction is found in the Hebrew Bible, where God announces to His chosen people:

> If you will earnestly heed the commandments I give you this day, to love the Lord your God and to serve Him with all your heart and all your soul, then I will favor your land with rain at the proper season – rain in autumn and rain in spring – and you will have ample harvest of grain and wine and oil. I will assure abundance in the fields for your cattle. You will eat to contentment. Take care lest you be tempted to forsake God and turn to false gods in worship. For then the wrath of the Lord will be directed against you. He will close the heavens and hold back the rain; the earth will not yield its produce. You will soon disappear from the good land which the Lord gives you.[7]

Other examples abound. Muslims in Nigeria in 1973 interpreted the drought of that year as a sign of "the wrath of Allah against mankind." For Christians in late Elizabethan England, the famine of the 1590s "showed that God was angry with the people."[8] In Botswana in the nineteenth century it was widely believed that a prolonged drought was caused by the incursions of Christianity, especially after a renowned rainmaker, upon being baptized, abandoned his rainmaking practices. When, after a series of disastrous years, the local missionary (David Livingstone) left and the tribe of the converted rainmaker also moved elsewhere, sure enough, the drought broke.[9]

Much of the reading I did relating to comparative religion was written by anthropologists. It is now widely accepted that the core religious practice of the Boxers as they fanned out across the North China plain in the spring and summer of 1900 was spirit possession – a transformative religious experience in which a god (or spirit) descends and enters the body of an individual who then becomes the possessing god's instrument.[10] There are many descriptions of the possession ritual both by contemporary eye-witnesses and by former Boxers (in oral history materials collected mainly in the 1950s and 1960s); some accounts describe the physical and behavioral characteristics of possessed Boxers, others the sense of empowerment derived from the trance experience. Boxer spirit possession, as the following firsthand account (from Chiping, Shandong) suggests, was closely tied to the martial arts, to Boxer invulnerability claims, and to the stock operatic characters who formed part of the cultural world of even the lowliest Chinese farmer from early childhood:

> When we took up Spirit Boxing [Shenquan], we were first told…to write down on a piece of red paper our names, home villages, and how many we were. The six of us then kneeled down and burned incense; we didn't burn white paper. We requested teachers. I requested Sun Bin. They requested Liu Bei, Zhang Fei,* and such people. We requested the gods to attach themselves to our bodies. When they had done so, we became Spirit Boxers, after which we were invulnerable to swords and spears, our courage was enhanced, and in fighting we were unafraid to die and dared to charge straight ahead. This is how it was when the six of us became Spirit Boxers.[11]

The anthropological literature on spirit possession, both within China and in many other parts of the world, is extensive; reading in it helped me to place Boxer possession in a wider context, thereby clarifying its meaning and functions within the movement. Anthropologists often view spirit possession as a response to crisis, either individual or collective. When faced with personal crises, individuals in all parts of China have for centuries sought out the services of spirit mediums.[12] These people, when in the possessed state, serve as intermediaries between ordinary human beings and the supernatural. They heal the sick, exorcise evil spirits, predict the future, mediate interpersonal conflicts, enable barren women to become pregnant. Although mediums perform a range of different services and spirit mediumship has assumed different forms in different parts of the Chinese culture area, in general the accent is on *communication* between the supernatural and human worlds. Spirit mediumship is a "helping profession," and the individual spirit medium, by virtue of his or her training and aptitude, is not infrequently seen as performing a protective function on behalf of the local community, safeguarding the community against the whole array of dangerous and malevolent forces to which ordinary people are subject.

---

* Sun Bin was a one-legged warrior of the Warring States period (403–221 B.C.E.). Liu Bei was a political leader, Zhang Fei a general, during the Three Kingdoms period (third century C.E.). Liu and Zhang were also characters in the *Romance of the Three Kingdoms*.

Although the physical symptoms accompanying trance, as experienced by the Boxers, seem very much like those presented by Chinese spirit mediums,[13] suggesting a common neurophysiological basis, the sociocultural meaning of Boxer spirit possession was fundamentally different. Prior to the winter of 1898–9, it is true, the Spirit Boxers in northwestern Shandong (the direct antecedents of the Yihe Boxers)* were much concerned with healing the sick, especially after the disastrous flooding of the Yellow River that took place in August and September, 1898. Also, even after this date, as the purpose of Boxer possession shifted increasingly to invulnerability (as a consequence of the rising levels of violence between Boxers and Christians), possession trance continued to be seen as serving a protective function with regard to the community.

In other respects, however, Boxer possession functioned in very different ways from the possession accompanying Chinese spirit mediumship. For one thing, even before the winter of 1898–9, possession among the Spirit Boxers was a *mass*, not an individual, phenomenon. And, for another, although the Boxers in their placards and public notices and on their flags frequently referred to their role as protectors of the Qing dynasty or of China (Figure 3.6),[14] one senses very strongly that, on a personal level, the overwhelming object of Boxer invulnerability rituals was less community protection than *self*-protection.

Erika Bourguignon, looking at possession trance globally, distinguishes between societies, such as Palau (in the western Pacific), in which possession trance plays a predominantly *public* role, serving the needs of the community, and societies – the Shakers of St. Vincent in the West Indies or the Maya Apostolics of Yucatán – in which the function of trance is a mainly *private* one, focusing on its importance for the individual, "who believes himself 'saved' as a result of the experience and...derives euphoria and personal strength from it."[15] Bourguignon sees these ideal-typical functions of trance, the public and the private, as endpoints of a continuum and she recognizes that, in some societies, possession appears to serve both roles simultaneously. Certainly this was the case with the Boxers. In fact it would not be wide of the mark to argue that the broad range of individual (private) needs spirit possession satisfied within the context of the Boxer movement (the precise mix varying from one Boxer to another) constituted a major reason for the ease with which Boxer possession developed into a mass (public) phenomenon in the last years of the nineteenth century. Self-preservation, in an immediate sense, and national preservation, on a more abstract level, were mutually reinforcing.

---

* There were many different forms of Chinese boxing: Spirit Boxing (Shenquan), Plum Flower Boxing (Meihuaquan), Red Boxing (Hongquan), Monkey Boxing (Houquan), and so on. The group that launched the uprising of 1899–1900 and that are known to Westerners as the "Boxers" were the Yihe Boxers (Boxers United in Righteousness).

Figure 3.6 Boxer flag. Inscribed on the flag is the most widely encountered Boxer slogan, "Fu-Qing mieyang" (Support the Qing, destroy the foreign).

Source: Zhang Haipeng, ed., *Jianming Zhongguo jindaishi tuji* (Beijing: Changcheng Chubanshe, 1984).

Anthropologization of the West

Anthropologists are trained to view the peoples they study nonjudgmentally and are prepared, at least implicitly, to subject themselves to the same standards of ethnographic scrutiny they apply to others. In regard to religious phenomena in particular – conversion experience, spirit possession, magic, and so on – they do not assume, as a stated or unstated given, the superiority or greater perfection of the religious experience and practice of their own community. Whatever they may believe and value on a personal level, they are disciplined to keep such beliefs and values from intruding, any more than is absolutely necessary, into their professional judgments.

In *History in Three Keys* I adhere to this code of anthropological practice as faithfully as possible, resulting in an assessment of Boxer thought and behavior that differs sharply from that of most Chinese historians. First, in contrast with almost all Chinese historians, I scrupulously avoid using pejorative terms like "superstitious" or "ignorant" or "backward" to describe the beliefs and practices of the Boxers.[16] To define such beliefs and practices as "superstitious" is, in my view, to adopt an essentially adversarial stance toward them, making it more difficult to acquire a deeper appreciation of how they appeared to the Boxers themselves and the functions they served in the Boxers' intellectual and emotional worlds.

Second, in my development of various aspects of the experiential world of the Boxers, I make it a point wherever possible to counteract the Boxers' exceptionalism, to remove them from the realm of the strange and exotic. In part I do this by paying close attention to the extraordinary emotional climate that characterized North China in 1900 – the unusual levels of excitement, anger, jitteriness, and above all fear and anxiety that prevailed among all groups, Chinese and foreign, in the context of the problems and dilemmas confronting Chinese society at the time. Emotions are a great leveler. In part also I show that in important respects the Boxers' responses to the problems they faced were not all that different from the responses of people in other cultures, including the cultures of Europe and America, when faced with comparable difficulties.

Let me supply a few examples. We have already seen how common it is the world over to view drought as supernatural in origin. Predictably, among people who hold to such a view, both in China and elsewhere, a characteristic response to drought is direct propitiation of the gods through prayer or other rain-inducing ceremonial practices. Our intuition, however, prompts us to reserve such a response to "backward" societies with low educational attainments; it is not something we would anticipate encountering, say, in modern secular America, with its general trust in scientific explanation of the physical world and its extraordinary techno-logical capability. How surprising, then, to discover that when a serious drought hit the Midwest in the summer of 1988, Jesse Jackson, then campaigning for the Democratic nomination for President, prayed for rain in the middle of an Iowa cornfield, and an Ohio florist flew in a Sioux medicine man from one of the Dakotas to perform a rainmaking cere-mony, which thousands came to watch.[17]

Another example has to do with magic and how people in different cultures respond when magic doesn't work. Chinese, as well as foreigners, who have written on the Boxer movement, either as contemporary witnesses or latter-day scholars, have consistently ridiculed the movement's vaunted magical powers. This mocking stance has, for reasons that are plain enough, been displayed with greatest frequency in connection with the Boxers' invulnerability claims. "If the bandits' magic can protect against gunfire," the staunchly anti-Boxer official Yuan Chang intoned, "how is it that on the seventeenth and eighteenth days [of the fifth month of *gengzi*, i.e. June 13–14, 1900], when the bandits launched repeated assaults against the legation quarters on East Jiaomin Lane (Legation Street), the foreign soldiers' firing instantly killed several bandits?"[18] The American missionary Luella Miner, after reporting that a band of 30–40 Boxers had scattered when fired on by marines in Beijing on June 14, quipped: "These bullet-proof Boxers don't seem to like the smell of foreign powder!"[19] Chinese scholars, while honoring the Boxers for their patriotic resistance to foreign aggression, have been equally dismissive of Boxer magical claims. "The 'magical powers' of the Boxers weren't magic at all," writes one historian,

> they were simply a combination of traditional *qigong* [deep-breathing exercises], sorcery, and martial arts. Although that acclaimed mystery of mysteries, the Boxer technique of rendering oneself impenetrable to swords and spears, had a credible component, it was mostly a matter of deliberate exaggeration and artful deception.[20]

There are a number of points to be made here. First, we have compelling evidence that the Christian antagonists of the Boxers operated from a perspective, with respect to magicoreligious protection, that was broadly similar to that of the Boxers themselves: Chinese Catholic survivors in southeastern Zhili apparently believed that the appearance of the Virgin Mary above their church was instrumental in safeguarding them from a number of Boxer attacks between December 1899 and July 1900,[21] and foreign missionaries (Protestant as well as Catholic), threatened by fire, regularly attributed life-saving shifts in the direction or strength of the wind to the hand of God.[22] (See Chapter 4 of this volume.)

Second, I would argue that the empirical-efficacy test applied by all critics of Boxer magical beliefs, generally leading to the conclusion that these beliefs were ineffective, largely misses the point. When the rites of medieval Catholics failed to result in miracles, people didn't stop performing them. When Protestant prayers for deliverance in the summer of 1900 went unanswered, the Christian faith of those who survived often became even stronger. Prayers and other ceremonies designed to induce rain sometimes "work" and sometimes don't, yet it seems an invariable rule the world over that when drought conditions prevail the stock of rain-makers goes up. Empirical efficacy, as a test of magicoreligious validity, is the ultimate cheap shot and as such has been universally used to discredit other people's beliefs. And yet people, even of "high cultural level," continue to believe. They continue to make, as hardheaded psychologists who study superstition are apt to put it, "false correlations between a particular act and a particular result."[23] Why?

This is a difficult question, and it is answered differently in different religious settings. One answer questions the very premise on which the challenge to magicoreligious ritual is often founded, to wit, that such ritual must be immediately and discernibly efficacious. Thus, Mary Douglas writes of the Dinka herdspeople of the southern Sudan: "Of course Dinka hope that their rites will suspend the natural course of events. Of course they hope that rain rituals will cause rain, healing rituals avert death, harvest rituals produce crops. But instrumental efficacy is not the only kind of efficacy to be derived from their symbolic action. The other kind is achieved in the action itself, in the assertions it makes and the experience which bears its imprinting." "So far from being meaningless," Douglas adds, "it is primitive magic which gives meaning to existence."[24]

In responding to the same question, Christian missionaries at the turn of the century, although they would not have disagreed entirely with Douglas's formulation (assuming replacement of the phrase "primitive magic" by the term "prayer"), would certainly have put the emphasis elsewhere. Prayer, for Christians, might indeed inform existence with subjective meaning. But the inner logic of events, in objective terms, was knowable only to God. God could be counted on to "bring forth the good to the *greatest number*,"[25] and one could be certain that, whatever transpired, in the end it would be for the furtherance of His Kingdom. But, in the daily workings of human life, His plan was often beyond comprehension, and all Christians could do in the face of this was trust in it absolutely, even when their prayers were of no avail.

The Boxers had yet other ways of accounting for the inefficacy of their rituals without imperiling the belief system on which they were based. Sometimes, when Boxer rituals failed to work properly, it was explained in terms of the insincerity or spiritual inadequacy (or impurity) or insufficient training of the person enacting them. But much more often the Boxers pointed to sources of pollution in the external environment (the most powerful of which were things relating to women, most especially uncleanness in women) – countervailing magical forces that had the power to destroy the efficacy of the Boxers' own magic.[26] (Another source of Boxer confidence, of course, was that sometimes the world responded to Boxer actions as the Boxers anticipated it would. After Boxers killed all fifteen foreign Protestants in Baoding, Zhili, on June 30 and July 1, 1900, according to Luella Miner, a heavy rain fell, breaking the local drought and confirming, from the Boxer point of view, the rightness of their cause and conduct.[27])

For all that separated the Dinka, the Christians, and the Boxers, in the ways in which they dealt with the issue of ritual efficacy, there was one thing that drew them – and perhaps all other religious practitioners – tightly together. Their religious and magical practices had as a paramount goal the affording of protection and emotional security in the face of a future that was indeterminate and fraught with danger and risk. Through their rituals, each sought to exercise some degree of control over the uncertainty – or, as I called it earlier, the outcome-blindness – that is one of the defining marks of human experience.[28]

Conclusion

In Part 1 of *History in Three Keys*, where I reconstruct the history of the Boxer uprising as a sequence of interconnected events, although some of my specific interpretations may differ from those of Chinese historians, my basic approach does not. In Part 3, where I explore the mythologization of the Boxers in twentieth-century China, I pursue a line of inquiry that no Chinese historian to my knowledge has yet pursued, but I doubt it is something a Chinese historian could not *imagine* doing. Part 2, however, is different. How?

Some of the specific methodological differences are suggested in the body of this chapter. But there are others – perhaps deeper and more fundamental – that I want to try to identify here. One has to do with the way in which I go about "anthropologizing the West" in the book. The ultimate objective of this process – the phrase is borrowed from the anthropologist Paul Rabinow[29] – is the creation, as far as is humanly possible, of a level playing field between the Western inquirer and the non-Western object of his/her inquiry. Rabinow calls on Western anthropologists to accomplish this end by showing how culturally specific and exotic the West's own understanding of reality has been. I fully share Rabinow's objective. However, I seek to achieve it by emphasizing how unexotic, even universally human, was the Boxers' understanding of reality. I don't adopt this as a monocausal explanation of Boxer behavior. I believe culture also to be very important and pay a great deal of attention to its shaping influence. But, on an emotional level, whether the reference is to anxiety resulting from drought or belief in the protective power of magic/religious ritual or susceptibility to unusual levels of credulousness in time of crisis or fear of death, I firmly believe that certain universal psychological mechanisms play a vitally important part in human behavior, and I emphasize this in my book far more than has generally been the case in Chinese writing on the Boxers.

A second important difference between my approach and that of Chinese historians stems from the fact that the Boxers are not part of my history in the same sense that they are part of Chinese history. In China, in the twentieth century, where the West has been by turns hated as an imperialist aggressor and admired for its mastery of the secrets of wealth and power, the Boxers, because they attacked both the West and its modern secrets, have presented a complicated problem. When the West is defined as aggressor and exploiter, Boxer resistance to it has been deeply satisfying to patriotic Chinese and readily treated in laudatory terms. But when the West is seen as the wellspring of modern life, Boxer machine-bashing – the Luddite-like attacks on Western telegraphs, railways, and steamships (Figure 3.7) – has often been a source of acute embarrassment and roundly condemned. The Boxer uprising, in short, is a part of Chinese history that carries a uniquely powerful emotional charge. It resonates deeply with unresolved issues in the Chinese quest for a modern identity that both embraces and rejects the culture of the West, and it is therefore hard for Chinese – historians included – to deal with it in an even-handed, detached way. Like the Civil War for American historians or 1789 for French, the Boxers force Chinese historians to take sides.

Figure 3.7 Boxers destroying railway.
Source: Li Di, *Quan huo ji* (preface dated 1905).

I certainly do not wish to imply that, because I am an American historian, I am able to be completely dispassionate in my treatment of the Boxer uprising. The Boxers have been an emotional issue for Westerners too (albeit in quite different ways), and early Western accounts of the uprising were hardly detached or unbiased. Recent Western studies have, however, gone quite far in reversing older biases, not only by evincing greater empathy for the Boxers but also by adopting a more critical view of Western conduct in China at the end of the nineteenth century.[30]

There is a broader factor as well that is important in my own case: it has to do with the historiographical tradition in which I operate, as compared to that of most Chinese historians. I have no desire or need to derive from the Boxer episode lessons for the present. Nor am I concerned with seeing the Boxers as a negative or positive model for later generations. My interest as a historian is at once less instrumental and more humanistic. I believe that the overriding aim of historical writing, like that of good fiction (though the two are certainly not the same), should be to provide insight into the human condition. My main concern therefore in approaching the history of the Boxer uprising is to discover how a diverse collection of individuals – foreign as well as Chinese, Christians as well as Boxers – responded to the circumstances in which they found themselves in North China in 1900. For me, recovering as far as possible the experience of the participants in the Boxer episode, reconstructing their thoughts and feelings, and trying to understand and explain why they behaved as they did is what I care most about as a historian.

Notes

This chapter originally appeared in Chinese: "Yi renleixue guandian kan Yihetuan" (trans. Lin Liwei), *Ershiyi shiji* (Twenty-first century) 45 (February 1998). The English version presented here contains minor changes only.

1 *History in Three Keys* has been translated into Chinese under the title *Lishi sandiao: Zuo wei shijian, jingli he shenhua de Yihetuan*, trans. Du Jidong (Nanjing: Jiangsu renmin chubanshe, 2000). The book's main themes were previously introduced in Ke Wen [Paul A. Cohen], "Lijie guoqu de san tiao tujing: zuo wei shijian, jingyan he shenhua de Yihetuan" (Three avenues to understanding the past: the Boxers as event, experience, and myth), trans. Lin Tongqi, Xiao Yanming, and Zhu Hong, *Shijie hanxue* (World sinology) 1 (May 1998): 122–32.

2 See, in particular, Joseph Esherick's pathbreaking book *The Origins of the Boxer Uprising* (Berkeley: University of California Press, 1987).

3 In interesting contrast, Zi Zhongyun, in her review article "Lao wenti xin shijiao" (New perspectives on an old problem), *Dushu* (Reading), January 1998, pp. 122–30, places far greater weight on Part 3, dealing with the range of ways in which the Boxers were remembered in China in the course of the twentieth century.

4 Li Yuanshan, age 79, in Nankai daxue lishixi (Nankai University history department), ed., *Tianjin Yihetuan diaocha* (The Tianjin Boxer survey) (Tianjin: Tianjin guji chubanshe, 1990), p. 142.

5 Guan He, *Quanfei wenjian lu* (A record of things seen and heard concerning the Boxer bandits), in Jian Bozan *et al.*, eds., *Yihetuan* (The Boxers), 4 vols. (Shanghai: Shenzhou guoguang she, 1951) 1: 482.

6 Chen Zhenjiang and Cheng Xiao, *Yihetuan wenxian jizhu yu yanjiu* (Explications and studies of Boxer writings) (Tianjin: Tianjin renmin chubanshe, 1985), p. 49.

7 Deuteronomy 11: 13–21.

8 Both examples are cited in David Arnold, *Famine: Social Crisis and Historical Change* (Oxford: Basil Blackwell, 1988), p. 15.

9 R.K. Hitchcock, "The Traditional Response to Drought in Botswana," in Madalon T. Hinchey, ed., *Symposium on Drought in Botswana* (Gabarone, Botswana: Botswana Society in collaboration with Clark University Press, 1979), p. 92.

10 For a long time it was commonly believed that Boxer possession was a form of hypnotism or mesmerism. See Arthur H. Smith, *China in Convulsion*, 2 vols. (New York: Fleming H. Revell, 1901), 2: 661; Dai Xuanzhi, *Yihetuan yanjiu* (A study of the Boxers) (Taibei: Zhongguo xueshu zhuzuo jiangzhu weiyuanhui, 1963), pp. 21–33.

11 Xie Jiagui, age 86, Chiping county, December 1965, in Lu Yao *et al.*, comps., *Shandong Yihetuan diaocha ziliao xuanbian* (Selections from survey materials on the Shandong Boxers) (Jinan: Qi-Lu, 1980), p. 200.

12 Chinese spirit mediumship is discussed in a wide range of Western works (most of them by anthropologists). See, for example, Alan J.A. Elliott, *Chinese Spirit Medium Cults in Singapore* (London: Athlone, 1990 [originally published in 1955]); Jack M. Potter, "Cantonese Shamanism," in Arthur P. Wolf, ed., *Studies in Chinese Society* (Stanford: Stanford University Press, 1978), pp. 321–45; David K. Jordan, *Gods, Ghosts, and Ancestors: The Folk Religion of a Taiwanese Village* (Berkeley: University of California Press, 1972), pp. 67–86; and Margery Wolf, *A Thrice-Told Tale: Feminism, Postmodernism, and Ethnographic Responsibility* (Stanford: Stanford University Press, 1992).

13 See, for example, the descriptions of spirit-medium trance recorded in Potter, "Cantonese Shamanism," pp. 322–9, 334–6; Elliott, *Chinese Spirit Medium Cults*, pp. 63–5; Jordan, *Gods, Ghosts, and Ancestors*, pp. 75–6.

14 This was one of the two main ideas contained in the most famous of the Boxers' slogans: "Fu [Bao] Qing mieyang" (Support [protect] the Qing, destroy the foreign).

15 "An Assessment of Some Comparisons and Implications," in Erika Bourguignon, ed., *Religion, Altered States of Consciousness, and Social Change* (Columbus: Ohio State University Press, 1973), pp. 326–7.

16 Examples of otherwise excellent Chinese studies that use such terms freely are: Li Wenhai and Liu Yangdong, "Yihetuan yundong shiqi shehui xinli fenxi" (A social-psychological analysis of the Boxer movement era), in *Yihetuan yundong yu jindai Zhongguo shehui* (The Boxer movement and modern Chinese society) (Chengdu: Sichuan sheng shehui kexueyuan chubanshe, 1987), pp. 1–25; Yang Tianhong, "Yihetuan 'shenshu' lunlüe" (A summary discussion of the "magical powers" of the Boxers), *Jindaishi yanjiu* (Studies in modern Chinese history) 5 (1993): 189–204; Chen Zhenjiang and Cheng Xiao, *Yihetuan wenxian jizhu yu yanjiu*; Wang Zhizhong, " 'Hongdengzhao' kaolüe" (A brief examination of the "Red Lanterns"), *Shehui kexue* (Social science) (Gansu) 2 (1980): 63–9, 85.

17 Boston radio station WEEI, June 19–20, 1988. The consensus of the onlookers in Ohio, according to the radio announcer, was to believe in rather than doubt the potential efficacy of the rainmaking ceremony.

18 Memorial of gengzi 5/22 (June 18, 1900), in *Yihetuan* 4: 162. Other examples of elite Chinese mockery of Boxer invulnerability claims are noted in Cohen, *History in Three Keys*, pp. 331–2, n. 3.

19 Journal, Beijing, June 14, 1900, in Luella Miner Papers (North China Mission), Box 1, File 1, American Board of Commissioners for Foreign Missions, unpublished papers, Houghton Library, Harvard University. Nigel Oliphant, describing an encounter that took place on June 14 between Boxers and British marines in the capital (very possibly the same as that recounted by Miner), reported that, after being fired on by the British, the Boxers

> all threw themselves on the ground, praying, according to the Boxer custom, to be saved from the bullets, and the marines, thinking they were praying for mercy, ceased fire. Then one of their leaders rushed forward with a huge poleaxe and was shot dead by the sergeant. Then the whole crowd retreated.
>
> Oliphant, *A Diary of the Siege of the Legations in Peking During the Summer of 1900* (London: Longmans, Green, 1901), p. 13.

20 Yang Tianhong, "Yihetuan 'shenshu' lunlüe," p. 194.

21 Albert Vinchon, S.J., "La culte de la Sainte Vierge du Tche-li sud-est: Rapport présenté au Congrès marial de 1904," *Chine, Ceylan, Madagascar: Lettres missionnaires français de la Compagnie de Jésus (Province de Champagne)* 18 (March 1905): 132–3. Richard Madsen says that, in interviews elsewhere in the province with Chinese Catholic descendants of families that lived through the Boxer experience, he heard stories of a similar nature. Personal communication, August 1, 1995.

22 Bishop Favier, sequestered in the Northern Cathedral in Beijing, reported that when retreating Boxers on June 15 set fire to the houses adjoining the cathedral on the south, the cathedral itself and its occupants were "preserved by God, who changed the direction of the wind in our favor." Diary, June 15, 1900, in J. Freri, ed., *The Heart of Pekin: Bishop A. Favier's Diary of the Siege, May–*

August 1900 (Boston: Marlier, 1901), p. 26. For additional examples see Cohen, *History in Three Keys*, p. 337, n. 69.

23 Jane E. Brody, "Lucking Out: Weird Rituals and Strange Beliefs," *New York Times*, January 27, 1991, p. S11.

24 Mary Douglas, *Purity and Danger: An Analysis of the Concepts of Pollution and Taboo* (New York: Routledge, 1991), pp. 68, 72.

25 Sarah Boardman Goodrich, letter, Tong Cho [Tongzhou], May 25, 1900. See also Goodrich's letters of May 28, May 30, and June 3, 1900. In Miscellaneous Personal Papers, Manuscript Group No. 8, Box No. 88, China Records Project, Divinity School Library, Yale University (unpublished).

26 See Cohen, *History in Three Keys*, pp. 128–34.

27 Miner, "Last Rites for the Pao-ting-fu Martyrs," *The Advance*, August 1, 1901.

28 Gustav Jahoda writes of "superstition" – and I would make the same claims for religious and magical ritual generally – that it provides "at least the subjective feeling of predictability and control," thereby reducing the anxiety that is apt to be aroused in threatening situations marked by uncertainty as to probable outcome. *Psychology of Superstition* (Harmondsworth, Middlesex, England: Penguin, 1969), pp. 130, 134.

29 In his "Representations Are Social Facts: Modernity and Post-Modernity in Anthropology," in James Clifford and George E. Marcus, eds., *Writing Culture: The Poetics and Politics of Ethnography* (Berkeley: University of California Press, 1986), p. 241.

30 See, in particular, Esherick, *The Origins of the Boxer Uprising*; also James Hevia, "Leaving a Brand on China: Missionary Discourse in the Wake of the Boxer Movement," *Modern China* 18.3 (July 1992): 304–32.

4 Boxers, Christians, and the gods

The Boxer conflict of 1900 as a religious war

The Boxer uprising of 1898–1900, so called because of the martial arts practices of its participants, was a major antiforeign explosion and watershed event in Chinese history. It has often been portrayed in the West as a struggle between the forces of progress, civilization, and enlightenment, on the one hand, and barbarism, savagery, superstition, and xenophobia, on the other. In China, over the past century, it has been quite differently viewed, above all by those in the Marxist camp, who have shown a strong inclination to define the conflict as one between foreign imperialism and the Chinese people's patriotic resistance to this force. In researching my book on the Boxer episode,[1] mainly focusing on the spring and summer of 1900 when the struggle between the Boxers and their foreign and Chinese Christian adversaries reached peak intensity, I was struck by the degree to which, at the time, this struggle – as well as the circumstances surrounding it – was understood by both sides in profoundly *religious* terms. As a corollary to this, I also noted the general tendency of each party to the conflict to view *itself* as acting in behalf of a supernatural force that was authentic and good – God or the gods – and the other side as representing false gods that were, at bottom, either powerless or the very embodiment of evil.

I would like here to present some of the evidence I uncovered supporting the understanding of the Boxer–Christian conflict as a religious encounter. I will focus on three themes: the religious construction of drought, the religious construction of war, and the strong predisposition of both Boxers and Christians to denigrate each other's religious beliefs and assumptions. In my conclusion I will comment briefly on the more general issue, clearly raised in this case, of how historians define and categorize the events they study.

Religious constructions of the world: drought

The climactic months of the Boxer uprising in the spring and summer of 1900 took place against a backdrop of severe drought that extended over much of the North China plain and created conditions of extreme anxiety

for the farming population of the region. Although the experience of
foreign missionaries, especially those stranded in isolated parts of the
North China countryside, was very different from that of Chinese farmers,
the missionaries too faced a situation defined by life-and-death uncertainty, and they too hoped desperately – and prayed – for rain. Unlike the
farmers, however, the immediate object of the missionaries' fear was death
not from hunger but at the hands of hungry Chinese.

This fear and the corresponding one on the Chinese side were nicely
expressed by Rowena Bird, an American Congregationalist, in letters and
journal entries written from the northern Chinese province of Shanxi only
weeks before her death (on July 31). On June 25 Bird wrote:

> These are most trying times – famine threatens the people with starva-
> tion – the dry, hot weather makes all ill, and the Boxers are
> threatening the destruction of the country by robbing and killing
> missionaries and Christians.... The country is full of the wildest
> rumors and threats. The people have nothing to do but talk and they
> talk of killing the foreigners and Christians and we feel that the end
> may not be far off for any of us...things grow worse and worse and if
> the rains hold off it is hard to say what violence may not ensue. We
> know God could send relief thru rain if He thot best, and we know all
> our interests are in His hands.[2]

In Zhili province, it was much the same story (Figure 4.1). Mrs. F.E.
Simcox (American Presbyterian) wrote in mid-April from the city of
Baoding: "There is great need of rain. The ignorant attribute this drought
to the foreigners who have 'offended heaven.'" In a letter of June 2, also
from Baoding, Horace Pitkin, after describing the growing threat in the
area to Protestants and Catholics alike, commented with terse urgency:
"Dry as powder – oppressive duststorm – God give us rain. That would
quiet things a moment.... We can't be sure of a single day's life. Pray for
us. Pray for rain." The rains finally came, but only (as we saw in Chapter
3 of this volume) after the killing of all fifteen foreign Protestants in
Baoding on June 30 and July 1.[3]

Fundamentally the same analysis was also made in the reports of the
foreign diplomatic representatives in Beijing to their governments.[4] In one
important respect, however, the understanding of the diplomats differed
from that of the missionaries: it was cast in completely secular terms. For
Christians at the close of the nineteenth century God's hand was everywhere. If He wanted His flock to survive, He would deliver them from
danger. If He wanted the missionaries to continue in their work, He would
see to it that their material needs were satisfied. And if, as Rowena Bird
had written, "He thot best," He "could send relief thru rain."[5] Conversely,
if the Christians faced a deadly threat like that of the Boxers, it was not
because God was asleep on the job. The Boxer uprising took place because

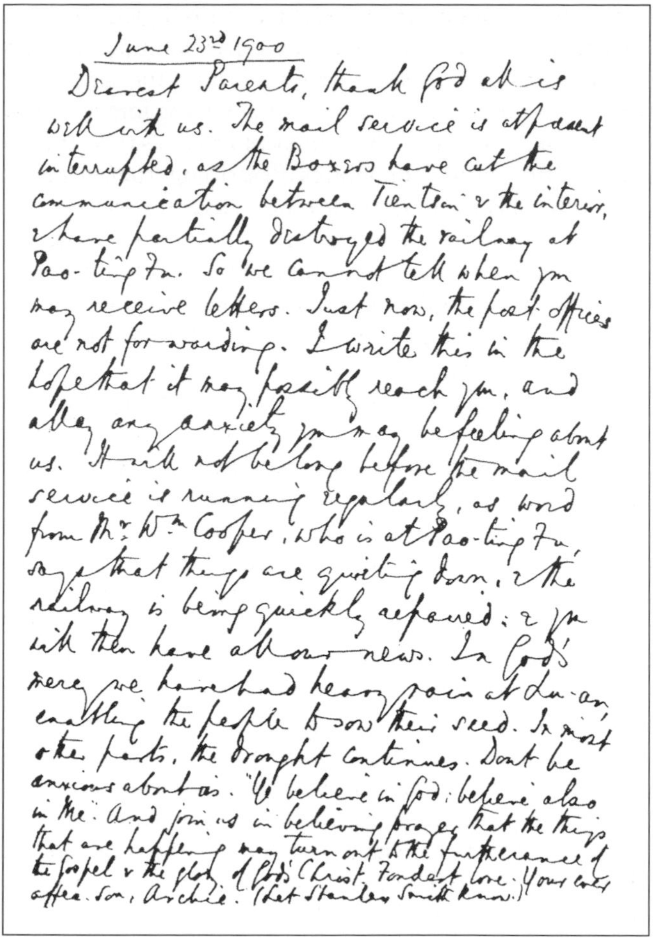
June 23rd 1900
Dearest Parents, thank God all is well with us. The mail service is at present interrupted, as the Boxers have cut the communication between Tientsin & the interior, & have partially destroyed the railway at Pao-ting Fu. So we cannot tell when you may receive letters. Just now, the post offices are not forwarding. I write this in the hope that it may possibly reach you, and allay any anxiety you may be feeling about us. It will not be long before the mail service is running regularly, as word from Mr Wm Cooper, who is at Pao-ting Fu, says that things are quieting down, & the railway is being quickly repaired; & you will then have all our news. In God's mercy we have had heavy rain at Lu-an, enabling the people to sow their seed. In most other parts, the drought continues. Don't be anxious about us. "Ye believe in God: believe also in Me." And join us in believing prayer that the things that are happening may turn out to the furtherance of the gospel & the glory of God's Christ. Fondest love. Your loving affec. son, Archie. (Let Stanley Smith know.)

Figure 4.1 Report on drought. In a missionary's postcard to his parents, dated June 23, 1900, note is taken of the continuation of the drought in south and central Zhili.

Source: Archibald E. Glover, *A Thousand Miles of Miracle in China* (London: Hodder and Stoughton, 1904).

He had permitted it to take place. His dealings were sometimes "mysterious," and it was not always easy for mere mortals to understand why He allowed certain things to happen. But good Christians knew that, although it was necessary in such circumstances to walk "by faith, not by sight,"[6] in the final analysis everything that transpired "must be," as one missionary put it, "among the 'all things' which are working together for the good of God's kingdom, and of China."[7]

What is remarkable is the degree to which contemporary Chinese – non-Boxers as well as Boxers – also viewed everything that happened in the world, including whether it rained or not, as being in the control of Heaven or "the gods." In fact, although the Chinese construction of reality differed greatly in specifics from that of the missionaries, in a number of broad respects it formed almost a mirror image of the missionaries' construction. Where the missionaries saw themselves as representatives of the Lord, sometimes describing themselves as "God's soldiers"[8] and often believing quite literally that they had been called by Jesus Christ to go to China to labor for that country's salvation, in jingles repeated and notices circulated throughout North China in 1900 the Boxers were often portrayed, in comparably salvific (as well as martial) terms, as "spirit soldiers" (*shenbing*) sent down from Heaven to carry out a divine mission or, which amounted to the same thing, as mortals whose bodies had been possessed by spirits (thereby rendering them divine) for the same purpose.

Again, where the missionaries constructed the Boxer movement as a satanic force, whose capacity for evil knew no bounds, the Boxers (and, one presumes, millions of Chinese sympathizers who were not active participants in the movement) saw the missionaries, and by extension all other foreigners (as well, of course, as Chinese Christians), as the root source of evil in their world, the immediate occasion for the anger of the gods. As pointed out in Chapter 3 of this volume, the explanation of the drought found in Boxer notices was embedded in a full-blown religious structuring of reality; the notices also provided participants in the movement with a clear program of action designed to mollify the gods and restore the cosmic balance. Such notices began to be widely circulated at least as early as the beginning of 1900. In February of that year the following text was reported to have been "posted everywhere" in North China:

> On account of the Protestant and Catholic religions the Buddhist gods are oppressed, and our sages thrust into the background. The Law of Buddha is no longer respected, and the Five Relationships [of Confucianism] are disregarded. The anger of Heaven and Earth has been aroused and the timely rain has consequently been withheld from us. But Heaven is now sending down eight millions of spiritual soldiers to extirpate these foreign religions, and when this has been done there will be a timely rain.[9]

Boxer notices were often written in doggerel, which made them easier to circulate orally. A portion of one of the most widely disseminated examples went as follows:

> They proselytize their sect,
> And believe in only one God,
> The spirits and their own ancestors
> Are not even given a nod.

Their men are all immoral;
Their women truly vile.
For the Devils [foreigners] it's mother–son sex
That serves as the breeding style.

...

No rain comes from Heaven.
The earth is parched and dry.
And all because the churches
Have bottled up the sky.

The god[s] are very angry.
The spirits seek revenge.
En masse they come from Heaven
To teach the Way to men.[10]

The writings of the Boxers were numerous and diverse, and not all of them attempted to link foreign religious incursions, heavenly anger, and drought. A great many of them, however, did.[11] While it is entirely possible that some of the authors of these writings, as well as some rank-and-file Boxers, did not in fact subscribe to the analysis contained in them, the likelihood is that the great majority did. There is every reason to believe, moreover, that this judgment held true for the population at large as well. "There come the foreign devils, that[']s why we don't have any rain,"[12] a missionary reported hearing a street boy call out on a visit to the Chinese city of Tianjin in May 1900.

As noted in Chapter 3 of this volume, the linkage between drought (or famine) and heavenly anger was displayed not only in China but in many other cultures as well. "Whatever the precise cause," generalizes David Arnold,

> there was no doubting the divine provenance of famine.... The involvement of the elements – the failure of the rains, the unseasonal frosts and floods – seemed to place causation beyond human reach and to provide sober confirmation of man's subordination to god and nature.[13]

Still, while the basic premise that natural disasters are to be accounted for by some supernatural agency acting in response to human wrongdoing appears with great frequency, the particularities of a society's response to such disasters, the "structures of meaning" (to use Clifford Geertz's language) within which it interprets them,[14] will be shaped by the special cultural forms and historical experience of that society. While in more ordinary times in China the human agency responsible for the disruption of cosmic harmony might typically have been identified as the misconduct of native officials, in 1900, at a time of increasing foreign pressure and mounting crisis in China's foreign relations, it was not surprising to find the blame for drought shifted from the domestic to the foreign arena.

The same sort of analysis may be applied to the instructions for crisis remedy that we find in many of the Boxer notices. The first recourse for people faced with drought, in China as elsewhere, is to offer up prayers and perform a range of rain-inducing rituals (Figure 4.2). But when such conventional means fail to produce relief, and the anxiety occasioned by the drought deepens, people often resort to more heroic measures. The generic element here is scapegoatism, the identification of a human agency deemed responsible for the crisis and the punishment of that agency. The forms of scapegoatism, however, vary enormously in different cultural and historical settings. "When the monsoons failed in Gujarat in western India," Arnold tells us, the local people "suspected Bania traders of stopping the rain deliberately so as to profit from the resultant dearth and high prices. To break this spell the[y]...forced a Bania to hold a water pot on his head at which they fired arrows until the pot broke and released the rains."[15] Far more extreme measures were taken in late medieval European millenarian movements, as analyzed by Norman Cohn. In 1420 in Bohemia, Cohn writes,

> people saw themselves as entering on the final struggle against Antichrist and his hosts.... No longer content to await the destruction

Figure 4.2 Rain god. The Chinese prayed and offered sacrifices to a variety of gods in time of drought. The one whose rainmaking responsibilities were most specific is shown here, standing amid the clouds with a watering can in his hands.

Source: C.A.S. Williams, *Outlines of Chinese Symbolism and Art Motives*, 2nd rev. edn. (Shanghai: Kelly and Walsh, 1932).

of the godless by a miracle,...preachers called upon the faithful to carry out the necessary purification of the earth themselves.... "Accursed be the man [stated one widely circulated tract] who withholds his sword from shedding the blood of the enemies of Christ. Every believer must wash his hands in that blood."[16]

The crisis remedy proposed by the Boxers in 1900 revealed a close kinship to that described by Cohn for the millenarian movement of 1420.[17] In one placard after another, the Chinese people were enjoined to kill off all foreigners and native Chinese contaminated by foreigners or foreign influence. Only after this process of physical elimination of every trace of the foreign from China had been completed would the gods be appeased and permit the rains once again to fall (Figure 4.3).

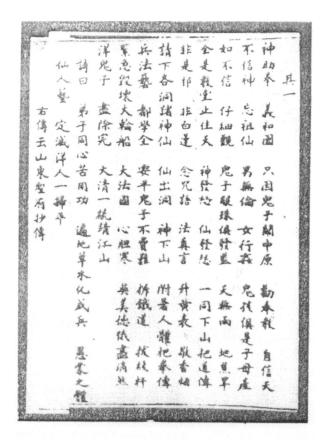

Figure 4.3 Boxer notice. The link between elimination of foreign influence and termination of the drought is clearly drawn in this notice, which was one of the most widely circulated in the spring and summer of 1900.

Source: Chen Zhenjiang and Cheng Xiao, *Yihetuan wenxian jizhu yu yanjiu* (Tianjin: Tianjin Renmin Chubanshe, 1985).

Religious constructions of the world: war

The gods who withheld rain were often seen as angry, jealous, vengeful gods – gods who were prepared to punish an entire community of believers if representatives of this community either turned to other gods or violated established rules of behavior. When, on the other hand, believers perceived themselves not as harborers of miscreants but as innocents at risk in situations marked by danger, they expected their gods to perform a protective function. This function was plainly evidenced in both Boxer and Christian understandings of the role of supernatural agency in the context of war.

The beliefs and practices of the Boxers in this realm – the array of magicoreligious means the Boxers used to control their immediate environment, to make it less dangerous, more predictable – were especially impressive. The two areas of activity in which Boxer magic was deployed most extensively were, not surprisingly, also the ones in which the danger, either to individual Boxers or to the Boxer cause, happened to be greatest. I refer to fighting, mainly against Chinese Christians and foreign expeditionary forces, and to the destruction by burning of churches and the homes and shops of native Christians. The need for magical protection in the case of the former activity was self-evident. In the case of the latter, it was more indirect, having to do with the Boxers' relationship to the population of a given locale. If the Boxers were able to burn down Christian buildings through magical means, this would redound to the credit of the movement and garner local support. If, on the other hand, the fires they set, by whatever means, spread to the homes and shops of non-Christians, the Boxers ran a substantial risk of incurring popular wrath (Figure 4.4).

The Boxers were best known for the invulnerability to foreign weapons they acquired when possessed by their gods.[18] But apart from possession-conferred invulnerability, they were also reported to have command of a wide range of other magical skills in combat situations. Frequently, as they were about to go into battle, they chanted rhymed invulnerability incantations, such as the following (which was widely used in the area northwest of Beijing in the summer of 1900): "Disciples in the world of men, stop up the barrels of guns; guns in unison sound, bullets scatter all 'round."[19] Many Tianjin residents apparently accepted the claim that when a rank-and-file Boxer received a bullet or shell wound the Boxer leader had only to rub it and it healed instantly, and the additional claim that when a Boxer was killed in action it was only necessary to recite an incantation to restore him to life. In Beijing it was said that when the Boxers went into battle, men and horses were more than ten feet tall and the swords of the former were so numerous that it was impossible to resist them. Like their brothers in Tianjin, moreover, when bullets struck their clothing, they rolled off like raindrops, not injuring them in the slightest.[20]

The top Boxer commanders in the Tianjin region, Cao Futian and Zhang Decheng (Figure 4.5), were alleged to have exceptional magical powers. They were able to make themselves invisible and to disappear into

Figure 4.4 Boxers setting fire to a church.
Source: *Quanfei jilüe* (Shanghai: Shangyang Shuju, 1903).

the earth. They had the power to be in two places at once. While they slept their souls roamed about and reconnoitered foreign troop deployments. When Cao Futian went into battle, he carried in his hand a millet stalk two feet long which, he said, was really a precious sword given him by the Jade Emperor (the top god in the Chinese pantheon); all he had to do was point the stalk in the enemy's direction and one after another their heads fell to the ground.[21]

No less powerful than the magic of Boxer leaders was that of the female auxiliaries of the Boxers, the Red Lanterns (Figure 4.6). These girls and young women, it was maintained, were able to protect the Boxers during combat (Figure 4.7). They could send swords flying through the air without looking and from a distance lop off enemy heads. They were also able to hurl bolts of fire and, using their magic, make off with the screws holding

Figure 4.5 Boxer leader Zhang Decheng in a sedan chair. The banner next to Zhang's sedan chair is inscribed "Number One Unit Under Heaven," the name of the famous Boxer headquarters Zhang founded in a town west of Tianjin in spring 1900.

Source: *Jing-Jin quanfei jilüe* (Hong Kong: Xianggang Shuju, 1901).

Figure 4.6 Red Lantern. This is a rare photograph of a Red Lantern, portraying realistically a rather plain-looking teenaged girl in a studio setting.

Source: Li Di, *Quan huo ji* (n.d., preface dated 1905).

Figure 4.7 Red Lanterns assist in the siege of the Northern Cathedral in Beijing. The Red Lantern to the left rear (holding a lantern in her hand) has flung a magical rope between the opposing sides, protecting the Chinese combatants in the middle from the crossfire.

Source: V.M. Alekseev, *Kitaiskaia narodnaia kartina: Dukhovnaia zhizn' starogo Kitaia v narodnykh izobrazheniiakh* (Moscow, 1966).

together the foreigners' artillery. When the Red Lanterns stood erect and did not move, their souls left them and engaged in battle. They were not daunted by weapons of any sort. Foreign guns were paralyzed in their presence.[22] They also had extraordinary healing and restorative powers. A former Red Lantern from the Tianjin region recalled that, once the senior member of her Red Lantern unit had gone into trance, all she had to do was clap her hands in the direction of a sick person and the person became well.[23]

The incendiary activities of the Boxers were, from the Boxer point of view, not something separate from the larger conflict in which they were engaged; indeed, given the primitive state of their weaponry, arson was, quite literally, the most potent form of firepower generally available to the Boxers.[24] The trouble was that arson in China at the turn of the century, especially in cities like Tianjin and Beijing, where homes and shops were often flimsily constructed and crowded together in close proximity, was exceptionally hard to control. The Boxers, therefore, had to take special magical measures to contain the fires they set in these cities. One contemporary chronicler, who was more receptive to Boxer claims than most Chinese elites, insisted that the Boxers had a remarkable capacity to know which homes belonged to Christians and which did not and that, by burning slips of paper and invoking the help of their gods, they were able to ensure that only the former were burned down. As an example, he recounted an incident in which the Boxers in early June set fire to two churches. One of the churches was located very close to a government granary. The local magistrate knelt and prostrated himself in the direction of the fire and prayed to the gods to protect the granary. Suddenly, there appeared in the air a god in golden armor, who stood atop the flames and then disappeared. Neither the granary nor the homes on either side of the church were damaged. Everyone said it was Guandi (the God of War) making his power manifest.[25]

There were also accounts of more powerful incendiary techniques available to the Boxers. It was reported, for example, that when they destroyed a section of the Beijing–Baoding railway on May 28, they simply went along the tracks pointing stalks of *gaoliang* and shouting "burn, burn" ("*shao, shao*"), whereupon the tracks burst into flame.[26] A former Boxer from Tianjin recalled that, when the Boxers burned churches in that city, all they had to do was point at their target and it would catch fire.[27]

The most potent incendiary magic of all was, arguably, that possessed by the Red Lanterns, whose specialties were flying and controlling the strength and direction of the wind. On June 18, during the fighting in Tianjin, a dust storm made the blaze in the foreign section of the city (caused by Chinese gunfire) burn with great intensity. Boxer supporters, according to an eyewitness, circulated the word that the fires had been set by the magic of the Boxer teacher and that Red Lanterns perched on the northeastern corner of the city wall, by waving their red fans, had made the fires burn all the more fiercely. Upon hearing this, people repeatedly offered up prayers to the Buddha.[28]

The most impressive claims with respect to Red Lantern incendiary magic related to the ability of these women, by waving their fans, to fly. After becoming accomplished at this, they soared through the sky to other lands, where they set fire to foreign buildings and homes.[29] By mid-June, according to one tally, the Red Lanterns had by this means already destroyed sixteen of eighteen foreign countries.[30]

From the perspective of the Boxers, the fighting they were engaged in in the summer of 1900 was not to be understood as a military conflict in the conventional sense. Much more fundamentally, it was to be seen as a contest to determine whose magical skills – and by extension, in the case of foreign and Chinese Christian adversaries, whose gods – were more powerful and would prevail. When they experienced setbacks, therefore, the Boxers attributed them not to their adversaries' superior firepower but, almost invariably, to their more effective magic. Bishop Favier (Figure 4.8), the white-bearded leader of the Catholic defenders of the

Figure 4.8 Bishop Favier

Source: J. Freri, ed., *The Heart of Pekin: Bishop A. Favier's Diary of the Siege, May–August 1900* (Boston: Marlier, 1901).

Northern Cathedral in Beijing, which the Boxers had besieged for weeks without success, was transformed into a "devil prince" (*guiwang*), 200 years of age, who, in addition to being highly skilled as a strategist, practiced sorcery, was expert at divination, and had gained complete ascendancy over the minds of the other "devils."[31] And repeatedly, we are told, Boxer efforts to overpower churches in southeastern Zhili province were thwarted by the apparition of a white-clad woman, whose presence stopped them in their tracks and deprived them of their powers.[32]

There are indications, it is interesting to note, that the Christian adversaries of the Boxers interpreted the world from a roughly analogous religious perspective. As we saw in Chapter 3 of this volume, Chinese Catholics in southeastern Zhili alleged that the appearance of the Virgin Mary above their church (the Boxers' "white-clad woman") was instrumental in protecting them from a series of Boxer assaults between December 1899 and July 1900.[33]

Foreign missionaries, also, were quick to claim divine support in combat-related settings. Sarah Goodrich reported in her journal that the children of the besieged foreigners in the legations in the capital held a prayer meeting on Sunday, July 1, 1900, at which they "especially prayed for our brave men on the wall, and for Mr. Hall who is a great favorite of theirs, their 'lady-bug.' " Later on the same day Hall sustained a minor wound on the knee. "Just the moment before the ball struck him," Goodrich continues, "he lost his balance and fell over backward, and thus saved his life." At dinner Hall said "with much feeling, 'I am sure it was the children's prayers that saved me.' "[34]

When a force of several thousand Boxers threatened to overpower a Catholic village in southeastern Zhili in July 1900, the local missionary prayed for heavy rains that would form a cordon of water around the village and prevent the Boxers from entering. His prayers were answered by a terrific storm, which had exactly the desired effect. It was assumed, without question, that the storm had been sent by the Virgin Mary.[35]

Much like the Boxers and Red Lanterns, missionaries menaced by fire habitually interpreted life-saving shifts in the direction or strength of the wind as manifestations of God's will. Sarah Goodrich wrote of the besieged in the legation quarters: "We have had many wonderful answers to prayer, twice at least in turning the wind away from us when it seemed as if our houses must certainly catch fire."[36] And Bishop Favier, sequestered in the Northern Cathedral, reported that when retreating Boxers on June 15 set fire to the houses adjoining the cathedral on the south, the cathedral itself and its occupants were "preserved by God, who changed the direction of the wind in our favor."[37] "Overshadowing every other impression made by the events of the past Summer," one missionary concluded, "is the indelible impression that God's hand move[d] through it all. The final result is His will."[38]

Mutual religious denigration

In a religious conflict in which each side viewed the aid and protection of its god or gods as essential if it was to prevail, there was a strong imperative on the part of both Christians and Boxers in 1900 to discredit each other's magicoreligious claims. On one point, however, the two sides differed significantly. Where the Christians, ever the religious exclusivists, were convinced that only they had true religious power and that Boxer magicoreligious pretensions were completely unfounded, the Boxers, even as they laid siege to particular Christian religious claims, were quite capable of crediting their adversaries with a high level of supernatural power.

Christian missionaries at the turn of the century certainly believed in the power of Satan to create havoc in the world and had no hesitation in defining the Boxer movement as (in the words of one of them) "the work of the devil, saturated with superstition and witchcraft, reeking with cruelty, diabolical to the last degree, an open revolt against Jehovah and his Anointed."[39] But the faith that Christ had conquered Satan assured Christians that in their own struggles the stakes were eternal and final victory guaranteed.[40] Certainly the characterization of the Boxers as a "diabolical sect...directly instruments of the devil" (to quote Bishop Favier) did not translate into acceptance of Boxer supernatural claims, for which the missionaries lost few opportunities to announce their utter contempt.[41] A Shanxi missionary, referring to the spirit-possession rituals of the Boxers, described young Boxers as being "worked up to a frenzy of evil by men skilled in such works of old, called wizards."[42] Another missionary, in Beijing, wrote that the Boxers "nerve[d] themselves to their work by a species of self hypnotism, in which state they say they can feel no pain."[43] Yet another, elaborating on the same theme, insisted that the majority of Boxers were under a "hypnotic or mesmeric spell," and described them as poor coolies whom the leaders of the movement had subjected to occult "magnetic influences" by which they had been "led astray."[44]

This denigratory stance was displayed toward the entire spectrum of Boxer magicoreligious pretensions. But, not surprisingly, it was most commonly encountered in reference to the Boxers' invulnerability claims. Thus, F.W.S. O'Neill of the Irish Presbyterian Mission in Manchuria wrote in early July 1900:

> Young girls also enter the [Boxer] Society, and they especially are said to be bullet-proof. On the occasion of [the] first attack at Tiehling [Tieling] the Chinese troops were led by a maiden on horseback. She was shot in the head, and died, of course. But the story was that she became alive again.[45]

Along more general lines, the American missionary publicist Arthur Smith observed that, while among the Chinese the marvels allegedly performed by the Boxers were "almost universally regarded as real and solid evidences of supernatural power,...the Christians had a tendency to attribute them to the direct agency of the devil."[46]

Like the missionaries, the Boxers, in addition to building up their own supernatural constructions of reality, also did all in their power to tear down the other side's. In their writings they perpetuated anti-Christian rhetoric that, in some respects, could be traced back as far as the sixteenth century and had reemerged as an important dimension of anti-Christian sentiment in the mid-nineteenth century. This rhetoric was partly *cultural*, insofar as it caricatured the ways in which Western Christian culture differed from Chinese; insofar as it portrayed Westerners as subhuman and depicted them (not only in printed materials but also in anti-Christian posters) as sheep, goats, and pigs (the latter especially in the case of Jesus), it was overtly *racial* in nature (Figures 4.9 and 4.10).[47]

Figures 4.9 and 4.10 Anti-Christian posters.
Figure 4.9 shows foreigners worshiping the pig Jesus (the characters inscribed on the pig's side are those for Jesus). The text in the center describes Jesus as having been exceptionally licentious and power-hungry in his day. When punished for his crimes by being nailed to a cross, he assumed the form of a pig and died. Chinese may be protected against the greed and lust of Jesus' latter-day followers (the missionaries) by chiseling crosses into their doorsills and steps. The character for "pig" in Chinese is homophonous with that for "Lord," although the tones are different. The character for "grunt" is homophonous with that for "religion, teaching." Thus, the "religion of the Lord of Heaven" (Catholicism) becomes the "grunt of the pig of heaven." In this poster, as well as others, characters referring to Christianity or the foreigners are printed in green in the original, and foreigners and native Christians are depicted wearing green hats. "Green hat" (*lümao*) in the Chinese vernacular is an epithet for "cuckold."

Boxer denigration of the claims of Christianity in general and the alleged power of Jesus in particular is also reported with some frequency in contemporary missionary writings. In the Beijing area, we are told, a crowd of soldiers and Boxers gathered around a young Chinese Christian woman and, jeering and laughing, shouted "kill her, kill her, and see if her body will rise again and go to Jesus Christ."[48] Another missionary reported being taunted by a mob shouting "Your God cannot save you. Jesus is dead; He is not in the world; He cannot give real help. Our...[God of War] is much stronger; he protects us, and he has sent the Boxers to pull down your house and to kill you."[49] Another told of his treatment after being captured by Boxers in northwest China:

> They heaped the most awful curses on the name of Jesus, making me shudder at their horrible blasphemies. When I asked them for a drink of water they said, "Ask your Jesus for water." When all hope of life seemed past, I asked them to let me see and speak with my wife before

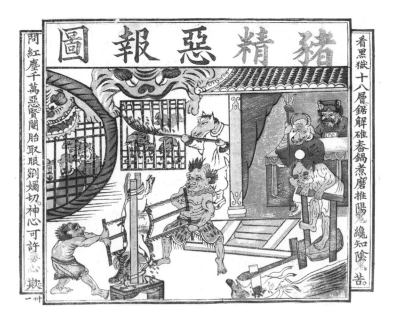

Figure 4.10, titled "The Terrible Punishment of the Pig Incarnate [Jesus]," depicts Jesus (being sawed in two) and a missionary (being pounded with a pestle) in a Chinese hell. The text on the left (referring to Jesus' Christian followers in China) reads: "You who in this life have committed a thousand times ten thousand malicious acts, who have castrated boys, removed the fetuses from pregnant women, gouged out people's eyes, and cut off women's nipples – do you think that the gods will permit themselves to be taken in by your viciousness?"

Source: Both posters are from *Jinzun shengyu bixie quantu*, as reprinted in *The Cause of the Riots in the Yangtse Valley: A "Complete Picture Gallery"* (Hankow, 1891).

I died. They said, "Ask your Jesus whether you may see her," and brutally kicked me on the head.[50]

There is a remarkable parallel between Chinese and foreign efforts in 1900 to invalidate each other's religious beliefs by calling attention to their inability to provide protection in the face of danger and the similar efforts made in the sixteenth century by Protestants and Catholics in France. In 1561, according to Natalie Davis, a Protestant crowd cornered a baker guarding the holy-wafer box in a church in Paris. "Messieurs," the baker pleaded, "do not touch it for the honor of Him who dwells here." The Protestants' reply, before killing the baker, was: "Does your God of paste protect you now from the pains of death?" Easily a match for the Protestants, a crowd of Catholics in Orléans in 1572 taunted its prospective victims with the following challenge: "Where is your God? Where are your prayers and Psalms? Let him save you if he can."[51]

When, seemingly deaf to anxious prayers, God failed to provide protection in the summer of 1900, foreign missionaries routinely took refuge in the view that, in the daily workings of human life, His plan was beyond comprehension, and it was the mark of the good Christian that, even in the face of this incomprehension, he or she still trusted in God's goodness absolutely. Boxers (and possibly also some Chinese Christians) accounted for the inefficacy of their magicoreligious rituals in quite different ways. When Boxer rituals failed to have the desired effect, it was sometimes explained (as we saw in Chapter 3 in this volume) in terms of some failing on the part of the individual performing them. Far more often, however, the Boxers identified countervailing magical forces in the environment (above all, female pollution) that they believed had the capacity to thwart their magical powers.

Not only did the Boxers differ from the foreign missionaries in regard to their understanding of why magicoreligious rituals sometimes didn't work; they also had very different notions concerning the general availability of magicoreligious capacity. In the magicoreligious world in which the Boxers (and many non-Boxer Chinese) lived, the potentiality existed for everyone, regardless of what god or gods they worshiped, to have access to supernatural power. The crucial question, therefore, as already suggested in my discussion of the Boxers' understanding of warfare, was whose supernatural power in a given situation was more efficacious. During the drought in the summer of 1900 a missionary reported that the local official of the town in Shanxi province where she and her husband were stationed was "so eager...to obtain rain that, finding his prayers in the temple had failed, he even secretly asked my husband how to pray to the God of Heaven and Earth."[52] Even more to the point, another Shanxi missionary reported the following:

Various stories were set afloat as to the power of the missionaries to prevent rain, ascribing almost superhuman strength in the way of controlling the elements. Clouds were constantly being driven away by fierce winds, which led to the story – thoroughly believed by all the people – that we went into our upper rooms and drove the clouds back by fanning with all our might. The story was changed as regards another group of missionaries in the province, that they were naked when doing the fanning.[53]

One of the more intriguing things about this report is its clear implication that Chinese at the time saw no bar to attributing to foreigners the same kind of supernatural powers they believed to be possessed by certain Chinese (in this instance, the wind-manipulation magic of the Red Lanterns).

Other examples abound. A Chinese teacher in Shanxi stated that there was an organization of Christian women in the capital of the province who were called White Lanterns and had magic so powerful it could overcome that of the Boxers and Red Lanterns.[54] Arthur Smith accounted for the Boxer penchant for cutting their victims to pieces – and often burning them – by citing the popular belief (which he claimed was widely prevalent) that Christians would rise from the dead within three days "unless energetic steps were taken to prevent it."[55] Finally, in addition to the examples cited earlier, the Boxers attributed to the foreigners a broad range of magical powers in combat situations, mostly focused on the foreigners' use of females to counteract the Boxers' own magical powers. The Boxers regularly attributed the casualties they suffered in fighting with the foreigners in Tianjin to the latter's placement of a naked woman in the midst or in front of their forces, which broke the power of the Boxers' magic.[56] The story was also circulated and widely believed by the populace that a naked woman straddled each of the many cannon mounted in the buildings in the foreign quarter of Tianjin, making it impossible for the "gunfire-repelling magic" (*bipao zhi fa*) of the Boxers to work properly.[57]

In Beijing, the most frequent references to foreign manipulation of the polluting power of women were in connection with the Boxers' siege of the Northern Cathedral, in which approximately 3,400 people, mostly Chinese Catholics, more than half of them women and girls, had taken refuge in June.[58] Among the reasons the Boxers are said to have offered for their repeated failures to take the cathedral and the heavy losses they suffered in these attempts were the following: naked women had come out of the building; the defenders had hung the skins of women (*furen pi*) and other "dirty things" (*huiwu*) from the spires; naked women were nailed to the church façade; countless naked women with "dirty things" in their hands stood on top of the walls; the foreigners had cut open the bellies of pregnant women and nailed them to the building; the Catholic defenders had a "ten-thousand woman flag" (*wan nü mao*), woven from women's pubic hair, which, when they used it to direct the fighting from the church steeple, prevented the Boxers' gods from possessing them.[59]

Conclusion

To summarize, Christians and Boxers both understood their encounter in the summer of 1900 in religious terms. But their respective understandings were not entirely symmetrical. The most critical difference, I believe, centered on the question of exclusivity. Christians generally interpreted the Boxer movement as the incarnation of evil, a characteristic expression of the traditional satanic role of opposition to God.[60] At the same time, supremely confident that only they, through the workings of God, were in possession of authentic supernatural power, the Christians consistently disparaged any and all Boxer magicoreligious claims. The Boxers, as we have seen, viewed matters quite differently. They might or might not regard their magicoreligious powers as more potent than those of the foreigners – on this point there was room for difference. But never, for a moment, did they see themselves as the exclusive possessors of such powers.

Of course, just because both the Boxers and the Christians saw the conflict in which they were engaged as an expression of religious agency does not mean that this was the only way in which they were capable of experiencing it. Certainly, the antiforeignism of the Boxers, although often situated in a religious matrix, had an existence apart from religion; moreover, there is no reason to doubt that at least some Boxers were in certain circumstances motivated by genuinely patriotic sentiments. On the Christian side as well, the fact that the conflict was seen as religiously determined did not keep missionaries from also understanding it as an encounter between civilization and barbarism, the forces of progress and the forces of reaction, although even here the hand of God was believed to be at work, it being widely assumed by Christians at the turn of the twentieth century that progress – and the Western civilization that embodied it – was itself the expression of God's will.[61]

Historical events, as we all know, are subject to multiple readings. Sometimes these multiple readings reflect variant themes in a society's history. Among the meaning contexts in which historians have placed the witchcraft outbreak in late seventeenth-century Salem, for example, are: "the history of the occult, the psychopathology of adolescence, the excesses of repressive Puritanism, and the periodic recrudescence of mass hysteria and collective persecution in Western society."[62] Sometimes, on the other hand, new readings result from subsequent developments that, in one way or another, alter the meaning(s) of prior events. The atomic bombing of Hiroshima is often described as the opening act of the nuclear age, but, obviously, the possibility of so describing it hinges entirely on a nuclear age in fact having materialized in the post-Hiroshima years. Or, to take a simpler case, the Great War didn't become World War I until another war, World War II, erupted years later.

Clearly, historians are at liberty to interpret past events in different ways. But not all interpretations are equally valid. The question therefore arises: how do we decide which interpretations are better, which worse? This is not the place to look into this question in depth. But hopefully we can agree that, at the very least, valid interpretations of past events must somehow reflect or otherwise relate to the realities of the world in which the events occurred (whether or not these realities were consciously perceived at the time), and conversely that they must avoid insinuating into these realities meanings that, however plausible, are without substantial empirical support. In my study of the Boxer conflict I have come increasingly to the conclusion that the characterization of the Boxer movement as "anti-imperialistic and patriotic" (*fandi aiguo*), almost universally the view of mainland Chinese historians, is not justified by contemporary evidence and distorts and misrepresents the diverse and complex motives impelling the Boxers to behave as they did.[63] On the other hand, I find a degree of empirical support, on the foreign side, for the view of the conflict as one between the forces of progress and the forces of reaction, and a good deal of evidence, on the Chinese side, in support of the view that hatred and fear of foreigners (and of all things foreign) was of paramount importance. Both of these views were, however, wrapped at the time in religious language and rested on a bedrock of religious premises about how the world operated. Therefore, if we are to gain a fuller and more accurate understanding of the Boxer–Christian conflict, as it was experienced by those who took direct part in it, the religious assumptions guiding participants on both sides must be assigned a far more central place than has hitherto been the case.

Notes

This chapter was originally presented as a talk. It was subsequently published in Chinese: "Yihetuan, Jidutu he shen: Cong zongjiao zhanzheng jiaodu kan 1900 nian de Yihetuan douzheng" (trans. Li Li, Tao Feiya, and Xian Yuyi), *Lishi yanjiu* (Historical research) 1 (February 2001). The English version presented here contains minor changes only.

1 Paul A. Cohen, *History in Three Keys: The Boxers as Event, Experience, and Myth* (New York: Columbia University Press, 1997).
2 Journal entry, in Alice M. Williams Miscellaneous Papers (Shansi Mission), file 12, American Board of Commissioners for Foreign Missions, Houghton Library, Harvard University (hereafter ABCFM). See also Bird's letter of June 24, 1900 to her brother, *ibid.*
3 Simcox, letter, April 12, 1900, Paotingfu [Baoding], *China Supplement* (October 1900), p. 279, excerpted toward end of Mrs. S.P. Fenn, "Peking Siege-Book" (n.p.), in Miscellaneous Personal Papers, Manuscript Group No. 8, Box No. 68, China Records Project, Divinity School Library, Yale University (hereafter CRP); Pitkin, letter, June 2, 1900, in Sarah Boardman Goodrich, "Journal of 1900," June 6, 1900, pp. 6–7, in Miscellaneous Personal Papers, Manuscript Group No. 8, Box No. 88, CRP; Miner, "Last Rites for the Paoting-fu Martyrs," *The Advance*, August 1, 1901.
4 See, for example, the dispatch from American minister Edwin H. Conger to Secretary of State John Hay, May 8, 1900, in United States, *Papers Relating to*

the Foreign Relations of the United States, 1900 (Washington, D.C.: GPO, 1902), p. 122. Conger had earlier linked the drought to mounting problems (including Boxer-related unrest) in northwestern Shandong (dispatch to Hay, December 7, 1899, *ibid.*, p. 77). See also the dispatch of British minister Claude M. MacDonald to Foreign Secretary Salisbury, May 21, 1900, in Great Britain, Parliamentary Papers, *China No. 3 (1900)* (London, 1900), p. 105.

5 Bird, journal entry, June 25, 1900; see also Dwight H. Clapp, diary letter, Taigu, Shanxi, July 7 and 15, 1900, in Alice M. Williams Miscellaneous Papers (Shansi Mission), file 12, ABCFM; Luella Miner, journal, Beijing, June 25, 1900, in Luella Miner Papers (North China Mission), ABCFM.

6 Miner, journal, Tongzhou, June 7, 1900.

7 Miner, journal, Beijing, June 23, 1900; Clapp, diary letter, Taigu, Shanxi, July 13, 1900; see also Clapp's comment, after voicing his fears for the safety of missionaries elsewhere in Shanxi:

> Ah this is serious business for poor China! But in the end [it] will be for the furtherance of the Kingdom of God. Of this I feel sure. I have felt for many years that Satan would stir up a great persecution for China one of these days & it is coming now. It is a time of testing & sifting too.
>
> Diary letter, Taigu, Shanxi, July 6, 1900.

8 Sarah Boardman Goodrich, letter, Tung Cho [Tongzhou], May 28, 1900, in Miscellaneous Personal Papers, Manuscript Group No. 8, Box No. 88, CRP. (I have inserted an apostrophe in the original, which reads "Gods soldiers.") Murray Rubinstein describes the "military cast of mind" as "an inherent element in the mission enterprise." See his "The Wars They Wanted: American Missionaries' Use of *The Chinese Repository* Before the Opium War," *The American Neptune*, 48.4 (Fall 1988): 271.

9 *The Boxer Rising: A History of the Boxer Trouble in China* [reprinted from the *Shanghai Mercury*], 2nd edn. (Shanghai: Shanghai Mercury, 1901), p. 9.

10 The translation is Esherick's, in his *The Origins of the Boxer Uprising*, p. 299. The original may be found in *Yihetuan shiliao* (Historical materials on the Boxers) (Beijing: Zhongguo shehui kexue, 1982), *shang*, p. 18; Chen Zhenjiang and Cheng Xiao, *Yihetuan wenxian jizhu yu yanjiu* (Explications and studies of Boxer writings) (Tianjin: Tianjin renmin chubanshe, 1985), p. 34. For two other almost identical notices, see *ibid.*, pp. 30–3; Sawara Tokusuke and Ouyin, *Quanluan jiwen* (A record of things heard concerning the Boxer disorders), in Jian Bozan *et al.*, eds., *Yihetuan* (The Boxers) (Shanghai: Shenzhou guoguang she, 1951) (hereafter *YHT*) 1: 112. A shorter version of the text translated by Esherick was circulated orally in the Shandong–Zhili border area. See Zhang Zhizhen (84), Liyuantun, Nangong, Hebei, 1960, in Lu Yao *et al.*, comps., *Shandong Yihetuan diaocha ziliao xuanbian* (Selections from survey materials on the Shandong Boxers) (Jinan: Qi-Lu, 1980), pp. 315–16; Chen Zhenjiang and Cheng Xiao, *Yihetuan wenxian jizhu yu yanjiu*, pp. 31–2.

11 For a sampling, in addition to the ones already cited, see Qiao Zhiqiang, comp., *Yihetuan zai Shanxi diqu shiliao* (Historical materials on the Boxers in the Shanxi area) (Taiyuan: Shanxi renmin chubanshe, 1980), pp. 1, 4–5; *Shanxi sheng gengzinian jiaonan qianhou jishi* (A complete account of the church difficulties in Shanxi province in 1900), in *YHT* 1: 510; and, especially, Chen Zhenjiang and Cheng Xiao, *Yihetuan wenxian jizhu yu yanjiu*, pp. 22–3, 26–8, 41–2, 47–8, 49–50, 84.

12 Emma Martin, diary, May 15, 1900, p. 29, in Miscellaneous Personal Papers, Manuscript Group No. 8, Box no. 137, CRP.

13 Arnold, *Famine: Social Crisis and Historical Change* (Oxford: Basil Blackwell, 1988), pp. 15–16. During the disastrous flooding that struck parts of the American Midwest in the summer of 1993, a Des Moines woman responded to President Clinton's visit to a stricken area as follows: "He can't play with God and nature. He'll do what he can. But this happened because God wanted it." *New York Times*, July 15, 1993, p. B10.

14 Clifford Geertz, "Thick Description: Toward an Interpretive Theory of Culture," in his *The Interpretation of Cultures* (New York: Basic Books, 1973), p. 12.

15 Arnold, *Famine*, p. 77.

16 Cohn, *The Pursuit of the Millennium: Revolutionary Millenarians and Mystical Anarchists of the Middle Ages*, rev. and expanded edn. (New York: Oxford University Press, 1970), p. 212.

17 This kinship is noted in Mark Elvin, "Mandarins and Millenarians: Reflections on the Boxer Uprising of 1899–1900," *Journal of the Anthropological Society of Oxford* 10.3 (1979): 121.

18 People in other cultures have also relied on invulnerability magic for protection in combat. In the religious rioting unleashed by the Islamic sect the 'Yan Tatsine against Nigerian security forces in 1980, the insurrectionists were said to have used rituals, tattoos, invincibility charms, and "magic sand" to protect themselves against the bullets of their adversaries. Paul M. Lubeck, "Islamic Protest under Semi-Industrial Capitalism: 'Yan Tatsine Explained," *Africa*, 55.4 (1985): 370, 386. Earlier in the twentieth century, the Lugbara followers of the Kakwa prophet and diviner Rembe, after performing specified rituals, went into battle "berserk and believing in the power of the *Yakan* water to turn bullets into water." John Middleton, "Spirit Possession Among the Lugbara," in John Beattie and John Middleton, eds., *Spirit Mediumship and Society in Africa* (New York: Africana Publishing, 1969), pp. 227–8.

19 Chen Zhenjiang and Cheng Xiao, *Yihetuan wenxian jizhu yu yanjiu*, pp. 153–4. The original Chinese reads: "Dizi zai hongchen, bizhu qiangpao men; qiangpao yiqi xiang, shazi liangbian fen."

20 Tang Yan, *Gengzi xixing jishi* (A record of the imperial progress westward in 1900), in *YHT* 3: 471; see also Zhongfang Shi, *Gengzi jishi* (A record of the events of 1900), in *Gengzi jishi* (A record of the events of 1900) (Beijing: Zhonghua shuju, 1978), p. 12. In Shanxi, according to China Inland Mission missionary Olivia Ogren, it was reported that as soon as foreign troops attacked, the Boxers would "fly away to heaven, out of the reach of bullets." Ogren, "A Great Conflict of Sufferings," in Marshall Broomhall, ed., *Last Letters and Further Records of Martyred Missionaries of the China Inland Mission* (London: Morgan and Scott, 1901), p. 72; also *ibid.*, p. 65.

21 Anon., *Tianjin yiyue ji* (An account of one month in Tianjin) (hereafter *TYJ*), in *YHT* 2: 148, 151. Someone told Liu Mengyang in late June that when Cao Futian found himself downstairs in a foreign building with a lot of foreigners upstairs, he threw a metal coin upstairs and the heads of the foreigners instantly fell to the ground. The same person informed Liu that he had personally seen Cao decapitate a bunch of foreigners in a building simply by waving a stick at them. The person who claimed to have witnessed this told Liu: "I saw it with my own eyes. It's not fabricated." Liu Mengyang, *Tianjin quanfei bianluan jishi* (An account of the Boxer bandit disorders in Tianjin), in *YHT* 2: 24.

22 *Yu nan riji* (A daily record of my encounters with misfortune), in *YHT* 2: 163; Liu Mengyang, *Tianjin quanfei bianluan jishi*, pp. 9, 36. Before his unit left the Tianjin area to take part in the fighting in the capital, one former Boxer reported, they all went to the home of the top local Red Lantern, the Holy Mother of the Yellow Lotus (Lin Hei'er), to ask for magic charms to make

them invulnerable to firearms. Guo Shirong (75), Boxer, Nankai daxue lishixi (Nankai University history department), ed., *Tianjin Yihetuan diaocha* (The Tianjin Boxer survey) (Tianjin: Tianjin guji chubanshe, 1990), p. 146.

23 Zhao Qing (72), Jinghai county, Fourth Sister-Disciple, *ibid.*, p. 144; *TYJ*, p. 146. It was claimed, according to Liu Mengyang (*Tianjin quanfei bianluan jishi*, p. 36), that the Holy Mother of the Yellow Lotus, by smearing incense ash on wounds, was able to stop the pain and close the wound.

24 As was clearly recognized by foreigners at the time. "During the whole of yesterday," Elwood G. Tewksbury, Arthur H. Smith, and W.T. Hobart wrote from Beijing in a letter of June 15, "the entire horizon was filled with smoke from the countless fires in every direction, *and this most dangerous weapon the Boxers hope to use constantly and effectively against us*" (emphasis supplied). Cited in Sarah Boardman Goodrich, June 18 entry of "Journal of 1900," p. 18. During the first days of the siege of the legations, W.E. Bainbridge wrote: "Under cover of their troops, the Boxers resorted to their favorite weapon and for an entire week we were in the center of a circle of raging flames." Bainbridge, "Besieged in Peking," p. 24, unpublished, in Lou Hoover Papers, Boxer Rebellion: Diaries, Herbert Hoover Presidential Library, West Branch, Iowa.

25 Liu Yitong, *Minjiao xiangchou dumen wenjian lu* (A record of things seen and heard concerning the mutual hatred of the people and the Christians in the capital), in *YHT* 2: 183, 185. See also *ibid.*, pp. 190–1, where the Boxers, by mumbling some phrases and waving their banners, are reported by Liu to have protected a grain shop in the Xidan area of the capital.

26 Liu Yitong, *Minjiao xiangchou dumen wenjian lu*, pp. 183–4. In a slight variation on the same story, Guan He heard that the Boxers pointed their swords at a certain portion of track, which then immediately caught fire. See his *Quanfei wenjian lu* (A record of things seen and heard concerning the Boxer bandits), in *YHT* 1: 468.

27 Sun Shaotang (75), Nankai daxue lishixi, *Tianjin Yihetuan diaocha*, p. 156.

28 Liu Mengyang, *Tianjin quanfei bianluan jishi*, p. 17. The extreme skeptic Guan He gave a quite different account of Red Lantern wind-management skills. Tianjin people, according to Guan, all said that in order for the fires burning in the city to reach the foreign concession area a northwest wind was needed. Yet, day after day, the wind blew only from the southeast. Red Lanterns, therefore, mounted the city wall and, using their magic, called on the wind to shift its direction, after which they announced that by the next morning at the latest the winds would become northwesterly. But the next day the winds were southeasterly as before. Guan He, *Quanfei wenjian lu*, p. 478.

29 According to one account, Red Lanterns learned to fly by placing a copper dish filled with water before a god and walking around it continuously crying out "fly." After doing this for forty-eight days they were able to fly. Hu Sijing, *Lü bei ji* (Writings from the back of a donkey), in *YHT* 2: 488. For a slightly different version of this training procedure, which took only five days to master, see *TYJ*, p. 141.

30 *TYJ*, p. 141. At one point, according to Liu Mengyang (*Tianjin quanfei bianluan jishi*, p. 37), it was reported (and widely believed) in Tianjin that a Mongol prince had occupied Russia with his army and half of the Japanese capital had been burned down by Red Lanterns using their magical skills.

31 Liu Yitong, *Minjiao xiangchou dumen wenjian lu*, p. 194. According to Liu (*ibid.*), on June 28 Prince Duan, the staunchest supporter of the Boxers at court, had personally mounted the steeple of the cathedral and captured and killed the devil prince, so that the Boxers should henceforth experience little difficulty in vanquishing the other defenders. Zhongfang Shi's account of

Favier (*Gengzi jishi*, p. 28), although less bizarre than that of Liu Yitong, also speaks of an "old devil" inside the cathedral who specialized in harming people with his black magic. It is reasonable to assume, therefore, that in one form or another this belief was widely circulated at the time.

32 Albert Vinchon, S.J., "La culte de la Sainte Vierge au Tche-li sud-est: Rapport présenté au Congrès marial de 1904," *Chine, Ceylan, Madagascar: Lettres des missionnaires français de la Compagnie de Jésus (Province de Champagne)* 18 (March 1905): 132–3.

33 *Ibid.*

34 Goodrich, "Journal of 1900," July 1, 1900, p. 33.

35 Vinchon, "La culte de la Sainte Vierge," p. 133. Although it was not likely to have been known to the missionary, water, it was widely believed on the Chinese side, had the power to nullify the Boxers' magic.

36 "Journal of 1900," June 28, 1900, p. 29.

37 Diary, June 15, 1900, in J. Freri, ed., *The Heart of Pekin: Bishop A. Favier's Diary of the Siege, May–August, 1900* (Boston: Marlier and Company, 1901), p. 26.

38 Mary Porter Gamewell, "History of the Peking Station of the North China Mission of the Woman's Foreign Missionary Society of the Methodist Episcopal Church," p. 64, in Miscellaneous Personal Papers, Manuscript Group No. 8, Box No. 73, CRP.

39 Luella Miner, journal, Beijing, June 17, 1900.

40 Elaine Pagels, *The Origin of Satan* (New York: Random House, 1995), p. 181; see also *ibid.*, pp. 180, 182, 184.

41 Favier, letter, Beijing, May 18, 1900, reproduced in Freri, *The Heart of Pekin*, p. 8. From western Shanxi, Edith Nathan (China Inland Mission) wrote: "Truly these 'Child Boxers' are devilish, and a device of the devil. We in England know little of what the power of Satan can do over the mind of a child." Letter, July 12, 1900, in Broomhall, ed., *Last Letters*, p. 34.

42 May Nathan (China Inland Mission), letter, early to mid-July, 1900, western Shanxi, *ibid.*, p. 38.

43 Theodora M. Inglis, letter, Beijing, May 30, 1900, in Fenn, "Peking Siege-Book," pp. 1–2.

44 Newspaper clipping, excerpted in *ibid.*, p. 35.

45 Quoted in Robert Forsyth, comp. and ed., *The China Martyrs of 1900* (London: Religious Tract Society, 1904), p. 276; see also the account of John Ross (United Presbyterian Church), in *ibid.*, pp. 302–3. The Tianjin correspondent for the *North-China Herald* reported (in a dispatch dated June 8) that a lot of foreigners in the city eagerly awaited the attack of the Boxers, so they could prick the bubble of Boxer invulnerability claims (which "Chinese of all classes believe"). *North-China Herald and Supreme Court and Consular Gazette*, June 20, 1900, p. 1113.

46 Smith, *China in Convulsion*, 2 vols. (New York: Fleming H. Revell, 1901), 1: 172–3.

47 For additional anti-Christian posters, see *Jinzun shengyu bixie quantu*, as reproduced in *The Cause of the Riots in the Yangtse Valley: A "Complete Picture Gallery"* (Hankow, 1891); also Paul A. Cohen, *China and Christianity: The Missionary Movement and the Growth of Chinese Antiforeignism, 1860–1870* (Cambridge: Harvard University Press, 1963).

48 From the account of Miss G. Smith (London Missionary Society), as quoted in Forsyth, *The China Martyrs of 1900*, p. 354.

49 The account of Mr. Argento, in *ibid.*, p. 246.

50 Quoted in Olivia Ogren, "A Great Conflict," p. 77.

51 Natalie Zemon Davis, *Society and Culture in Early Modern France* (Stanford: Stanford University Press, 1975), p. 157.
52 Ogren, "A Great Conflict," p. 65; see also Forsyth, *The China Martyrs of 1900*, pp. 148–50.
53 C.W. Price, diary, between June 15 and 23, 1900, Fen Chou Fu, Shansi [Fenzhou, Shanxi], as excerpted in E.H. Edwards, *Fire and Sword in Shansi* (Edinburgh and London: Oliphant Anderson and Ferrier, 1903), pp. 269–70.
54 Liu Dapeng, *Qianyuan suoji* (Sundry information from the Qian garden), in Qiao Zhiqiang, *Yihetuan zai Shanxi*, p. 30.
55 Smith, *China in Convulsion* 2: 660.
56 Liu Mengyang, *Tianjin quanfei bianluan jishi*, p. 16; *TYJ*, p. 153.
57 *TYJ*, p. 151.
58 Freri, *The Heart of Pekin*, pp. 29–30.
59 Liu Yitong, *Minjiao xiangchou dumen wenjian lu*, pp. 184, 191, 193–4; Hua Xuelan, *Gengzi riji* (A diary of 1900), in *Gengzi jishi*, p. 109; Zhongfang Shi, *Gengzi jishi*, p. 28. For another example of foreign use of pregnant women to foil Boxer invulnerability magic, see Liu Yitong, *Minjiao xiangchou dumen wenjian lu*, p. 189. Hua Xuelan, the source of the allegation concerning the ten-thousand woman flag, heard it in conversation with friends after dinner and hesitated to vouch for its accuracy. Although this was among the more bizarre of the stories that circulated at the time, none of which probably had much basis in fact, I am persuaded that, in the atmosphere of excitement, uncertainty, and anxiety that prevailed in North China in the summer of 1900, the level of acceptance of such accounts not only among the Boxers but among the population at large was very high.
60 Neil Forsyth, *The Old Enemy: Satan and the Combat Myth* (Princeton: Princeton University Press, 1987), pp. 4–5.
61 Paul A. Cohen, "Christian Missions and Their Impact to 1900," in John K. Fairbank, ed., *The Cambridge History of China*, vol. 10: *Late Ch'ing, 1800–1911*, Part 1 (Cambridge: Cambridge University Press, 1978), pp. 588–9.
62 Paul Boyer and Stephen Nissenbaum, *Salem Possessed: The Social Origins of Witchcraft* (Cambridge: Harvard University Press, 1974), p. xi.
63 This point is more fully developed in the conclusion to Chapter 9 of *History in Three Keys*.

5 Ambiguities of a watershed date

The 1949 divide in Chinese history

Dates, especially those major year markers that we customarily refer to as watersheds or turning points in the flow of historical time, are inherently unstable, their meanings shifting in response either to new understandings of the events leading up to them or to later developments that were largely if not entirely unforeseen when the original meanings were established. A good example is the year 1949. This year, until not too long ago, was widely seen as constituting a radical breach in the continuity of Chinese history; it also (sociologically speaking) marked a sharp divide within the field of China scholarship, at least in the United States, with different people for the most part studying the pre- and post-1949 periods, asking different questions, relying on different source materials, reading different books, and more often than not attending different conferences.

The sharpness of the 1949 break was greatly reinforced by the tendency of those scholars whose work was primarily concerned with post-1949 China (most of them, especially during the early years, political scientists, economists, and sociologists) to view it from a systemic rather than a historical perspective, emphasizing the structural features China shared with other social systems of a comparable nature (such as, to take the most prominent instance, the Soviet Union).[1] There was nothing intrinsically wrong with such thinking; indeed, it continues to play an important part in the analyses of social scientists to this day. The problem was an extrinsic one: the fact that its practitioners often failed to see the importance of supplementing the systemic approach by paying serious heed to what had happened in Chinese history prior to 1949. In an article published in 1988, I attempted to do just this with reference to the early post-Mao era, looking at the reforms of that time from a historical rather than a systemic vantage point.[2] Although not discounting the important changes that had taken place in China with the advent of Communist rule, I put a good deal of emphasis on certain broad patterns that could be discerned in the Chinese reform process from the late nineteenth century through the Yuan Shikai and Guomindang years, all the way to the time of Deng Xiaoping's ascendancy. The year 1949, from this perspective, certainly did not disappear. But, with the reforms of the 1980s and the attendant "collapse of communism" (a phenomenon that became even more marked after Deng's time), its meaning shifted perceptibly, becoming increasingly complicated and ambiguous.

In the present essay I want to take another look at 1949, this time from a somewhat broader perspective. I will start out by touching on certain aspects of the issue of continuity vs. discontinuity as it bears on the 1949 divide; then I will explore some of the factors that I believe from the outset reinforced the notion of this year as a radical break in time; finally, I will suggest that it has been the weakening of these very factors in recent years that, as much as anything, has encouraged the more complex under-standing of 1949 that we have today.

1949: continuity vs. discontinuity

One tangled aspect of the continuity–discontinuity issue, as it surfaces in 1949, is the whole question of how it relates to the revolution that was supposed to have taken place in that year. If there was indeed a revolution – the ultimate discontinuity – how do we square this with the very substantial continuities growing numbers of scholars have discerned between pre- and post-1949 China? If, on the other hand, there wasn't a revolution, what did happen in 1949? How do we identify and label the very great changes that unquestionably occurred as a direct or indirect result of the Communists coming to power? And, more generally, would it be preferable to think of the Chinese revolution not as something that happened at a single point in time, but as a long-term political and social process made up of multiple revolutionary transformations?

One way of cutting through this tangle is to reframe the problem. Instead of asking *whether* a revolution took place in (and after) 1949, it may make more sense to ask what *kind* of revolution – or revolutions – occurred. Certainly, if we look at some of the more radical social changes that accompanied the Communist rise to power – the physical (and socio-logical) elimination of the landlord and rich peasant classes in the countryside, or the introduction of rural collectivization in the mid-1950s, or, in urban China, the destruction of the nascent bourgeoisie and severe reduction in the freedom of intellectuals, and of professional and manage-rial elements, to operate and express themselves socially and culturally[3] – or the transformative experiences of the period from the late 1950s until the mid-1970s – above all, the Great Leap Forward and the Cultural Revolution – we can talk of a specifically *Communist* or *Marxist–Leninist* or *Maoist* revolution. But many of the most dramatic and sweeping changes that occurred in the first years of Communist rule represented the realization of what I would call a consensual Chinese agenda. That is, they were changes that would have been supported by the Guomindang – and even in some instances the rulers of the late Qing – as well as the Communists.

Among the changes I have in mind are the following: the complete elimination of the last remnants of foreign imperialism; the incorporation into
the Chinese nation of the entire territory embraced by the Qing empire,
with the exception of Mongolia,[4] and the reestablishment of full central
government control over this territory after over a hundred years of
partially curtailed sovereignty; the greatly enhanced capacity of the central
government to gain control (through the elimination of middlemen) of
revenues extracted from the farming sector;[5] the reestablishment of
domestic peace after decades of civil and foreign warfare; the more than
doubling of the size of the workforce; the rapid extension of education at
all levels, with particular attention to raising literacy rates; the dramatic
improvement in public health; and, partly owing to this last change, a
rapid growth in population.

The changes noted in the preceding paragraph were of major import. In
their impact on the lives of hundreds of millions of Chinese people, they
were without question of the most far-reaching nature. But, although
brought about by the Communists and certainly viewed by Mao and his
colleagues as part of their revolutionary program, they did not really
constitute a "Communist" revolution in any substantive sense. Add to the
revolutionary changes of the early 1950s the enormous forces of change
unleashed in the post-Mao era, starting in the late 1970s – changes that
overturned some of the most striking innovations of the Mao years – and
arguably we are presented with yet another revolution,[6] this one in certain
respects more a continuation (or resumption) of developments that had
their beginnings *prior* to 1949 than of developments that came out of the
1949–76 period (the years of Mao's rule). So, one point I would make,
although it is somewhat awkward sounding, is that in the years after 1949
China experienced not just one revolution but a number of different revolutions, partly overlapping and partly in conflict with one another.

Let me return to the notion of a "consensual Chinese agenda." I take
this phrase to embrace, in its broadest sense, not only a set of *goals* that
most Chinese, regardless of political affiliation, would support (such as the
elimination of imperialism, or the establishment of domestic peace and
stability, or the creation of a strong military or development of the Chinese
economy), but also certain *means* or *methods* or *instrumental strategies*
that Chinese of differing political commitments would agree were appropriate for the realization of specified goals. So far so good. The trouble is
that the consensus that exists with respect to such goals on a fairly high
level of abstraction or generality often breaks down when the focus shifts
to the specific content of the goals to be realized. *Formal continuity*, in
such situations, may well coexist with *substantive discontinuity*.

David Wang, for example, observes that "[f]or all the ideological antago-
nism between the two regimes, there were striking similarities between the
Nationalist and Communist ways of administering literary activities in the
1950s." Among both Nationalists and Communists there was substantial

consensus that it was right and proper for the state to exercise control in the realm of literary production and distribution. But after 1949 (before 1949 as well, only focusing on different themes) there was a complete lack of consensus concerning the *contents* of the literature to be permitted, Communist writers celebrating the Communist victory in the civil war and the huge changes that had taken place in China in the aftermath of that victory, Guomindang writers embracing one or another form of anti-Communist stance, including the notion that 1949 signaled the loss of the Chinese mainland to foreign – that is, Soviet – control.[7] Some would argue that, even at the instrumental level, although there were similarities the literary policies of the Communists and the Guomindang after 1949 were hardly identical, with much more creative freedom being permitted to writers on Taiwan than to those on the mainland. This may be so, but it is a fact that as late as the early 1960s, when I was living in Guomindang-ruled Taiwan, there was nothing even faintly approaching a free marketplace of ideas in the literary realm: the works of most major twentieth-century Chinese writers (Lu Xun, Lao She, and Shen Congwen, to name only a few) were banned from circulation and unavailable in bookshops and libraries.

Essentially the same point may be made with respect to the film industry. On the level of specific content, important shifts took place from the late 1940s to the early 1950s. But, on a more formal level, we can identify a continuity of some importance, namely the state's assumption that the film industry needed to be placed under a greater or lesser degree of control – greater in the case of the Communists, lesser in that of the Guomindang – to ensure, at the very least, that films would be free of content that opposed or undermined government policy.[8]

Obviously, a major reason for the above-noted formal continuity between the strategies pursued by the Chinese Communist Party and the Guomindang was that both were beneficiaries of a centuries-old political tradition that, at least in theory and often in practice, gave the state considerable control over society (including the literary and intellectual realms). Beyond this, there is the important fact that both political organizations were structured along Leninist lines, with the consequence that they both viewed it as their prerogative to exercise a substantial degree of societal control. To cite one further instance of this, as we shall see in the next chapter, the Guomindang, when it came to power in the late 1920s, assumed complete supervision over national anniversary observances and, behaving in almost every respect like the Chinese Communist Party in its marking of anniversaries after 1949, used these occasions to promote its own political agenda. The one respect in which the Guomindang differed from the Communists, of course, was in the content of its agenda, which was explicitly and stridently anti-Communist.[9]

General statements about the past (above all, I think, statements about the meaning of this or that "turning point" or "watershed") tend to have a larger mythic component than more bounded statements and, as such, reflect to a higher degree the passions and concerns of the persons making them and the times in which they live. This can be a problem, inasmuch as the passions and concerns of the present have a way of changing abruptly and without warning, and when this happens the general assertions about the past that embody such passions and concerns quickly lose their currency. The meaning of the past – and I include here watershed dates – is not, in other words, fixed for all time; it is forever subject to a future marked by indeterminacy.

The point is nicely made by Vera Schwarcz in her commentary on Joseph Levenson's characterization of the meaning of the intellectual and political developments known in China as the May Fourth Movement of 1919. In his essay "The Day Confucius Died," Schwarcz writes,

> Levenson had tried to endow the event of 1919 with a decisive, epoch-making significance not unlike that assigned to it by Mao Zedong in his distinction between "new" and "old" democracy. For Levenson, May Fourth marked a point of no return between tradition and modernity, between Western inspired solutions to China's dilemmas and the once universal truth claims of Confucianism.

Ironically, not too many years after Levenson wrote his essay (1961), Confucius was dragged through the streets of Cultural Revolution Canton in effigy, a clear sign that his influence in China was not moribund at all. Reflecting this and other realities, scholarship on May Fourth, according to Schwarcz, had by the 1980s moved away from the bloated language of earlier times and was less likely to embody such extreme claims as Levenson's.[10]

In like fashion, the effect that unforeseen future developments can have on perceptions of the past complicates our efforts to plumb the meaning of 1949. As suggested earlier, some fairly sharp discontinuities characterizing the periods immediately prior to and after this year were substantially moderated, if not completely reversed, in the post-Mao era or even in some respects (such as the opening to America) as early as 1970 (when Mao was still very much alive), so that by the late 1980s one can point to important continuities – or at least resonances – with the period of Guomindang rule on the mainland, in particular the 1930s. One clear example of this is the relationship between foreign influences and freedom, on one hand, and foreign influences and control, on the other, as it affected scientific and technical personnel, artists, students, and other social groups. In the case of the student community, for example, foreign influences were a source of liberation and empowerment in both the 1930s and the 1980s, insofar as they opened up the minds of young Chinese to new worlds of experience. But in both decades they also created a line of tension and potential conflict between students and the government, exposing the former to not infrequently shrill, uncomprehending criticism from the latter. The government's periodic lashing out against such expressions of "spiritual pollution" as rock and roll in the 1980s was a clear echo of criticisms of Western popular culture leveled in the 1930s, when Minister of Education Chen Lifu warned sinisterly that "Hollywood films lay traps of decadence" and the head of the Board of Education of Shanghai stigmatized imported movies as "propaganda pieces of American commercial culture!"[11]

In both the 1930s and the 1980s there was also competition between officials, on one hand, and students and intellectuals, on the other, over who had the greater standing to speak on behalf of nation and society. And there were tensions between a *modernization* that was collective in orientation and focused above all on the achievement of greater wealth and power for the nation – something both a Chiang Kai-shek and a Deng Xiaoping could support with enthusiasm – and a *modernism* centered on individual liberation and creative freedom, which both Chiang and Deng felt distinctly uncomfortable about and periodically lashed out against. In the broadest sense, all of these resonances had to do with conflictual interaction between the state and one or another sector of society, thus pointing to larger issues of state–society relations that plagued China in the 1930s and continued to plague China in the 1980s and on into the 1990s. (A similar point is made in Chapter 6 of this volume.)

Apart from such resonances between decades separated by half a century, the 1980s (and 1990s) also witnessed the *reappearance* of a variety of phenomena that had existed in one form or another up to 1949 and then been eradicated in the immediate post-1949 era: the rise of the household sector and the market, rich peasants, entrepreneurs, extensive foreign trade and investment, prostitution, links between native places (*guxiang*) within China and regional associations (*tongxianghui*) overseas, American influence on Chinese higher education, the sending of Chinese to the West to study, and so on. We have to be very careful, however, not to think of such phenomena as simple continuities or even, strictly speaking, revivals. Labels can be highly misleading. To understand any historical phenomenon in any period, we need to look at it in the context of the reality in which it is embedded in that time period.

Let me offer a few examples. When the multifaceted ties between overseas Chinese and their native places, which had been sundered by the Communists after 1949, were revived in the late 1970s, the terminology describing these ties remained the same. But, as Elizabeth Sinn clearly shows, there were significant substantive differences from the pre-1949 period. The most conspicuous of these was the unprecedented effort of mainland authorities at all levels in the 1980s to put overseas (and Taiwanese) Chinese talent and wealth to work in support of China's new development plans. In response to this mainland "offensive," fifty-four new *tongxianghui* were founded in Hong Kong between 1979 and 1990, a major motivation being to take advantage of the new opportunities for trade and investment that were rapidly opening up in China. (Significantly, a sizable proportion of these new Hong Kong *tongxianghui* were Fujianese, a consequence partly of the growing population of Fujianese in Hong Kong and the economic development of Fujian province, but also of the need to strengthen contacts with Taiwan, with its extensive human and capital resources, the exploitation of which in the 1980s had become a major Chinese objective.) The unparalleled expansion of trade and investment prospects on the mainland that led to the creation of new regional associations in Hong Kong during these years also, of course, encouraged existing associations to renew and strengthen their *guxiang* ties in the hope of sharing in the bounty. In the upshot, although fresh life was certainly injected into many of the older functions of the Hong Kong *tongxianghui* during the 1980s, the enormous expansion of the mainland economic involvement of these organizations also added an important new dimension to their nature and purpose.[12]

The resumption of Chinese study abroad during the Deng Xiaoping era presents another instance of apparent continuity combined with significant change. (I will confine my discussion here to the United States, although at various points in the course of the twentieth century substantial numbers of Chinese also pursued studies in Japan, Europe, and the Soviet Union.) The total number of *liuxuesheng* (literally, "returned students") going to America during the entire century from 1854 to 1953 (mostly in the latter half of this period) has been estimated (very roughly) at 21,000,[13] and the great majority of these, because of prewar America's extremely restrictive immigration laws regarding Chinese nationals, had no choice but to return to China, where during the republican period they often achieved great prominence in diplomacy, industry, finance, higher education, and other fields.[14] When, after a hiatus of thirty years, such study resumed in the post-Mao era, the numbers of Chinese students (still universally referred to as *liuxuesheng*) and scholars annually entering the United States grew, from 1,330 in 1979 to 13,491 in 1990, resulting in a total of 102,468 entrants in just over a decade.[15] Apart from the enormous difference in numbers, moreover, unlike in the pre-1949 period, a very large proportion of this later generation of Chinese students and scholars have not (especially since the late 1980s) returned to China (although this has been less true of senior scholars). Part of the reason for this, of course, has been a substantial easing of American immigration restrictions, especially after the Tiananmen events of 1989; but economic, political, and "quality of life" factors in China have also affected the decisions of many Chinese to remain, at least temporarily, in the United States.[16] This pattern may be changing, in response to a growing improvement in the Chinese economy's capacity to absorb and adequately reward highly trained individuals.[17] But even if the brain drain were to be decisively reversed, as happened over time in Korea and Taiwan,[18] it seems unlikely, given the enormous changes that have engulfed China during the past quarter-century, that returned students would ever play the same range of roles that they played in the 1920s, 1930s, and 1940s.[19]

One last example has to do with foreign trade and investment. "Foreign firms, investments, loans and personnel dominated important parts of the modern sector of China's economy in the early republic," Albert Feuerwerker has written, but "the modern sector...was only a minute portion of the Chinese economy as a whole. Foreign and Chinese modern enterprise both grew steadily, but neither bulked very large before 1949." "The overall poverty of the Chinese economy," he adds, "fundamentally limited the impact of foreign merchants and their goods."[20] During the first three decades of the Communist period, foreign trade played only a minor role in China's planned economy and there was general opposition among Chinese leaders to foreign investment.[21] With the accession of Deng Xiaoping and a new commitment to the integration of China into the world economy, however, this situation changed radically. China's trade volume, which in the 1970s represented less than 1 per cent of total world trade, grew to US$69 billion by 1985, and ten years later to US$281 billion; by 2001, when it reached US$509.8 billion, China had become the fourth largest trader in the world (counting the European Union as a single trader and combining exports and imports of merchandise and commercial services). Equally stunning, Chinese exports, mostly manufactures, rose from US$9.75 billion in 1978 to US$266.2 billion by 2001, and there was comparable growth, especially from the latter half of the 1980s, in foreign investment activity.[22] In contrast with the pre-1949 years, moreover, foreign trade and investment since the 1980s have had a sizable impact on the Chinese economy as a whole. (Chinese exports, for example, have generated much of the foreign exchange that has enabled China to buy needed foreign technology and equipment.[23]) But the more general point to be made, as before, is that ostensibly the same phenomena – foreign trade and investment – had entirely different implications in the pre-1949 and post-1978 periods, as a result of the very different historical settings in which they operated. Not only did the Chinese economy grow at an extremely rapid pace after 1978; it also underwent a profound structural transformation, as the proportion of people of working age engaged in agriculture dropped, from 70.5 per cent in 1978 to 54 per cent in 1994, and China took significant strides toward becoming an industrial urban society.[24]

The point I have tried to make in the preceding paragraphs in connection with such complex processes as *tongxianghui–guxiang* relations, Chinese study abroad, and foreign trade with and investment in China may also, I am convinced, be made in regard to such occupational categories as rich peasants, prostitutes, and entrepreneurs. These groups were an important part of the Chinese social scene in the decades prior to 1949, were suppressed and became largely moribund during the Mao years, and then reemerged in the 1980s. But my guess is that if we were to conduct a serious study of their place in society in the 1980s as compared to, say, the 1940s we would find that there were enormous differences between the two, masked to some extent by the shared vocabulary with which we refer to them.

Watershed dates, as earlier suggested, are not stable in nature. Like all historical phenomena, the meaning and valence we assign to them are affected by new developments and understandings that emerge sometimes many years after the original date. This can work in opposite ways, moreover. Sometimes a discrete event that, in itself, is fairly ordinary and in other circumstances might well get lost in the historical shuffle becomes invested with major significance once historians begin to piece together the origins and evolution of the larger event of which it is part. The Marco Polo Bridge incident of July 7, 1937, instead of being a forgettable skirmish between Chinese and Japanese troops in North China, like many previous such skirmishes, is transformed into the first act in a drama known to the Chinese as the War of Resistance and to much of the rest of the world as World War II.[25] In other instances, as in the 1949 divide, the meaning of an event ("the Chinese revolution") that once seemed huge becomes more ambiguous over time. Certain Communist or Maoist features of the changes that took place in the middle of the twentieth century or shortly thereafter – the encouragement of class warfare, for example, or farm collectivization – continued in place through the Mao years before being reversed. Other changes that resulted from the Communist victory in the civil war but that were not the fulfillment of a specifically Communist agenda (such as the eradication of the last vestiges of imperialism or the rapid extension of popular literacy) remain in place to this day. And still other changes, those that took place during the post-Mao years (as discussed immediately above), resonate in some respects with developments of the pre-1949 period. The year 1949, in short, looks very different depending on the point in later time from which it is viewed.

Historical origins of the 1949 divide

If there have been significant continuities, resonances, and points of correspondence (however much qualified) between aspects of Chinese life that predated and postdated 1949, how did the sense of 1949 as a total break, a complete rupture in historical time, come into existence in the first place? Certainly, as I have noted, vitally important changes did in fact take place in the immediate post-1949 years (although some of these, most notably land reform, got their real start a few years prior to 1949). And this is part of the answer. But the *actual* changes that occurred were greatly reinforced in people's minds by a number of other factors that were conspicuous features of the environment in the 1950s, 1960s, and 1970s.

One such factor – and this was perhaps the most important of them – was the master narrative the Chinese Communists themselves constructed to define the meaning of 1949. This master narrative, although primarily targeting the Chinese populace, was also effectively promoted globally by the Chinese propaganda apparatus. It was superimposed on the changes that had actually taken place in China as a result of the Communist victory in the civil war; and, increasingly, as memories dimmed it shaped and simplified (if it did not entirely displace) these actual changes in people's minds. As everyone who went to China in the 1970s and asked people to tell their life stories will recall, the 1949 break (framed as "before liberation" and "after liberation") was, in popular rhetoric, absolutely fundamental.[26] It established the line between darkness and light, between suffering and joy, between oppression and empowerment, the transition from the first to the second term in each case being depicted as a precious gift from "our beloved savior Chairman Mao" and the Communist Party that embodied his will and every wish. This master narrative, highlighting the sharp dichotomy between the pre-1949 and post-1949 Chinese worlds, was woven into the very fabric of Chinese life and encountered at every turn. It was arguably the principal foundation stone on which the legitimacy of the Chinese party-state existed after 1949. The Chinese leadership therefore had a powerful vested interest in its perpetuation, regardless of the changes that did or did not occur in fact. In time, the notion of 1949 as a profound divide in historical time became an important component of Chinese consciousness and, as such, a very real factor influencing Chinese thinking and behavior, with little or no concern evinced for the degree to which its content accorded with reality. (For an analogous discussion of the meaning of the Opium War in Chinese consciousness, see Chapter 7 in this volume.)

Western academics, especially perhaps American social scientists, also developed a strong vested interest in 1949 as a major historical divide. The reasons, however, were quite different from those governing Chinese Communist thinking. Initially, it is well to keep in mind, there wasn't much post-1949 China to deal with in any case; also, as of mid-century the number of social scientists specializing in China was extremely small. Moreover, even when such persons began gradually to emerge as a significant academic force after the 1960s, we find that for the most part they paid little attention to developments prior to 1949; indeed, precious few of them were equipped by training to do research of any sort on the republican era. Another way of putting this, to elaborate on a point made earlier, is that the initial crop of social scientists generally were taught to approach societies as systems. Inasmuch as Communist societies were a particular variety of system (often further defined as exemplifying the "totalitarian model"), their natural tendency was to study them comparatively, looking at the features any given Communist society shared with other such societies. Since 1949 was the inaugural year of the Communist system in China, the idea of this year as a decisive break, a new beginning, was greatly reinforced. It was further magnified, as we have seen, by the fact that the post-1949 period tended, until fairly recently, to be largely the preserve of social scientists, while historians concentrated their labors on the period prior to this date.[27]

The Cold War, by greatly inflating the importance of communism and crudely mythologizing the distinction between the "communist" and the "free" worlds, created yet another vested interest in the concept of 1949 as radical break. The one change that took place in 1949 that no one seriously contests was that the Communists came to power on the Chinese mainland and the Guomindang retreated to Taiwan. In the United States the Communist victory in the civil war was defined by not a few Cold Warriors as the most significant event by far of all the events that had taken place in that year. China, with its enormous population, had been "lost" to "communism," and it was not uncommon, even among people like U.S. Secretary of State Dean Acheson (who should have known better), to portray China's Communist leaders as having "foresworn their Chinese heritage and...publicly announced their subservience to a foreign power, Russia."[28] Coming in the wake of the 1948 Czechoslovakia coup d'état and the Berlin Blockade, the Alger Hiss and other cases of alleged Soviet espionage, the upset victory of the Democrats in the U.S. presidential election (1948), and in 1949 the explosion of a Soviet atom bomb, ending America's nuclear monopoly, China's turn to communism created a level of fear, suspicion, and a sense of betrayal, above all in the United States (which in the early stages of the Chinese civil war had been allied with the Guomindang and therefore had a significant stake in the outcome), that it is hard to imagine in the early twenty-first century.[29]

To be sure, the Cold War was not just a frame of mind. Within a year of the establishment of the People's Republic of China in October 1949, China had become formally allied with the Soviet Union and the Korean War had broken out. The Cold War, moreover, was the defining feature of the system of international relations that developed throughout the world beginning in the late 1940s and a major contributing factor in most of the wars fought in the ensuing decades. But I am mainly interested here in the state of mind that the Cold War engendered in the West (again especially in America) – a state of mind that made it difficult if not impossible to hold, much less publicly articulate, a nuanced view of the world. To suggest that the world might be a more complicated place than Cold Warriors asserted was to imply that communism was not the evil monster they said it was, thereby laying oneself open to the charge of being soft on it, which in the United States in the 1950s and early 1960s (and a good deal longer in Guomindang-controlled Taiwan) was a dangerous thing to be accused of. Since neither the Chinese world nor the Western academic world existed in isolation from the Cold War environment,[30] this environment had the effect of reinforcing the importance already attached, for other reasons, to the 1949 divide in these worlds.

Conclusion

In recent years, all of the sources of a powerful and historically decisive 1949 divide that I've been discussing have undergone significant change. The Chinese Communist master narrative focusing on the profound contrast between the bad old society that existed before 1949 and the good new society that came into being after this date has by no means disappeared. It may still be found in official and officially inspired rhetoric. But its influence on Chinese consciousness has weakened palpably since the late 1970s, owing partly to the emergence in intellectual circles of a more affirmative stance toward aspects of the pre-1949 past and the dramatic resurgence, at the popular level, of a whole range of older beliefs and practices that an earlier generation of Communists (and Nationalists) had attempted to stamp out; partly to the open criticism of major phases of the Maoist era that, beginning in the late 1970s, it became possible to articulate; and, perhaps most importantly, to the reintegration of China into the world economy, its rapidly growing exposure to global cultural influences of all kinds, and the reversal of the most distinctive features of post-1949 socialism.

The sociology of Western scholarship has also undergone major changes during the past decade or two. As the period of post-1949 Chinese history has expanded (it is now more than a half-century long), social scientists, even those with minimal training in pre-1949 China, have been forced to think in more historical terms. Meanwhile, newer generations of social scientists have emerged that include individuals with a significantly stronger historical foundation and the ability to carry on research in pre-1949 materials.[31] For their part, historians of twentieth-century China have, with the augmented heft of the post-1949 era, become increasingly unwilling to allow social scientists to exercise near-monopolistic rights over it.[32] These changes together have resulted in growing intellectual cross-fertilization between historians and social scientists, one consequence of which has been an increased disposition on the part of both to see China before and after 1949 in less starkly dichotomous terms. A splendid example of this trend is the volume *Chinese Village, Socialist State* (1991), whose authors, Edward Friedman, Paul G. Pickowicz, and Mark Selden, explicitly reject the view of 1949 "as a complete rupture with the past, the end of the old order and the beginning of the new" and, in their probing examination of the impact of the state on a rural area in Hebei province, pay much attention to "deep continuities that transcend the founding of the People's Republic."[33]

Finally, the break-up of the Soviet Union and the collapse of East European communism, by bringing an abrupt end to the Cold War, removed the most powerful ideological support of the notion of 1949 as simple discontinuity – a shift that has, if anything, been reinforced by the increasingly "uncommunist" look of many aspects of Chinese life during the Deng and post-Deng years.

This retreat or eclipsing of forces that in an earlier time magnified the salience of 1949 has clearly encouraged the tendency of recent years to reduce its prominence as a historical breach. Some may be tempted, in these circumstances, to turn complete discontinuity into complete continuity, or to substitute for the concept of a revolution that changed everything the equally unpersuasive concept of a revolution that changed nothing, indeed that wasn't a revolution at all. This would be bad history. The challenge, instead, is to develop a picture of 1949 that is adequately complex, certainly more complex than the one we had in the 1950s and 1960s. This picture should acknowledge and probe the ways in which 1949 did indeed signal abrupt and important change, as well as the ways in which it did not. It should encompass the idea of multiple revolutions stretching both backward and forward from 1949, each making its distinctive contributions to the overall process of revolutionary change that has engulfed China for the past century and more. It should analyze (as I attempted briefly in the first portion of this chapter) the variety of ways in which historical processes can be continuous and discontinuous, sometimes at the same time. And, perhaps most important, it should be sensitive to the degree to which the past is ever hostage to an unforeseen and unforeseeable future, with the consequence that events and dates that have a certain meaning or cluster of meanings at one moment in time, at subsequent moments shed some of their earlier meanings and acquire new ones, their importance in the larger sweep of history undergoing a process of continual renegotiation, with results that are unpredictable and can sometimes be quite startling.

Notes

This chapter originated in comments made following a talk by Benjamin Schwartz at a conference, "China's Mid-Century Transitions: Continuity and Change on the Mainland and on Taiwan, 1946–1955," held at Harvard University, September 9–10, 1994. An earlier written version (with a slightly different title) appears in Jeffrey N. Wasserstrom, ed., *Twentieth-Century China: New Approaches* (London: Routledge, 2002). The present version is substantially enlarged.

1 This was true in some instances even of those with strong historical backgrounds. Thus, Franz Schurmann, in his pathbreaking study of the early years of the People's Republic, tended to approach his material from a comparative communism perspective. See Schurmann, *Ideology and Organization in Communist China* (Berkeley: University of California Press, 1966). For criticism of the systemic approach for its failure to take adequate account of contingent, contextual, and situational factors, see Paul A. Cohen, "Response to Introduction: Situational versus Systemic Factors in Societal Evolution," in Ramon H. Myers, ed., *Two Societies in Opposition: The Republic of China*

and the People's Republic of China after Forty Years (Stanford: Hoover Institution Press, 1991), pp. xlvii–liv.

2 Paul A. Cohen, "The Post-Mao Reforms in Historical Perspective," *Journal of Asian Studies* 47.3 (August 1988): 519–41. For an example of the systemic approach to the post-Mao reforms, see Chalmers Johnson, "What's Wrong with Chinese Political Studies?" *Asian Survey* 22.10 (1982): 919–33.

3 On the situation of Chinese intellectuals in the 1950s and 1960s, see the work of Merle Goldman, especially her *Literary Dissent in Communist China* (Cambridge: Harvard University Press, 1967) and her *China's Intellectuals: Advise and Dissent* (Cambridge: Harvard University Press, 1981). The sharp reduction in the political independence and occupational autonomy of professional and managerial elements after 1949 is dealt with in Deborah S. Davis, "Social Class Transformation in Urban China: Training, Hiring, and Promoting Urban Professionals and Managers after 1949," *Modern China* 26.3 (July 2000): 251–75.

4 The Guomindang on Taiwan went even further than this, insisting for many years in its official maps of China that Mongolia was still part of the Chinese realm.

5 This point is emphasized in Philip A. Kuhn, *Les Origines de l'état chinois moderne* (Paris: Édition de l'École des hautes études en sciences sociales, 1999), pp. 146–7.

6 Although some will argue that reform is fundamentally different from revolution, no matter how much change is involved, it has not been uncommon among China scholars to use the term "revolution" to describe the sweeping reforms launched in December 1978. See, for example, Jonathan D. Spence, *The Search for Modern China* (New York: W.W. Norton, 1990), p. 657; Merle Goldman, "The Post-Mao Reform Era," in John K. Fairbank and Merle Goldman, *China: A New History*, enlarged edn. (Cambridge: Harvard University Press, 1998), p. 410; Roderick MacFarquhar and John K. Fairbank, "Preface," in MacFarquhar and Fairbank, eds., *The Cambridge History of China*, Vol. 15: *The People's Republic, Part 2: Revolutions within the Chinese Revolution 1966–1982* (Cambridge: Cambridge University Press, 1991), p. xxi.

7 David Der-wei Wang, "Introduction," in Pang-yuan Chi and David Der-wei Wang, eds., *Chinese Literature in the Second Half of a Modern Century: A Critical Survey* (Bloomington: Indiana University Press, 2000), p. xviii; see also Wang's "Reinventing National History: Communist and Anti-Communist Fiction of the Mid-Twentieth Century," in *ibid.*, pp. 39–64.

8 See the unpublished paper of Corinne Cabusset, "Film Industry and Artists in the Process of Transition to Communism, 1948–1953," presented at the conference on "China's Mid-Century Transitions: Continuity and Change on the Mainland and on Taiwan, 1946–1955," held at Harvard University, September 9–10, 1994.

9 Chang Jui-te makes a similar point in regard to Taiwan and mainland commemorations of the fiftieth anniversary of the victory over Japan in the War of Resistance. See his "The Politics of Commemoration: A Comparative Analysis of the Fiftieth-Anniversary Commemoration in Mainland China and Taiwan of the Victory in the Anti-Japanese War," in Diana Lary and Stephen MacKinnon, eds., *Scars of War: The Impact of Warfare on Modern China* (Vancouver: UBC Press, 2001), pp. 136–60.

10 Schwarcz, "Remapping May Fourth: Between Nationalism and Enlightenment," *Republican China* 12.1 (November 1986): 25; Levenson's essay was a review of Chow Tse-tsung's *The May Fourth Movement: Intellectual Revolution in Modern China* (Cambridge: Harvard University Press, 1960). These two paragraphs are taken, with slight modification, from

Paul A. Cohen, *History in Three Keys: The Boxers as Event, Experience, and Myth* (New York: Columbia University Press, 1997), pp. 10–11.

11 Wen-hsin Yeh, *The Alienated Academy: Culture and Politics in Republican China, 1919–1937* (Cambridge: Harvard Council on East Asian Studies, Harvard University, 1990), p. 192.

12 Elizabeth Sinn, "Xin Xi Guxiang: A Study of Regional Associations as a Bonding Mechanism in the Chinese Diaspora. The Hong Kong Experience," *Modern Asian Studies* 31.2 (1997): 375–97, especially 388–97.

13 E-tu Zen Sun, "The Growth of the Academic Community, 1912–1949," in John K. Fairbank and Albert Feuerwerker, eds., *The Cambridge History of China*, Vol. 13: *Republican China, 1912–1949, Part 2* (Cambridge: Cambridge University Press, 1986), p. 364; Sun's numbers are extrapolated from Y.C. Wang, *Chinese Intellectuals and the West, 1872–1949* (Chapel Hill: University of North Carolina Press, 1966).

14 Weili Ye, *Seeking Modernity in China's Name: Chinese Students in the United States, 1900–1927* (Stanford: Stanford University Press, 2001), pp. 2, 7, 232, n. 38; Sun, "The Growth of the Academic Community," pp. 364–5.

15 Harry Harding, *A Fragile Relationship: The United States and China since 1972* (Washington, D.C.: Brookings Institution, 1992), p. 367.

16 The key work here is David Zweig and Chen Changgui, with the assistance of Stanley Rosen, *China's Brain Drain to the United States: Views of Overseas Chinese Students and Scholars in the 1990s* (Berkeley: Institute of East Asian Studies, University of California, 1995). Chen and Zweig draw attention to a number of factors other than economic ones that have had a significant bearing on the decisions of Chinese students in America not to return, the most important being the fear of unstable political conditions in China.

17 For analysis of factors contributing to a modest but steady growth in numbers of returnees after 1994, see David Zweig, *Internationalizing China: Domestic Interests and Global Linkages* (Ithaca: Cornell University Press, 2002), chap. 4. In their jointly authored book, Zweig and Chen maintain that for the brain drain to be reversed (as opposed to being merely moderated) there must be "an activist government strategy that creates a positive climate for returned students and is implemented by a strong leader...or ministry." Such a climate, they argue, would have to be accompanied by a change in attitude, one important difference between the Chinese case and that of Korea and Taiwan being China's "institutionalized mistrust of overseas scholars," which "undermines its ability to attract returnees." *China's Brain Drain to the United States*, p. 6.

18 As a result of better salaries, research facilities, and living conditions, 90 per cent of Korean and Taiwanese students stayed in the United States in the 1950s and 1960s; in the 1990s, according to Dwight Perkins, "90 percent or more returned home." "How China's Economic Transformation Shapes Its Future," in Ezra F. Vogel, ed., *Living with China: U.S./China Relations in the Twenty-First Century* (New York: Norton, 1997), p. 148.

19 To cite one example, the generation of American-educated students Weili Ye studied were among the first Chinese for whom "'modernity' became a *lived* experience," and they played an important part in introducing "modern" styles of living into the China of the 1910s and 1920s. Although American-educated students returning to China today (mainly to cities like Beijing and Shanghai) are often in a position to prosper and (less often) to exert influence in the academic or official worlds, there is little that they can teach their compatriots about "modern life." Ye, *Seeking Modernity in China's Name*, p. 5.

20 "The Foreign Presence in China," in John K. Fairbank, ed., *The Cambridge History of China*, Vol. 12: *Republican China 1912–1949, Part 1* (Cambridge: Cambridge University Press, 1983), pp. 192–3, 197. For statistics on foreign

trade and investment during the first three decades of the twentieth century, see Robert F. Dernberger, "The Role of the Foreigner in China's Economic Development, 1840–1949," in Dwight H. Perkins, ed., *China's Modern Economy in Historical Perspective* (Stanford: Stanford University Press, 1975), pp. 27, 29. "The foreign sector – foreign trade and direct investment – clearly made a positive *direct* contribution to the Chinese domestic economy," Dernberger writes, but "it was also a limited contribution – limited not only by the narrow geographical location, but also by a structure that restricted the favorable backward and forward linkages between the foreign sector and the domestic economy" (*ibid.*, p. 39).

21 Penelope P. Prime, "China's Economic Progress: Is it Sustainable?" in William A. Joseph, ed., *China Briefing: The Contradictions of Change* (Armonk, N.Y.: M.E. Sharpe, 1997), p. 74.

22 *Ibid.*, pp. 72–5; Perkins, "How China's Economic Transformation Shapes Its Future," p. 150; WTO News: 2002 Press Releases, Press/288 (May 2, 2002); *Chinese Business Review* 29.3 (May–June 2002): 28; annual figures on the growth of realized foreign direct investment between 1979 and 2000 may be found in *Economist Intelligence Unit Country Profile 2001: China*, p. 57.

23 Perkins, "How China's Economic Transformation Shapes Its Future," p. 150. More generally, Nicholas R. Lardy argues that since the inception of the economic reforms in 1978 "foreign trade has begun to exert a greater influence on the domestic economy than at any other period in China's history." See his *Foreign Trade and Economic Reform in China, 1978–1990* (Cambridge: Cambridge University Press, 1992), p. 1.

24 Perkins, "How China's Economic Transformation Shapes Its Future," pp. 142–4. On China's accelerating industrial growth in the 1980s, see Dwight H. Perkins, "China's Economic Policy and Performance," in MacFarquhar and Fairbank, eds., *The Cambridge History of China*, 15: 500–14.

25 Cohen, *History in Three Keys*, pp. 8–9.

26 For further discussion, along with specific examples, see Paul A. Cohen, *Report on the Visit of the Young Political Leaders Delegation to the People's Republic of China* (New York: National Committee on United States–China Relations, 1978), pp. 11–13.

27 There were, from an early point, significant exceptions to this rule on both ends. Merle Goldman, although trained as a historian, has done most of her work in post-1949 China (her first book appeared in 1967). Benjamin Schwartz, while primarily an intellectual historian whose scholarship spanned the entirety of the Chinese past, had a strong interest in Chinese Communism and began writing on post-1949 developments as early as the 1950s. On the other side, scholars such as Roy Hofheinz, Jr., and Elizabeth Perry, although political scientists by training, did important work (beginning in Hofheinz's case in the late 1960s) on the pre-1949 era. Despite these and other exceptions, however, the general division of labor here enunciated lasted at least through the 1950s and 1960s, and often a good deal longer.

28 Letter of Transmittal, July 30, 1949, in *United States Relations with China with Special Reference to the Period 1944–1949* (Washington, D.C.: U.S. Government Printing Office, 1949), p. xvi. Acheson stated further on that America's "historic policy of friendship for China" would

> necessarily be influenced by the degree to which the Chinese people come to recognize that the Communist regime serves not their interests but those of Soviet Russia and the manner in which, having become aware of the facts, they react to this foreign domination.
>
> *(Ibid.*, pp. xvi–xvii)

29 The American sense of betrayal was multidimensional: Americans felt betrayed by China, Republicans by Democrats, Democrats by Chiang Kai-shek and the Guomindang, and so on. For a classic contemporary statement of the right's sense of betrayal by the left, see Freda Utley, *The China Story* (Chicago: Regnery, 1951).

30 In the United States a major motivation for the rapid expansion of China studies (and for the funding that made it possible) starting in the mid-1950s was the perception of China as an adversary. Few would deny, moreover, that Cold War attitudes had a shaping influence on American study of both post- and pre-1949 China – the kinds of questions asked and the assumptions held – during the early postwar decades.

31 See, for example, the article by Beth Notar (an anthropologist), "Du Wenxiu and the Politics of the Muslim Past," *Twentieth-Century China* 26.2 (April 2001): 63–94, and that by Gardner Bovingdon (a political scientist), "The History of the History of Xinjiang," *ibid.*, pp. 95–139.

32 Symbolic of this shift was the decision of the editorial board of the journal *Republican China* to change its name to *Twentieth-Century China*, beginning with the November 1997 issue. "As we look back from our present vantage point near century's end," editor Stephen C. Averill wrote at the time, "it seems evident that for many topics of current scholarly interest, dates such as 1911 and 1949 now appear to be not so much rigid boundaries or barriers as useful signposts marking stages in complex, ongoing patterns of continuity and change." "Letter from the Editor: From *Republican China* to *Twentieth-Century China*," *Republican China* 22.2 (April 1997): 1.

33 Edward Friedman, Paul G. Pickowicz, and Mark Selden, with Kay Ann Johnson, *Chinese Village, Socialist State* (New Haven: Yale University Press, 1991), p. xxii. See also Joseph Esherick's effort to "think across the 1949 divide...by recognizing the social changes of the long 1940s as a harbinger of the early years of the PRC [People's Republic of China]", in his "War and Revolution: Chinese Society during the 1940s," *Twentieth-Century China* 27.1 (November 2001): 1–37 (quotation from p. 27).

6 Remembering and forgetting national humiliation in twentieth-century China

Patriotic Chinese in the twentieth century referred endlessly to the humiliations (*guochi*) their country had experienced at the hands of foreign imperialism beginning with the Opium War.[1] Indeed, in the republican era they even established days of national humiliation or shame (*guochi ri*) to mark the anniversaries of these painful episodes.[2] Such days, along with the sensitivity to national humiliation they reflected, constituted a major form of national remembering and, through much of the century, were the implicit or explicit focus of a vast *guochi* literature.[3]

This concern with national humiliation is well known. Much less familiar is a persistent sense of anxiety over what appeared to significant numbers of intellectuals as China's obliviousness to such humiliation. This anxiety took different forms in different periods. In the late Qing the complaint most often heard was that Chinese, unlike other peoples, were somehow impervious to feelings of national shame. Then, early in the republican period (the principal focus of this chapter), the problem shifted, in the view of many commentators, from imperviousness to forgetfulness. Chinese, it was now argued, after being subjected to acts of national humiliation, erupted in anger for a short time but then promptly forgot the source of their anger and retreated to their original condition of indifference. Anniversaries were regularly observed and formulaic memory markers widely circulated in society, but doubt was expressed whether such actions encouraged genuine remembering of the painful history to which they alluded. Also – and this is a form of "forgetting" that republican observers generally overlooked – anniversaries afforded a golden opportunity for different societal groupings to rework the past for their own purposes, tailoring it more closely to the needs and aspirations of the present.

In the final decade of the twentieth century, the problem with respect to the remembering of national humiliation assumed yet another guise. For the great majority of Chinese at century's end the humiliations of the past were no longer a matter of immediate, personal experience. Since an important source of legitimation for China's ruling Communist Party was its part in vanquishing imperialism in the 1940s – and the closure this brought to the country's "century of humiliation" – the challenge facing patriotic educators, in the climate of revived nationalistic feeling and weakened faith in Communism that characterized the 1990s, was to fill the minds of the young with narratives of the suffering and humiliation of the imperialist interval in China's history and entreat them to "not forget." Indeed, "do not forget" – *wuwang* – became the mantra of the *guochi* writing of this decade.

The late Qing: posing the problem

The fear that humiliating experiences, instead of serving as a constant goad to action, would quickly be forgotten was nothing new in China. It lay at the very heart of the well-known Spring and Autumn period saga of Goujian, King of Yue, who, after being defeated at Mount Kuaiji (in modern Zhejiang) by his arch-rival Fuchai, the king of Wu, was forced into servitude by him. Although during the Spring and Autumn period *guochi* referred to the humiliation not of a nation but of a ruling house,[4] the fear that the memory of past humiliation would fade with time was as acute then as it was to become in the twentieth century. Therefore, Goujian, after eventually being granted his freedom by Fuchai and returning to Yue, took numerous precautionary measures to ensure that he would not forget the bitterness he had experienced during his captivity or the humiliating defeat he had suffered at Mount Kuaiji three years before. He exchanged his soft silk-padded bedding for a pile of brushwood and in his room hung a gall bladder from the ceiling so that every time he raised his head he looked directly at it and whenever he ate or drank anything it had the taste of bile. Goujian even went so far as to have a new city constructed at Mount Kuaiji and to move his capital there, as a permanent reminder of Yue's defeat at the hands of Wu.[5]

Goujian managed, through these and other measures, to conquer the problem of forgetfulness. Over a twenty-year period he rebuilt the economic and military power of Yue and eventually destroyed the state of Wu and became the dominant leader of the China of his day. Forgetfulness and indifference, however, were not problems amenable to permanent solution. During the late Qing and the early years of the republic, they reemerged in a major way, and commentators, in their desperate efforts to awaken the Chinese public to this lamentable state of affairs, repeatedly alluded to the example of Goujian (Figure 6.1).

An early instance of this was an article published in 1904 in the newly founded general magazine *Dongfang zazhi*, the central theme of which was China's unresponsiveness to the repeated humiliations it had experienced at the hands of the foreign powers since the Opium War. The article, written by a member of the journal's editorial staff (under the pseudonym Fangshi), begins by positing a number of broad theorems concerning states. The author then observes: "It took twenty years for [Yue] to

Figure 6.1 Goujian. This depiction of a despondent Goujian reclining on a brushwood cot and gazing at the gall bladder suspended before him accompanied a lesson entitled "Guochi" in a repeatedly reissued mass education primer, first published in 1927.

Source: *Shimin qianzi ke*, 20th edn. (Shanghai: Shangwu Yinshuguan, 1929), vol. 2.

destroy Wu [*nian nian zhao Wu*].... This is what is meant by the determination to lie on brushwood and taste gall [*woxin changdan*] and to never forget past humiliation [*wuwang qian chi*]." But for such resolve to be carried to a successful conclusion a people must maintain its moral fiber and persevere even in the face of great difficulties. Hence, if one wants to know whether a state will flourish or decline, one must look to the character of its inhabitants.

That such was the case, Fangshi continued, was evident from China's current situation, which was marked by external troubles of unprecedented severity. The heart of the problem, which he referred to as the "white peril," was not that China was historically unique in being subjected to repeated humiliation; other countries had been exposed to comparable indignities. The problem lay in China's failure to react. When the Muslims in the tenth century [*sic*] seized the place where Jesus was buried in Palestine, Christians viewed this as a great humiliation. In response, showing a willingness to die for their religion, they launched the crusades lasting for almost two hundred years, and subsequently the countries of Europe underwent vigorous development. Again, when the Japanese, after shedding blood to obtain the Liaodong Peninsula in the War of 1894, were forced by Russia [*sic*] to return it, the entire population of Japan viewed this as a great humiliation. Never for a moment did they forget their hatred of the Russians, and now they have been victorious over them (referring to Japan's early triumphs in the Russo-Japanese War).

The contrast with China was stunning. When German soldiers violated the Temple of Confucius in Shandong in 1897, something the entire Chinese people should have experienced as the most egregious insult, there was not a whisper of protest. When the Russians occupied Manchuria, the final resting place of the rulers of the dynasty and an area of strategic importance, China offered no resistance. With no sense of shame in the face of humiliation, it treated a hostile act as if it were a friendly one. Even Korea, when Russian cavalry violated its borders recently, had attacked the Russians and forced them to retreat. If such a paltry little country could behave in this way, how was it that China was incapable of doing so? The answer, Fangshi concluded, lay in China's imperviousness to insult and humiliation. If the Chinese people were to avenge themselves against their enemies, they must first develop a clear sense of national shame.[6]

There are two things that are of particular interest about Fangshi's piece. First, the author makes it clear early on that in his view the Goujian story – Yue's destruction of Wu after twenty years of patient preparation during which Goujian goes to great lengths to keep from forgetting the earlier humiliation Wu inflicted on Yue – supplies the prototypical model for how China should respond to foreign imperialism in the early twentieth century.[7] Second, Fangshi argues that the most serious problem facing China is not the humiliation it has endured at the hands of the foreign powers – this was something all countries at one time or another experienced – but its failure to recognize humiliating acts as humiliating (Figures 6.2 and 6.3). This was a note sounded with growing urgency by Guo Songtao, Wang Tao, Liang Qichao, and other Chinese in the last decades of the Qing.[8] It suggested in no uncertain terms that the people of China, by not heeding the example of Goujian, bore substantial responsibility for their country's troubles.

The republican era: remembering and forgetting the Twenty-One Demands

Underlying Fangshi's argument is the assumption, pervasive throughout the twentieth century in China, that a people's consciousness – how it

Figures 6.2 and 6.3 National humiliation pictures. These pictures, exposing China's unprotesting acceptance of the humiliations inflicted by foreigners in the aftermath of the Boxer episode, are from a series published by the young Chen Duxiu in 1904 in one of China's first vernacular papers.
Figure 6.2: After the foreign forces took Tianjin in July 1900, "shameless" Chinese "who cared for nothing except saving their own skins" carried flags proclaiming that they were "people who submitted" (*shunmin*) to the foreign occupiers. The foreigners detested such persons and killed them anyway.

Source: *Anhui suhuabao, jiachen* 10/1 (November 7, 1904), no. 15.

construes the world in which it lives – is of decisive importance. This theme was taken up even more directly by the editor and future publisher Zhang Xichen (1889–1969) in an article of April 1915, also published in *Dongfang zazhi*. Entitled "Enduring Humiliations and Shouldering Burdens" ("Renru fuzhong"), the article underscores the importance of consciousness at the very outset: "When one understands what is humiliating about a humiliation and endures it, the humiliation is obliterated; when one understands what is burdensome about a burden and shoulders it, the burdensomeness is eased." During the past half century, Zhang tells us, China has endured numerous humiliations and shouldered huge burdens. Yet the foreign powers continue to impose additional humiliations and burdens at will. Must China accept this situation as permanent or is it a temporary one that may eventually be changed for the better?

Figure 6.3: Following their occupation of Manchuria, the Russians seized Chinese and forced them to repair the railways for them. They did not pay them regular wages and flogged them when their work was unsatisfactory, "treating them no differently from horses and oxen." (Chen Duxiu's family was involved in Manchuria at this time; he therefore had personal knowledge of the brutality of the Russian occupiers and was especially pained by the subservience of the local Qing authorities in the face of it.)

Source: *Anhui suhuabao, jiachen* 9/15 (October 23, 1904), no. 14.

In answer to this question, Zhang says that there are two things people who endure humiliations and shoulder heavy burdens need to know:

> First, they must reflect on the source of the humiliations and the burdens. A family must insult itself before others insult it. A nation must attack itself before others attack it. The fact that today the powers dare to impose humiliations on us and add to our burdens with impunity is surely something we have brought upon ourselves.... Second, they must not forget the humiliations endured and the burdens shouldered. The foreigners rebuke the people of China, saying that we are without feeling and are forgetful. Now when people are without feeling they don't experience humiliations as humiliating or burdens as burdensome, and when people have short memories they don't remember tomorrow the humiliations and burdens of today.

This is why the humiliations multiply daily and the burdens become ever more onerous. If in our enduring of humiliations we constantly think of ways to eradicate them, what humiliations will there be? If in our shouldering of burdens we continually devise ways to ease them, what burdens will remain?[9]

Zhang Xichen's article appeared a few months after the Japanese government's secret presentation to Beijing of the Twenty-One Demands on January 18, 1915. The demands were originally divided into five groups, the fifth of which, if assented to, would have required the virtual transfer of Chinese sovereignty to Japan. As a result of intense Chinese opposition and international pressure Japan eventually withdrew the fifth group. Within weeks of the publication of Zhang's article, his argument regarding the characteristic Chinese response to national humiliation was put to the test when, on May 7, Tokyo presented the remaining demands in the form of an ultimatum and, on May 9, the Yuan Shikai government acceded to them.[10]

The China of 1915 was very different from that of a decade before – between the early 1900s and the 1911 Revolution there had been a tremendous expansion of activist opposition to foreign encroachment[11] – and the immediate reaction to the Japanese demands and the Yuan regime's capitulation was anything but indifference. The problem in 1915 was one not of indifference but of staying power: how long the Chinese people (a term that throughout this chapter I use mainly to refer to the population of China's cities) could sustain a mood of anger and resentment and actions built around these emotions. Chinese newspapers began reporting the Japanese demands in late January 1915. By the end of February telegrams of protest against Japan and in support of the Chinese government were pouring into Beijing from the provinces. Chambers of commerce, educational associations, and the press were particularly active in encouraging resistance to Japan. Boycotts against Japanese goods were launched. In February Chinese students in Japan and America held rallies and submitted petitions. In March there were mass protest rallies in Shanghai and other cities. In April prominent bankers and businessmen in Shanghai established a National Salvation Fund (*Jiuguo chujin*), to which Chinese from all sectors of society, including the very poorest, made contributions.[12]

It did not take long in this heated atmosphere for Chinese to begin to portray the Japanese demands as a "national humiliation" and to enshrine either May 7 or May 9 as "National Humiliation Day," to be commemorated annually.[13] The slogan "Do Not Forget the National Humiliation" (*wuwang guochi*) was disseminated all over the country. At a meeting of students in Changsha, Hunan, a resolution was passed to request that newspaper and magazine publishers print the slogan above their newspaper's or magazine's name, that shops be urged to place it on the paper they packaged their products in and on their signs, that theaters print it on their programs and paper manufacturers on their stationery, that major publishers (such as Shangwu and Zhonghua) stamp it on the covers of their textbooks, and that schools inscribe it on their signs and flags.[14]

What seems especially noteworthy about all this talk of "national humiliation" is that it was concerned above all not with the rallies, boycotts, petitions, and fundraising efforts in progress at the time, but with people's consciousness. As early as May, in fact, intellectuals began to ponder seriously the question of how best to keep the memory of the Twenty-One Demands alive in the future. The educator Hou Hongjian (1871/2–1961) published an article in July in which he urged that the issue of national humiliation be incorporated into every part of the school curriculum.[15] At a meeting of Jiangsu school principals in June it was resolved that schools should hold assemblies devoted to the issue of national humiliation and make national humiliation souvenirs (*jinian-pin*).[16] In Beijing the Japanese ultimatum was read aloud to students every day so that they "would not forget the humiliation." Finally, to spread awareness of the national humiliation beyond the confines of the schools to the general public, it was proposed that popular "national humiliation songs" (*guochi ge*) be composed, that students on vacation travel about the countryside reading texts on *guochi* to illiterate farmers, that plays be performed to stimulate people's patriotism, and so forth.[17]

In the meantime, while all this consciousness-raising activity was going on, by mid-1915 the more immediate and direct expressions of China's response to the Twenty-One Demands were rapidly running out of steam. The protest rallies and petitions soon ceased. The boycott against Japanese goods was strongest from March through July, after which (only partly as a result of a government ban) it too declined in effectiveness. Fundraising in Shanghai dropped in June and petered out almost entirely after July; it did not last much longer in other cities. By September, the press, which had played an important part in arousing the ire of the urban populace, stopped discussing *guochi* altogether and moved on to other things.[18] Symbolic of the general weakening of concern, a magazine with the name *Guochi*, the sole purpose of which was to promote awareness of the national humiliation, ceased publication after the appearance of its first issue in June.[19]

In explanation of this palpable diminution of Chinese resistance, contemporaries pointed to the traditional political apathy and poor memories of the Chinese people. Zhang Xichen, as we have seen, had drawn attention to this problem even prior to May 1915. In the aftermath of the Japanese ultimatum, Ge Gongzhen (1890–1935) and other columnists, sounding the same note, warned of the serious problem Chinese had with remembering, their stubborn tendency, as soon as things got a little better, to erase from their minds the humiliating experience they had just been through.[20] Another writer, noting the lack of response to the humiliations suffered in 1894 and 1900, even though all Chinese knew perfectly well what had happened in those years, distinguished between two kinds of "not forgetting": the easy kind conveyed in writing and by word of mouth, and the truly efficacious kind that was inscribed in people's hearts.[21] And a gentleman in Beijing, addressing the problem of memory more idiosyncratically, made a collection of newspaper articles lamenting the situation in 1915 and promised that, if by May 7 of the following year the newspapers did not shed tears over the national humiliation, he would shed tears over the newspapers.[22]

What does all this anxiety about Chinese forgetting mean? Did people like Zhang Xichen and Ge Gongzhen who complained about Chinese forgetfulness think that their compatriots would *literally* forget the Twenty-One Demands? Obviously not. In point of fact, in the years after 1915 the social, political, and even economic landscape of China was fairly saturated with reminders of the Demands. My sense is that what really worried Zhang, Ge, and a host of other intellectuals in the period from 1915 to the mid-1930s was the quality of the remembering, the persistent indifference and passivity that they detected in the mood of the Chinese public.

This was one part of the problem of forgetting (to which I shall return). The other part, rather different in nature and seldom explicitly commented on by contemporaries, was that the remembering of the Demands in annual anniversary observances all too often was accompanied by a distortion – manipulation might be the more accurate term – of the content and import of what was to be remembered, to the point where it too contributed to an overall sense of memory debasement or loss. There was nothing especially unusual about this. Anniversaries everywhere create opportunities for people in the present to push agendas that have only the most tenuous links to the events the anniversaries are supposed to commemorate.[23] But it is a stunning paradox, nevertheless, in that occasions that are supposed to be all about remembering, instead become prime vehicles for forgetting.

This process of memory attrition or "forgetting" in connection with anniversaries assumed a number of guises during the years from 1915 to the outbreak of fighting between China and Japan in the 1930s. One form that it took might be termed "displacement," in the sense of the shifting of emotion associated with the original event to matters of more current concern that might or might not be related. This was seen most typically in the actions taken by students on subsequent anniversaries of the May 1915 events. Sometimes these actions were directly connected with Sino-Japanese relations, as in the case of the celebrated May Fourth Movement of 1919.[24] But it was also possible for the symbolic space of May 7 (or 9) to be used to energize or validate student actions over issues that, at least on the surface, had little if anything to do with Japan. This was clearly illustrated in the serious demonstrations that took place in

Beijing (and, to a lesser extent, other cities) on May 7, 1925. The background in this instance consisted in growing student unhappiness over the educational policies of the acting Minister of Education, Zhang Shizhao. When, on May 6, the Ministry of Education issued an order banning student commemoration of the May 7 anniversary, the students in the capital were outraged and, "transferring their anger" (*qiannu*) to Zhang, stormed his residence and caused extensive damage before finally being brought under control by the police.[25] It seems abundantly clear that, in this and comparable cases,[26] although anti-Japanese feeling was certainly part of the picture, it was greatly complicated, possibly in some instances even superseded, by another issue. I refer to the ongoing problem, seen throughout the republican decades, of students bridling at being prevented by those in authority (often viewed by them as corrupt and illegitimate to begin with) from giving full political expression to their feelings – a phenomenon by no means unheard of in other places and times – and using the space created by the anniversaries to give vent to their frustration. As one observer commented in regard to the Beijing student actions of May 7, 1925,

> if in this instance an order hadn't been issued curbing the students and prohibiting them from assembling, the students would have at most attended a lecture and staged a parade, passing the occasion in perfunctory fashion, as in the sacrificing of a sheep to announce the new moon [a figure of speech for a practice that has become routine].[27]

As the annual commemorations of the May 1915 events multiplied, the memory of them also became subject to a certain amount of commercial exploitation. Even prior to the first anniversary, companies had begun the practice of using the symbolism of 5–9 (May 9) in the names of tobacco, silk, and other products in order to discourage Chinese from buying Japanese goods (and, of course, at the same time to encourage them to buy their own).[28] Throughout the 1920s and on into the 1930s, the newspaper *Shenbao* ran ads linking the May 9 anniversary with everything from cigarettes and wine to towels, machinery, parasols, watches, straw hats, silk stockings, cotton cloth, tooth powder, and banking services (Figure 6.4). In an ad that appeared on May 9, 1920, a savings and deposit association urged readers to save and not squander their resources, as one way of wiping out the national humiliation.[29] A domestic products company announced in the May 8, 1924, issue that, by clipping and bringing in its ad, prospective customers, beginning on the following day (National Humiliation Day), would be able to purchase a whole range of top-brand products at wholesale prices.[30] Items were periodically promoted under the heading "May 9 National Humiliation Souvenirs."[31] In May 1925, on the occasion of the tenth anniversary of the Demands, *Shenbao* ran an ad

Figure 6.4 Advertisement for Patriotic (Aiguo) cigarettes. This Nanyang Brothers Tobacco Company ad superimposes the characters for "May 9" over those for "Patriotic Cigarettes," so that the opening injunction ("Please, sir, do not forget") applies to both.

Source: *Shenbao*, May 9 and May 10, 1924.

for "National Humiliation Towels," the text of which maintained that in their daily use of the towels to wash their faces Chinese would be reminded of the need to wipe clean the national humiliation.[32] Another ad that played on the multiple meanings of *xue* (in this case, "to wipe clean" and "to whiten") and also on the homophones *chi* (meaning "humiliation") and *chi* (meaning "teeth") was one for a toothpowder called Xuechifen (powder for whitening the teeth), which appeared on May 9, 1931. "When you use Xuechifen each morning to brush your teeth," the ad declared, "you will naturally associate this in your mind with the great 'national humiliation' and ponder ways to wipe it clean."[33]

Among the more intriguing of the *Shenbao* ads was one for Golden Dragon cigarettes, a brand manufactured by the Nanyang Brothers Tobacco Company, which appeared in 1925 and 1926. The ad asked people not to forget May 9. It explicitly identified the smoking of Golden Dragon as a patriotic act. An inset showed a group of people standing under a tree on the branches of which were hung strips of paper with *guochi* written on them. The ad even incorporated an image of a modern-day Goujian seated uncomfortably on a pile of brushwood and holding a gall bladder up to his mouth[34] (Figure 6.5).

There may have been a degree of genuine patriotic sentiment behind notices of this sort, and certainly, as was clearly revealed in the aftermath of the terrorist attack in New York City on September 11, 2001, there was nothing peculiarly Chinese about the tendency to wrap oneself in the flag while exploiting painful memories for individual or corporate advantage.[35] My strong conviction, nevertheless, is that whatever patriotism may have informed the *Shenbao* ads, it generally took a backseat to economic self-interest.[36] It is further arguable that by trivializing the memory of the May

Figure 6.5 Advertisement for Golden Dragon (Jinlong) cigarettes.
Source: Shenbao, May 7–11, 1925; May 9, 1926.

1915 events the ads ironically contributed to the very process of "forgetting" that they repeatedly inveighed against.[37]

Political self-interest also played an important part in reframing the memory of past humiliation. Although my focus here has been on how the Twenty-One Demands, in particular, were remembered, in the context of the mounting anti-imperialist sentiment of the 1920s the anniversaries of May 7 and 9 were soon joined by a profusion of other national humiliation anniversary days.[38] Initially, the observance of these days was decentralized and followed no set pattern. Schools and businesses would often close for the day, flags were flown at half-mast, banqueting and other forms of entertainment were curtailed, notices with slogans written on them were displayed in shop windows, schools held assemblies at which speeches were given explaining the origins and meaning of the anniversary, and students sang national humiliation songs (*guochi ge*)[39] and paraded through city streets passing out leaflets and urging citizens "not to forget the national humiliation."[40]

With the Guomindang's attainment of national power in 1927, however, the process of commemorating national humiliation days underwent an abrupt and decisive change. The party promoted these days assiduously, periodically issuing detailed instructions on how they were to be observed in schools, factories, offices, army units, party branches, and other organizations. According to one set of instructions, anniversary meetings were to begin at 7 a.m. and last for one hour. After the singing of the party anthem, everyone was to bow three times before the party flag, the national flag, and the portrait of Sun Yat-sen. This was to be followed by a reading of Sun's deathbed testament, five minutes of silence, and finally a lecture on the subject of the anniversary, which was to adhere closely to the propaganda points supplied by the Party Central Committee. There were to be no street demonstrations.[41]

With some variation in detail, this was the format that was followed in the observance of the May 7 and May 9 National Humiliation Days from 1927 on. There are a number of points to be made concerning it. First, the Guomindang now stage-managed the entire commemorative process, rendering it far less free form, far more formulaic, than in the pre-1927 years. Second, the contents of the speeches and slogans central to the process focused at least as much on inciting hatred of the Communists (and the USSR) and inculcating allegiance to the Nanjing government, the Guomindang, and its Sun Yat-sen-centered reading of republican history as on reminding the Chinese people of the events of May 1915 and promoting anti-Japanese feeling[42] (Figure 6.6). Only by acceptance of the Guomindang's own agenda, it was clearly insinuated, would China succeed in wiping out the humiliations of the past. Third, as suggested by the ban on street demonstrations and the heightened security procedures now generally put into effect on National Humiliation Day anniversaries, Guomindang-managed commemorative activities were geared not only to

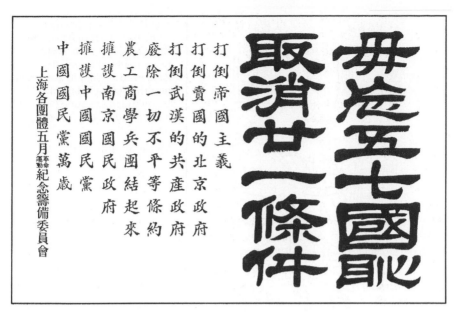

Figure 6.6 Guomindang notice of May 27, 1927. The large characters on the right state: "Do not forget the May 7 national humiliation. Abolish the Twenty-One Demands." The text on the left, incorporating the Guomindang's agenda in the period immediately following its establishment of control over Chinese Shanghai in April 1927, calls on Chinese to, among other things, overthrow the traitorous Beijing (warlord) government, overthrow the Communist government in Wuhan, support the National government in Nanjing, and support the Guomindang.

Source: *Shenbao*, May 7, 1927.

arousing patriotic sentiment but also to bringing such sentiment under tight official control, so as to keep it from causing problems for the state[43] (Figure 6.7).

Over the years, if we are to credit the frequent expressions of concern by patriotic Chinese intellectuals, memory of the Twenty-One Demands was also weakened by a process of routinization or repetition overload. Formulaic allusions to the humiliations of 1915 were encountered everywhere in urban China – on stamps, wall posters, stationery, in newspaper ads, playbills, school texts – raising the danger that people would become desensitized to the original hurt, that the very reminders with which they were inundated in their daily lives would numb them into forgetfulness.[44] Even prior to the assumption of Guomindang control, there are indications that the yearly anniversary observances, while providing an opportunity for emotional venting, had begun to function less as true vehicles for the recalling of the Twenty-One Demands than as a disguised form of forgetting. Time and again, Chinese commentators, internalizing a criticism originally voiced by foreigners, complained that their compatriots had "an enthusiasm

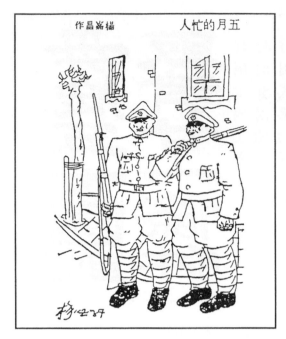

Figure 6.7 Yang Jiachang, "The busy men of May." By the late 1920s there were more national humiliation days in May than in any other month. On such days the Guomindang routinely put heightened security measures into effect.

Source: *Shenbao*, May 5, 1937.

for things that only lasted five minutes" (*wu fenzhong zhi redu*). One *Shenbao* reader, in alluding to this, wrote in 1921 that there were Chinese in his day who didn't even remember the date of the May 9 national humiliation. The whole point of marking the May 9 anniversary and holding commemorative meetings, he argued, was to keep people from forgetting this great national humiliation and to arouse them to exert themselves to wipe it clean, following the example of Goujian's lying on brushwood and tasting gall. But, instead, in six years' time the anniversary of May 9 had come to be observed as a happy occasion, as if it were China's National Day. It was time, therefore, to abandon the National Humiliation Day entirely and establish in its stead an Avenge Humiliation Day (*xuechi ri*).[45]

Others articulated similar views. "The commemoration of May 7," wrote an editorialist in May 1925 in the widely read *Guowen zhoubao* (National news weekly), "has become a spent force in recent years, like a shot of morphine the efficacy of which progressively diminishes the longer the elapsed time since the date of the shot"[46] (Figure 6.8). The commentator, Wu Songgao, also writing in May 1925, deplored the apathy (*mamu*) that was ubiquitous both within the government and among the people, and observed caustically that although the latter got all worked up and indulged in much cursing and scolding at the annual national humiliation meetings and took part in listless campaigns against Japanese products, when it came to building up the real strength of the nation or to developing their knowledge and understanding of current affairs they were shamefully remiss.[47] A similar complaint was voiced ten years later, in

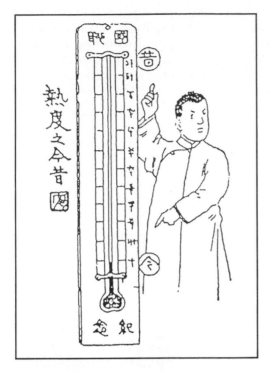

Figure 6.8 Measuring the heat of national humiliation anniversary observance. Published on the seventh anniversary of China's acceptance of the Japanese ultimatum, this cartoon depicts graphically the cooling of popular concern over time.

Source: Shenbao, May 9, 1922.

May 1935, by Wang Yunsheng, soon to be named editor of *Dagongbao* and a knowledgeable student of Japanese affairs. Wang bemoaned the deepening crisis in Sino-Japanese relations and wondered whether the situation had not already moved beyond considerations of national humiliation to touch on the very survival of China as a nation. "Every Chinese primary student knows that May 9 is National Humiliation Commemoration Day," he wrote, "but there are a great many Chinese citizens who do not appreciate the seriousness of the current national crisis and their responsibility to do something about it. This is a new national humiliation and also a great crisis."[48]

Anniversaries, even of such individual events as birthdays, weddings, and deaths, are a quintessentially social form of remembering. As such, it would be hazardous to assume that the kinds of forgetting they embody are the same as the kinds of forgetting encountered in individual memory.[49] Still, whether we are talking about social or individual memory, public memory or private, we are forced to confront the fact that memory is fragile, uncertain, malleable. The frequently encountered expressions of concern on the part of patriotic republican-era intellectuals over what they perceived as a propensity of the Chinese people to forget past humiliations point to one form of memory attrition. The fact that the anniversaries of May 7 or 9 were used by different elements in society to advance objectives often having only the most tenuous relationship to the original meaning of the anniversaries points to another. But in either case, although the "forgetfulness" implied was, in my judgment, very real – and my sense is that it characterized Chinese responses to humiliations other than the Twenty-One Demands as well – it certainly should not be taken to suggest that the Chinese people were steadfastly indifferent to the depredations of foreign imperialism.

The key word here is *steadfastly*. Prasenjit Duara, in a recent comment on the "simultaneous superficiality and depth of nationalist feelings," ventures a number of observations on the relationship between "nationalism and everyday life" that are pertinent in this regard. "Nationalism," he maintains, "is inculcated and can be intense, but its appearance is relational and contextual." Nationalist ideals are kept alive and become part of a person's sense of self via such mechanisms as the formal education system. But in people's actual lives these ideals often retreat into a passive mode and are given active expression only under special circumstances. To dramatize his point Duara presents a schematic depiction of the Chinese reaction to the May 1999 U.S. bombing of the Chinese embassy in Belgrade: "Day 1: Eat at McDonalds; Day 2: Throw rocks at McDonalds; Day 3: Eat at McDonalds"[50] (Figure 6.9).

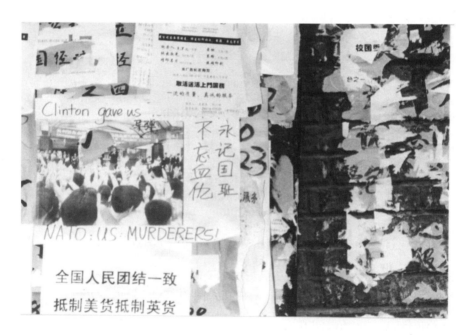

Figure 6.9 "NATO: U.S.: Murderers!"

Source: Photograph of May 10, 1999, by Jeffrey Wasserstrom.

Note: This is a collage of wall posters that were put up on the campus of Beijing University in the immediate aftermath of the Belgrade embassy bombing. The vertically written Chinese characters just to the left of center state: "Always remember the national humiliation, don't forget the blood debt."

A pattern remarkably similar to this seems to have characterized the aftermath of the May 1915 events. Following an initial period of manifest anger and indignation in the late winter and spring, by late summer the Twenty-One Demands, both literally and figuratively, had receded from the front pages. As Zhitian Luo observes in his excellent account of China's response to the Demands, a planned rally in Shanghai in early May 1916 to mark the first anniversary of China's capitulation to Japan was forbidden by the authorities and newspapers responded to the anniversary with apparent indifference. "Instead," Luo notes sardonically, "on May 9, 1916, Chinese and Japanese correspondents participated in a banquet for 'sincere friendship' held in a Japanese club in Peking."[51]

I find Duara's analysis insightful and persuasive. Indeed, it was precisely in order to counter the anesthetizing power of everyday existence, its power to induce forgetfulness, that Goujian took such extraordinary measures not to forget. Duara's observations, however, speak to an empirical reality; they don't really address the concerns of a succession of Chinese commentators who fretted about their compatriots' poor memory. One reason these people fretted, after all, was that China had its work cut out for it if it was to reverse the pattern of humiliation to which it had been so long subjected.[52] This was long-term work requiring great sacrifice on the part of the Chinese people, and the only way such sacrifice could be exacted was to instill in people's minds a clear and abiding sense of why it was necessary. What was needed, in other words, was not nationalism as momentary emotional eruption or ritualized commemorative observance, but nationalism as lasting commitment.[53] Here again the Goujian narrative is instructive. The deeper meaning of the measures Goujian took not to forget was that the people of Yue needed to be constantly reminded of the reason for the twenty-year program of reconstruction they had embarked on under his leadership. Comparable reminders were there in the republican period, too, in the form of national humiliation days and slogans like the ubiquitous "*wuwang guochi.*" But the other part of the Goujian story – the rebuilding process – was stalled during the 1920s, 1930s, and 1940s by internal political strife and external invasion, and in these circumstances there was a strong tendency for the reminders to become clichés, diminishing their capacity to motivate.

This was one reason – the absence of any sustained effort at reconstruction – for the periodic expressions of concern about Chinese forgetfulness. Another, brilliantly illuminated by Vera Schwarcz, was the commitment to remembering for its own sake. In China, Schwarcz tells us, those who were unable to forget the past were described as people "who did not drink Old Lady Meng's soup." These were the people – Lu Xun was one, the poet Yu Guangzhong and the novelist Zhang Xianliang were two others – who refused the Broth of Oblivion dispensed by Old Lady Meng, unwilling to succumb to the psychological forces that promoted "forgetting for the sake of ongoing life."[54]

Another such refuser was the writer Ba Jin, who, in the immediate aftermath of the Cultural Revolution, determined not to forget the horrors of the events he and others of his generation had just endured, wrote of his earlier efforts to remember the events of 1915:

> I can still remember buying "conscience stamps" when I was a boy of twelve or so to stick on my books. They were a little larger than normal postage stamps with a red heart in the middle and slogans on either side: "All of one heart"; "Never forget the national shame." Foreigners said we Chinese were like "a sheet of loose sand" with "an enthusiasm for things that only lasted five minutes," so we bought these stamps to jog our memories…. I stuck on my "conscience stamps" and kept the Days of National Humiliation, May 7 and May 9 1915, in mind…. But I must confess that after a while I forgot all about the stamps and only thought of them guiltily once in a while. Did my enthusiasm really only last for five minutes? Each time I castigated myself that memory was imprinted deeper in my mind. The National Humiliation is a thing of the past, and our young people today have no idea of the significance of "May 7" and "May 9." But I have not forgotten, nor do I wish to be a person who forgets things lightly.[55]

The 1990s: not forgetting past humiliations

If young people in 1979, the year in which Ba Jin penned these words, no longer understood the meaning of May 7 and May 9, how much more was this true of Chinese youth in the 1990s. Indeed, the loss of historical memory among the young was a major reason for the dramatic upsurge of writing on national humiliation in the final decade of the twentieth century. In important respects this writing – and other expressions of *guochi* sentiment – resonated with that of the republican era. There was an overriding emphasis on the shameful interlude of China's victimization at the hands of imperialism in the century following the Opium War.[56] And, especially among educated youth, there was an easily ignited sense of outrage over slights to Chinese dignity that, reminiscent of the attitudes of student activists in the 1920s and 1930s, incorporated one side of the Goujian story – the desire for revenge – but not the other and perhaps more critical side – the willingness to bide one's time while patiently making preparations for the future.[57]

But there were also significant differences between the two periods. For one thing, the *guochi* writing of the 1990s incorporated a very different master narrative. The emphasis was much less on the defects of the Chinese body politic that facilitated imperialist incursion and much more on the Chinese people's defiant struggle against it. "Modern Chinese history," Liang Yiqun tells us, "is not just a history of humiliation, it is also a history of resistance, of the wiping out of humiliation."[58] Another feature of the *guochi* literature of the 1990s that differentiated it from that of the republican years – and it is this feature that mainly concerns me here – was that it referred not to a problem that was ongoing in the present but to one that had existed in the past and then abruptly subsided with the Communist triumph in 1949. The emphasis, accordingly, was not on figuring out how China got into its existing predicament and what was required to get out of it; rather, it was on the importance of "not forgetting" the suffering and humiliation of the imperialist interval in China's history. If there was a problem in the present that needed addressing, it was the problem alluded to by Ba Jin: the eclipsing of the past in the minds of China's youth.

The explosion of writing on *guochi* at the end of the twentieth century was part of a broader phenomenon of resurgent nationalism that characterized these years. Many factors contributed to this revival of nationalistic sentiment.[59] First and foremost, in the aftermath of 1989 there was a felt, if unstated, need on the part of the Chinese government to come up with a new legitimating ideology to burnish the rapidly dimming luster of the original Marxist–Leninist–Maoist vision; in the eyes of Deng Xiaoping, Jiang Zemin, and other key leaders, the logical candidate for the fulfillment of this function was nationalism, to be inculcated via a multifaceted program of patriotic education.[60] Again, the negative response of many of the world's countries to the government's crackdown on the protest demonstrations of the spring of 1989, together with later actions taken by the United States in particular that many Chinese perceived as designed to thwart their longstanding goal of creating a strong nation, encouraged a hunkering-down, us-against-the-world mentality among elements of the Chinese leadership and populace (including many intellectuals). Then, of course, there was the fiftieth anniversary of the victory over Japan in World War II, drawing attention to ongoing sore spots in Sino-Japanese relations, and the run-up to, and celebration of, the resumption of Chinese sovereignty over Hong Kong in 1997, an event widely heralded in the Chinese press as *xuechi* or "the wiping away of a humiliation."[61] But if we train our sights on *guochi* writing as such, it is arguable that more important than any of these factors was the historical circumstance that by the 1990s a sizable majority of the Chinese population consisted of young and early middle-aged people who, born after 1949, had never directly experienced the onslaught of imperialism.[62] Since the victory over imperialism in the 1940s was a crucial part of the justification of Communist rule in China, these individuals had to be reintroduced to the imperialist past, to reexperience its bitterness and shame. It was to them that the upsurge of writing on national humiliation in the 1990s was mainly directed.

In his introduction (dated 1996) to a book entitled *Maps of Modern China's Hundred Years of National Humiliation*, a Beijing Normal University professor articulated several of these themes:

> Last year was the 50th anniversary of the victory of the world's people in the war against Fascism and also the 50th anniversary of the victory of the Chinese people in the War of Resistance against Japan. Next year will bring the 60th anniversary of the July 7th incident and also the joyous day of the return of Hong Kong to the motherland. Recalling the national humiliation at this time has special significance because for people who have grown accustomed to living in time of peace, especially the generation of youth born after the war, it is difficult to grasp the true meaning of national humiliation and the intense pain occasioned by the defeat of the nation and the destruction of the family, and because although the war has been over for 50 years some people in government circles in Japan still don't acknowledge Japan's aggression against China and continue to talk openly of the "liberation of Asia".... Past experience, if not forgotten, is a guide for the future. We need to review history and not forget the national humiliation![63]

I have examined some two dozen books on "national humiliation" published in the 1990s. Some of them, such as the ten volumes of a series entitled "Wuwang guochi lishi" (Don't forget the history of national humiliation), are quite specific in nature, focusing on topics like extraterritoriality, the Sino-Japanese War of 1894, the Mukden Incident of September 1931, and the Opium War and the first group of unequal treaties.[64] Others are broader in their sweep, covering the entire century from the Opium War to the Communist triumph.[65] Among the latter, there is a further distinction to be made between books that are expressly directed at a young readership and are written in a lively, popular style (often with copious illustrations) and texts of a more scholarly nature, clearly intended as reference works. [66]

Sometimes the content of these writings is keyed to events of current interest. For example, almost one-third of the mammoth 1,700-page work *Women zen neng wangji? Zhonghua minzu chiru shi* (How can we forget? The history of the humiliation of the Chinese nation) is devoted to the War of Resistance, reflecting the circumstance that it was published in 1995, the fiftieth anniversary of the defeat of Japan.[67] Virtually all of the 1990s publications on *guochi*, on the other hand, scholarly as well as popular, allude in their prefaces, introductions, and postfaces to the need to remind the young people of China of the century-long experience of humiliation at the hands of foreign imperialism and, equally important, of the crucial role of the Communist Party in ending this dark chapter in the country's history.[68] In a time of peace and growing prosperity, accompanied by diminishing support of Communist rule (partly, it must be noted, owing to the aggrieved feelings of significant numbers of Chinese who failed to share in the prosperity), this was the message that it was absolutely essential to impart.

Conclusion

As was noted at the beginning of this chapter, Chinese during the twentieth century repeatedly invoked the theme of national humiliation. Yet, at different historical junctures, patriotic intellectuals expressed concern either about their countrymen's complete indifference to this theme or their inability to keep it in focus for more than a short while or, late in the century, their fading memory of the imperialist interlude in China's recent history. What are we to make of this seeming contradiction between an obsession with national humiliation, on the one hand, and the recurrent apprehension over its not being treated with adequate seriousness or its threatened disappearance from the national consciousness, on the other? If the sense of national shame was so powerful, how is it that it was so readily muted or forgotten?

There is no simple, generic answer to this question. The three points in time I have dealt with were fundamentally different from one another, and within each time period, in a complex society, there were sizable differences from group to group and individual to individual. These differences clearly have to be taken into account in any effort to address the issue. It may be helpful, for this purpose, to distinguish for each period between the parts taken by state and society. During the late Qing, when the issue of national humiliation first began to emerge in public discussion, the state tended to be a silent bystander. To be sure, the foreign policy of the central government after 1900 was, as a number of scholars have shown, increasingly shaped by a nationalist agenda focused explicitly on the preservation and recovery of Chinese sovereignty.[69] But with a revolutionary movement in progress that defined nationalism in terms of the overthrow of the Manchus and the explosive growth in the first decade of the twentieth century of other forms of nationalism that, as often as not, were linked with demands for popular rights and political power-sharing,[70] the Qing had no great interest in the nurturing of Chinese nationalist sentiment. There was an important distinction to be drawn, in other words, between a nationalism-driven foreign policy, over which the state could exercise a modicum of control, and popular nationalism, which could easily spin out of control and turn against the dynasty. In the late nineteenth and early twentieth centuries the issue of national humiliation, with its potential to feed directly into popular nationalism, was raised almost exclusively at the society level, by a small (albeit rapidly growing) minority of Chinese intellectuals. People such as the author of the *Dongfang zazhi* article discussed at the beginning of this chapter were baffled and appalled by the unresponsiveness of the

overwhelming majority of their contemporaries to the repeated humiliations the foreign powers had inflicted on China since the Opium War and
regarded it as their urgent task to arouse Chinese society from its state of
indifference.

During the two decades or so that followed China's acceptance of the
Twenty-One Demands the situation was in some ways more complicated.
Initially, the anger and outrage triggered by this event seem to have been
widespread geographically (at least in urban centers) and to have cut
across social class lines. But by the summer of 1915, only a few short
months after the original issuance of the Demands, there was a conspicuous decline in political activism at all social levels and observers began to
worry out loud about the Chinese people's "precious 'ability to forget'"
(to cite the memorable words of Lu Xun).[71] In the ensuing years the
memory of the Twenty-One Demands was undermined, paradoxically, by
the numbing profusion of the very means – mainly anniversary observances and slogans – that were deployed for the purpose of keeping this
memory intact. It was further undermined by the economic and political
uses it was made to serve. Business firms, partly out of patriotic sentiment
but clearly also with a view to expanding sales and increasing profitability,
linked the public's purchase of their products to the wiping away of
national humiliation. Students, on anniversaries of the Demands, trans-
ferred the anger associated with the original event to whatever political
grievances happened to be uppermost in their minds at the time. And, after
coming to national power in the late 1920s, the Guomindang, partly to
establish and reinforce its own reading of postimperial Chinese history and
partly to keep anniversary observances, especially of the Twenty-One
Demands (but of other national humiliation days as well), from generating
political instability and jeopardizing the government's position *vis-à-vis* the
Communists and an increasingly aggressive Japan, sought to exercise
greater control over the entire commemorative process. The idea wasn't to
make all memory of China's past humiliation disappear, but rather to
assert the state's prerogative to serve as arbiter of what was to be remembered – and how. Popular nationalism was to be transformed into official
nationalism, a form of nationalism "the one persistent feature" of which
(to cite Benedict Anderson) "was, and is, that it is *official* – i.e. something
emanating from the state, and serving the interests of the state first and
foremost."[72]

This ambiguous relationship between popular and official nationalism
was also a factor in the 1990s. To a degree the two worked in tandem.
But, much as in the Guomindang period, in spite of significant contextual
differences there was also considerable tension between them.[73] Chinese
leaders welcomed popular nationalism to the extent that it served as a
substitute form of political validation and had a genuine interest in
reminding the Chinese people of past humiliations at the hands of the West
and Japan and in celebrating all instances (such as the Hong Kong rever-

sion and the victory over Japanese aggression in 1945) in which these humiliations were "wiped clean." But they feared a completely unfettered popular nationalism that might imperil the stability of the regime, undermine China's modernization efforts, and interfere with the government's foreign policy, especially in regard to the always sensitive relationships with the United States and Japan.[74] The government therefore prohibited mass gatherings (or other expressions of popular sentiment) relating directly or indirectly to national humiliation or, when the costs of complete prohibition were too steep, made every effort to keep such outpourings of popular feeling under tight state supervision.[75]

Where, then, does this leave us? In light of the widely variant ways in which national humiliation was experienced, remembered, manipulated, and forgotten in the course of the twentieth century, does it make sense, as I suggested earlier, to posit a simple contradiction between a national obsession with *guochi*, on one hand, and the tendency to disregard or forget it, on the other? I think not. On both ends, the actual situation was more complicated than this. First of all, although Chinese sensitivity to national humiliation was unquestionably a prominent theme throughout the century (and continues to be to this day), it did not have the same significance or salience in every period. Nor, at any given juncture, was it uniformly prevalent among all segments of the population, or equally energized even within a given segment at all times. "Obsession" may be too crude and imprecise a term to describe it.

Second (and this is closely related to the first point), the Chinese who at each historical moment were most vocal in leading the charge against their compatriots' propensity to ignore or forget were intellectuals who happened to feel very strongly about the repeated humiliations China had sustained. But although Chinese intellectuals in the last century operated within a venerable tradition of viewing themselves as the rightful custodians of China's national memory – at times tacitly competing, in this respect, with the state – there is no need to assume that the rest of the population (or, for that matter, all intellectuals) saw the world in exactly the same way. Many Chinese in the 1990s, including numbers of intellectuals, were happy to forget all about national humiliation and go out and get rich, and many others (farmers in the interior provinces and factory workers, in particular), left out of the country's growing material well-being, felt victimized less by foreign imperialism than by their own government's policies.

Third, there was the matter of differential generational experience. I've pointed this out with respect to the 1990s. But it was true as well of the early republic. When it came to remembering and forgetting, it made a great deal of difference whether one had experienced the Twenty-One Demands directly, as a conscious person, or only indirectly, as later transmitted via older members of society or the school system or the press. One couldn't really expect someone who was only a child in May 1915 or not yet born to look back upon the events of that time with the same kinds of feelings as someone who had experienced these events directly. There was likely to be an attrition of memory in either case, but a critical difference existed between the first-hand and second-hand remembering of the same experience.[76]

Fourth, although there was clearly a tension between remembering and forgetting in each of the periods I have discussed, as students of memory have pointed out (and historians have long known), all remembering takes place in the present and incorporates in itself a sizable component of the present.[77] It is a myth that memory has to do only with the past. It stands to reason, therefore, that as the political, social, intellectual, and international environments of China changed in the course of the twentieth century, the meanings of "remembering" and "forgetting" – as well as the nature of the tension between the two – also underwent significant change. Being indifferent to the repeated humiliations of one's own day, forgetting the initial outrage over a humiliation that occurred some time before (or linking the memory of this outrage to unrelated, or at best remotely related, purposes), and having to be taught in books about humiliations one had never personally experienced were quite different phenomena, reflective of the very different "presents" of the three time periods I have dealt with.

And, finally, I want to underscore the vast difference that existed between the late Qing/early republican tendency to view imperviousness or forgetfulness as a *Chinese* problem, something peculiar to the Chinese people, deeply ingrained in their culture, and the late twentieth-century perception of forgetting as contingent in nature, a problem that for historical reasons had belatedly turned up in China but was not in any inherent sense Chinese. Culture and history were alternative sources of forgetting, and they operated in different ways and with varying degrees of strength at different points in time.

Notes

This chapter originally appeared in *Twentieth-Century China* 27.2 (April 2002). I am indebted to Peter Gries, Mary Rankin, Mark Selden, Elizabeth Sinn, and the anonymous reviewer for *Twentieth-Century China* for their helpful comments; to Merle Goldman, Rudolf Wagner, and Vivian Wagner for alerting me to important source materials; and to Hue-Tam Ho Tai for insight into the Goujian story, memory, and other pertinent matters. I also benefited from audience comments following talks at the University of Hong Kong, Harvard University, and the Hong Kong University of Science and Technology, and from the suggestions of participants in conferences held in Oberflockenbach, Germany, in May 2001, and in Heidelberg in November of the same year.

1   In a book published several decades ago, Lucian Pye took special note of this phenomenon, finding it curious that the political leaders of the country, Nationalists and Communists alike, had, in their efforts to stimulate patriotic feeling, devoted such attention to detailing "the real and imagined ways in

which China ha[d] been humiliated by others" instead of turning to the charis-
matic appeals and themes of heroic glory that marked the nationalism of most
transitional societies. *The Spirit of Chinese Politics: A Psychocultural Study of
the Authority Crisis in Political Development* (Cambridge: MIT Press, 1968),
pp. 71–2.

2 National humiliation days were by no means the only anniversaries observed
during this time. There were also holidays of a more celebratory nature, such
as the anniversary of the 1911 Revolution, days of national mourning (notably
the anniversary of the death of Sun Yat-sen), and so on. Twenty-five such days
are covered in *Gezhong jinianri shilüe* (A concise history of the various
commemoration days), compiled and printed by the Political Training
Department of the Nanchang Field Headquarters of the Head of the Military
Affairs Commission of the National Government (Guomin zhengfu junshi
weiyuanhui weiyuanzhang Nanchang xingying zhengzhi xunlian chu) (1932?).
On the entire range of national anniversaries and the ways in which they were
observed, see Henrietta Harrison, *The Making of the Republican Citizen:
Political Ceremonies and Symbols in China, 1911–1929* (Oxford: Oxford
University Press, 2000).

3 The *guochi* literature of the 1990s is dealt with later in this chapter. For that of
the 1920s and 1930s, see Paul A. Cohen, "Commemorating a Shameful Past:
National Humiliation Days in Twentieth-Century China," unpublished paper,
presented at a conference on "Collective Identity, Experiences of Crisis and
Traumata," held in Essen, June 17–20, 1998.

4 For the locus classicus of *guochi* and a brief account of the difference between
its ancient and modern meanings, see Dai Yi's preface (*xuyan*), in Zhuang
Jianping, comp., *Guochi shidian* (A dictionary of national humiliation)
(Chengdu: Chengdu chubanshe, 1992), p. 1; see also Liang Yiqun's introduction (*qianyan*), in Liang Yiqun, Yang Jie, and Xiao Ye, eds., *Yibai ge guochi
jinian ri* (One hundred national humiliation commemoration days) (Beijing:
Zhongguo qingnian chubanshe, 1995), pp. 1–2.

5 The details of the steps taken by Goujian to counter forgetfulness vary from
one account to another. See, for example, Yang Muzhi and Huang Ke, comps.,
Zhongguo lishi gushi (Chunqiu) (Stories from Chinese history: Spring and
Autumn), third printing (Beijing: Zhongguo qingnian chubanshe, 1986 [orig.
edn. 1979]), pp. 120–1; Zheng Huixin, *Chunqiu wu ba* (The five hegemons of
the Spring and Autumn period) (Hong Kong: Zhonghua shuju, 1991), pp.
93–4; Zhao Longzhi, comp., *Goujian* (Goujian) (Taibei: Huaguo chubanshe,
1953), p. 12.

6 Fangshi, "Lun xue guochou yi xian li guochi" (To avenge ourselves against our
national enemies we must first foster a sense of national shame), *Dongfang
zazhi* (Eastern miscellany) 1.4 (June 8, 1904): 65–7. For another article, which
appeared in the same magazine later in the year and pursued some of the same
themes, see Kexuan (pseud.), "Guochi pian" (Essay on national humiliation),
ibid., 1.10 (December 1, 1904): 221–7.

7 One might indeed treat it as a paradigmatic narrative. J.D.Y. Peel argues that
for Protestant missionaries operating in West Africa in the nineteenth century,
and even more for their African converts, the Bible was "their supreme
paradigmatic history, through which they recognized new situations and even
their own actions." "For Who Hath Despised the Day of Small Things?
Missionary Narratives and Historical Anthropology," *Comparative Studies in
Society and History* 37.3 (July 1995): 595.

8 Guo Songtao had once expressed amazement at the palpable lack of indignation felt by his countrymen against the Western importation of opium. Xiao
Gongquan [Hsiao Kung-ch'üan], *Zhongguo zhengzhi sixiang shi* (A history of

Chinese political thought) (Taibei, 1961), 5: 684–5. The awakening of national shame was a frequent theme in *Ziqiang zhai baofu xingguo lun chubian* (Essays from the Self-Strengthening Studio on the safeguarding of China's wealth and the revival of the nation: first collection), compiled by Wang Tao shortly before his death (Shanghai, 1897). To Liang Qichao, at the beginning of the twentieth century, "it seemed as though the Chinese could look with equanimity on foreign invasion." Joseph R. Levenson, *Liang Ch'i-ch'ao and the Mind of Modern China* (Cambridge: Harvard University Press, 1965), p. 111.

9 Xuecun [Zhang Xichen], "Renru fuzhong" (Enduring humiliations and shouldering burdens), *Dongfang zazhi* 12.4 (April 1, 1915): 15. The phrase *renru fuzhong* often carries the meaning "to endure humiliation for the sake of accomplishing some larger purpose (or mission or task)." Here *renru* and *fuzhong* are coequal in value.

10 On the relationship of Chinese nationalism to the Twenty-One Demands, see Zhitian Luo, "National Humiliation and National Assertion: The Chinese Response to the Twenty-One Demands," *Modern Asian Studies* 27.2 (1993): 297–319. The Japanese side of the Twenty-One Demands is dealt with in Marius B. Jansen, *Japan and China: From War to Peace, 1894–1972* (Chicago: Rand McNally, 1975), pp. 209–23; for Yuan Shikai's response, see Ernest P. Young, *The Presidency of Yuan Shikai: Liberalism and Dictatorship in Early Republican China* (Ann Arbor: University of Michigan Press, 1977), pp. 186–92.

11 See Mary Backus Rankin, "Nationalistic Contestation and Mobilization Politics: Practice and Rhetoric of Railway-Rights Recovery at the End of the Qing," *Modern China* 28.3 (July 2002): 315–61.

12 For detailed accounts see Luo, "National Humiliation and National Assertion," pp. 300–9; Karl G. Gerth, "Consumption as Resistance: The National Products Movement and Anti-Japanese Boycotts in Modern China," in Harald Fuess, ed., *The Japanese Empire in East Asia and Its Postwar Legacy* (München: Ludicium Verlag, 1998), pp. 132–42.

13 Although eventually a multiplicity of national humiliation days were recognized and observed in China, initially there was only one National Humiliation Day, sometimes identified as May 7, sometimes as May 9. As an illustration of the confusion over the correct date, in the aftermath of the acceptance of the Japanese ultimatum, in circular telegrams, the Educational Association (*Jiaoyu lianhe hui*) announced its decision to commemorate the national humiliation annually on May 9, while the Beijing Chamber of Commerce fixed May 7 as the date of annual commemoration. Both telegrams may be found in the journal *Guochi* (National humiliation), No. 1 (June 1915): 4–6 (*jizai*); see also *Shibao*, May 16, 1915, p. 2. For a sarcastic foreign account of the date issue, see *North-China Herald and Supreme Court and Consular Gazette*, May 24, 1924, p. 289. The confusion between May 7 and 9 has been explained in various ways. Gerth asserts that May 7 was the focus of commemoration in North China, May 9 in the south, and sees this as symptomatic of China's political fragmentation at the time ("Consumption as Resistance," pp. 133–4, n. 36). Luo sees the confusion over the two dates as relating more closely to the degree to which people blamed the Yuan Shikai regime as well as the Japanese, those whose animus was directed mainly or exclusively at the Japanese favoring the May 7 date, those whose focus was on the culpability of the Yuan government in accepting the demands favoring May 9 ("National Humiliation and National Assertion," pp. 310–11). In the end, the ambiguity appears never to have been dispelled. In the days following the student demonstrations of May 4, 1919, in Beijing, both May 7 and 9 were identified as National

Humiliation Days in Shanghai. See *Shenbao*, May 6, 1919, pp. 1, 10; May 7, 1919, pp. 1, 3, 10; May 8, 1919, pp. 1, 10–11. The same confusion occurred again there in May 1927, after the Guomindang's establishment of control in the city. *Ibid.*, May 7, 1927, pp. 5–6; May 8, 1927, p. 5; May 10, 1927, pp. 13–14.

14 Zhichishe, comp., *Guochi*, n.d., reprinted in Shen Yunlong, ed., *Jindai Zhongguo shiliao congkan sanbian* (Third collection of materials on modern Chinese history), 23 *ji*, vol. 227 (Taibei: Wenhai chubanshe, 1979–86), p. 16 (*Wu yue jiu ri hou zhi quanguo yuqing*). See also Chow Tse-tsung, *The May Fourth Movement: Intellectual Revolution in Modern China* (Cambridge: Harvard University Press, 1960), p. 22; Min-ch'ien T.Z. Tyau, *China Awakened* (New York: Macmillan, 1922), p. 141.

15 Hou Hongjian, "Guoxue guochi laoku san da zhuyi biao li" (Illustrative charts displaying the three great principles: Chinese learning, national humiliation, and hard work), *Jiaoyu zazhi* 7.7 (July 1915): 23–6 (*zazuan*).

16 Hou Hongjian, "Shu Jiangsu sheng xiaozhang huiyi zhi gailüe" (A brief account of the meeting of the principals of Jiangsu province), *Jiaoyu zazhi* 7.8 (August 1915): 54 (*tebie jishi*).

17 Luo, "National Humiliation and National Assertion," pp. 311–12.

18 *Ibid.*, pp. 305–9, 312–14.

19 For an articulation of the magazine's purpose, see "Ben she jian ze" (Publisher's brief statement of principles) (inside front cover) and "*Guochi* chushi tebie guanggao" (Special advertisement on the occasion of *Guochi*'s initial appearance) (inside back cover).

20 Xiao, "Jinggao wu jianwang zhi guoren" (A respectful warning to my forgetful compatriots), *Shibao*, May 10, 1915, p. 2; Gongzhen [Ge Gongzhen], "Wuwang ci ci zhi chiru" (Do not forget the present humiliation), *ibid.*, p. 8; Yiming, "Guomin yongyong zhi xin jinian" (A permanent new anniversary for the Chinese people), *ibid.*, May 11, 1915, p. 1. One columnist likened the sudden mood changes of the Chinese public to the wind, which when active was capable of destroying everything in its path but when inactive left no trace of its ever having even existed. Leng, "Feng" (The wind), *Shenbao*, June 28, 1915, p. 2.

21 Zizhu, "He wei buwang?" (What does not forgetting mean?), *Shibao*, May 15, 1915, p. 1.

22 Luo, "National Humiliation and National Assertion," pp. 313–14. The man in question, Ding Yihua, asserted that the thing he most feared was his compatriots' predilection for abruptly switching from tears to laughter as soon as a crisis had passed. *Shenbao*, May 17, 1915, p. 6.

23 For further thoughts on anniversaries, see Paul A. Cohen, *History in Three Keys: The Boxers as Event, Experience, and Myth* (New York: Columbia University Press, 1997), pp. 219–21.

24 The May Fourth Movement – the student-led demonstrations that began in Beijing on May 4, 1919, in protest against the failure of the Versailles peace conference to transfer control of Shandong from Japan back to China – had originally been planned for May 7 ("National Humiliation Day") and, in the view of some, took much of its animus from the "continuing indignation" aroused by the Twenty-One Demands. Chow, *The May Fourth Movement*, p. 99; Chow cites the similar view of Paul Reinsch (*ibid.*). One Shanghai editorialist even suggested on May 5 that if the news from Versailles turned out to be accurate China would be in the position of commemorating a double national humiliation (*guochi zhi shuang jinian*). Mo (pseud.), "Shandong wenti jinghao" (Warning of possible bad news on the Shandong question), *Shenbao*, May 5, 1919, p. 7. At this point in time (at least in Shanghai) there was no

such thing as the "May Fourth Movement." The focus in the press was on the betrayal of Chinese interests at Versailles, which was consistently portrayed as a "national humiliation." This was also the view of 25,000 Beijing students, who on May 6 published a circular telegram calling on all Chinese citizens to hold national humiliation anniversary meetings on May 7 and "join in the common effort to guard against this desperate situation." *Ibid.*, May 6, 1919, p. 3; see also *ibid.*, May 6, 1919, p. 10; May 7, 1919, pp. 1, 10; May 8, 1919, pp. 10–11; May 9, 1919, pp. 10–11; May 10, 1919, pp. 10–11; May 11, 1919, p. 7. See also *North-China Herald*, May 10, 1919, pp. 370–1. On May 9 (the National Humiliation Day date generally observed in Shanghai) a *Shenbao* editorialist wrote that "this year we have a second national humiliation and an anniversary greater than any we have had since we started observing national humiliation days." Yong (pseud.), "Guochi" (National humiliation), *Shenbao*, May 9, 1919, p. 11. For another instance of plans for the May 7 anniversary (in this case consisting of preparations by educators and other civic leaders in Shanghai for a "citizens' assembly") feeding into the May Fourth Movement, see Jeffrey N. Wasserstrom, *Student Protests in Twentieth-Century China: The View from Shanghai* (Stanford: Stanford University Press, 1991), p. 52. For illustrations of seals that circulated during the May Fourth Movement, inscribed with such slogans as "Save the nation, wipe clean the humiliation" (*jiuguo xuechi*) and "An admonition to our countrymen, do not forget the national humiliation" (*jinggao tongbao wuwang guochi*), see Liu Jisheng, ed., *Guochi fen* (Indignation over national humiliation) (Jinan: Jinan chubanshe, 1990), p. 177. Although, as indicated above, there is a good deal of evidence indicating that in the early days of May 1919 the "May Fourth Movement" and National Humiliation Day were joined in the minds of many contemporaries, even including numerous students in Beijing, Rudolf Wagner has recently argued that the more activist students consciously refused to join in May 7 National Humiliation Day commemorative activities, on the ground that "mourning over one's shame" was a "meek and helpless" form of behavior "used only by slaves and defeatists." He further argues that, in the highly contested anniversary-date field of the new republican calendar, student radicals were intent upon establishing May 4 as a permanent "reminder to both the public and the government of the enduring legitimacy" of protest movements such as May Fourth. See his "The Canonization of May Fourth," in Milena Dolezelova-Velingerova and Oldrich Kral, eds., *The Appropriation of Cultural Capital: China's May Fourth Project* (Cambridge: Asia Center, Harvard University, 2001), pp. 67, 81–2.

25 The quoted phrase is in Lengguan [Wu Songgao], "Duiyu wuqi Beijing xuechao zhi ganxiang" (Reflections on the May 7 student upheaval in Beijing), *Guowen zhoubao* 2.18 (May 17, 1925): 2. See also the biography of Chang Shih-chao [Zhang Shizhao] in Howard L. Boorman, ed., *Biographical Dictionary of Republican China*, 4 vols. (New York: Columbia University Press, 1967–1971), 1: 107 (the date of May 7, 1926, given for the student rising, is incorrect); Gongzhan, "Guo neiwai yizhoujian dashi ji" (A record of the week's important events at home and abroad), *Guowen zhoubao* 2.18 (May 17, 1925): 26; Yanyan, "Wuqi xuechao zahua" (Random thoughts on the May 7 student upheaval), *ibid.*, p. 28; Harriet C. Mills, "Lu Xun: Literature and Revolution – From Mara to Marx," in Merle Goldman, ed., *Modern Chinese Literature in the May Fourth Era* (Cambridge: Harvard University Press, 1977), pp. 201–2; Xu Guangping letter to Lu Xun, May 9, 1925, in Lu Xun, *Lu Xun quanji* (The complete writings of Lu Xun), 16 vols. (Beijing: Renmin wenxue chubanshe, 1995), 11: 70–2; *North-China Herald*, May 16, 1925, p. 270. On the student actions of May 7, 1925, in Shanghai,

see Barry Keenan, *The Dewey Experiment in China: Educational Reform and Political Power in the Early Republic* (Cambridge: Council on East Asian Studies, Harvard University, 1977), pp. 94–5.

26 A similar pattern of student upheaval took place in May 1920 at a female normal school in Beijing. The students requested permission to have the day off from classes on May 7. When the principal refused their request on the ground that the Ministry of Education had issued orders forbidding it, the students, enraged, issued a public statement, in response to which the principal locked them in their classrooms. *Shenbao*, May 11, 1920, p. 6.

27 Yanyan, "Wuqi xuechao zahua," p. 28. The *North-China Herald* put it even more strongly: "Had it not been for some inexcusable bungling on the part of the Government, the acting Minister of Education, Chang Shih-chao [Zhang Shizhao] particularly, May 7 would have passed off without incident, and the subsequent demonstrations and rioting would not have occurred." May 23, 1925, p. 313.

28 Gerth, "Consumption as Resistance," pp. 136–7. Gerth (*ibid.*) reports an ad for "5–9 Brand Cigarettes."

29 *Shenbao*, May 9, 1920, p. 1 (Sunday Supplement).

30 *Ibid.*, May 8, 1924, p. 8.

31 See, for example, *ibid.*, May 9, 1924, p. 3; May 9, 1925, p. 1.

32 Slightly different versions of the ad are in *ibid.*, May 7, 1925, p. 13, and May 9, 1925, p. 13.

33 *Ibid.*, May 9, 1931, p. 11. Another ad, placed by a wine company (Zhangyu), linked not forgetting May 9 with not forgetting the finest of China's own wine-making (i.e. the wines produced by Zhangyu) and offered gifts of sample bottles of wine and candies (or fruits) to all patriotic customers who purchased a bottle of Zhangyu wine on May 6, 7, or 8. *Ibid.*, May 6, 1925, p. 1; May 7, 1925, p. 2; May 8, 1925, p. 2.

34 *Ibid.*, May 7, 1925, p. 12; May 8, 1925, p. 12; May 9, 1925, p. 12; May 10, 1925, p. 18; May 11, 1925, p. 17; May 9, 1926, p. 19. Another series of patriotic Golden Dragon ads, not expressly linked with National Humiliation Day, is in the May 3, 10, 17, and 24, 1925, issues of *Guowen zhoubao*. On Nanyang's incorporation of patriotic material in its advertising in order to compete more effectively with its main rival, the British–American Tobacco Company, see Sherman Cochran, *Big Business in China: Sino-Foreign Rivalry in the Cigarette Industry, 1890–1930* (Cambridge: Harvard University Press, 1980). Harrison observes that after the death of Sun Zhongshan (Yat-sen), Zhongshan became a popular brand name, and ads identifying the purchase of Zhongshan products as an expression of patriotism were common. See her *The Making of the Republican Citizen*, pp. 147–8; also *ibid.*, pp. 182–4.

35 Almost immediately after the attack people were turning a profit by peddling World Trade Center T-shirts ($5.50 for one that showed the towers and an American flag waving). Adam Gopnik, "Urban Renewal," *New Yorker*, October 1, 2001, p. 66. "Betting on a surge in American patriotism, countless wholesalers in New York City kicked into high gear the day after the…attacks." Lynette Holloway, "The Rush to Market Souvenirs," *New York Times*, December 8, 2001, p. A12. In the ensuing days and weeks numerous corporations took out full-page notices in the *New York Times* that were both patriotic and self-serving. The telecommunications giant Verizon, for example, published a message entitled "Let Freedom Ring." The notice begins: "Never before did a phone ringing sound so good as it did last week in lower Manhattan. And never before did the ringing of the opening bell sound as triumphant as on Monday morning at the Stock Exchange." It then goes on to detail the "crucial" role "thousands of Verizon employees" played in enabling

these and other things to happen. *Ibid.*, September 23, 2001, p. A17. See also the Pitney Bowes ad in *ibid.*, November 7, 2001, p. A7. The possible inappropriateness of the use of patriotic themes for corporate advantage did not go unnoted at the time. For criticism of Boeing in this respect, see Alessandra Stanley, "Jet Makers Use Patriotic Theme in Bid for Contract," *nytimes.com*, October 20, 2001. A more general assault on "profiteering in the name of patriotism" is found in a message from the Institute for America's Future and Citizens for Tax Justice, *New York Times*, November 6, 2001, p. A10.

36 Of course, even when companies used patriotic themes in their advertising for the purpose of advancing their own interests, they could still, to the extent that they were successful in persuading people to buy Chinese, end up benefiting the nation as well. Karl Gerth, in his work on the National Products Movement, argues for a growing Chinese commitment in the 1920s and 1930s to an "ethic of nationalistic consumption." See his "Consumption as Resistance."

37 The issue of when a particular form of evocation of a painful past becomes trivialization has been much debated. When the Birmingham diocese of the Church of England, in a promotional effort to make Christianity more relevant to the lives of young people, launched a series of ads featuring such slogans as "Body Piercing? Jesus had his done 2,000 years ago," other church groups reacted with horror, charging the diocese with "trivializing and secularizing the faith." The Church of England rejected the complaints. *Boston Globe*, September 1, 2001, p. A10.

38 The Guomindang in 1928 published an official list of twenty-six such days, indicating for each the date of the original humiliation, its causes, the adverse consequences for China, and the foreign country involved. The list is in the front matter of Liang Xin, *Guochi shiyao* (A concise history of national humiliation), sixth printing (Shanghai: Rixin yudi xueshe, 1933 [1931]), pp. 1–6. It was apparently first issued by the Ministry of the Interior. See Xu Guozhen, *Jin bainian waijiao shibai shi* (A history of the foreign affairs defeats of the past hundred years) (Shanghai: Shijie shuju, 1929), pp. 203–5.

39 The text of a relatively late example may be found in *Shenbao*, May 6, 1934, p. 15.

40 For examples of activities (pre-1927) relating to the anniversaries of the Twenty-One Demands in Shanghai, Beijing, Nanjing, and other cities, see *Shenbao*, May 10, 1917, p. 10; May 11, 1917, p. 10; May 10, 1918, p. 10; May 11, 1918, p. 11; May 7, 1919, pp. 3, 10; May 8, 1919, pp. 6–7, 10–11; May 9, 1919, pp. 10–11; May 10, 1919, pp. 10–11; May 11, 1919, pp. 7, 10; May 9, 1925, pp. 1, 13. See also *North-China Herald*, May 15, 1920, p. 375 (Canton); May 14, 1921, p. 461 (Shanghai); May 12, 1923, p. 363 (Peking); May 19, 1923, p. 439 (Changsha, Ichang); May 17, 1924, pp. 247 (Peking), 250 (Ichang); May 24, 1924, p. 289 (Wuchang); May 9, 1925, p. 234 (Shanghai).

41 These instructions, which were adopted by the Guomindang Central Committee on April 19, 1929, are found in *Chongbian riyong baike quanshu* (New edition of encyclopedia for everyday use) (Shanghai: Shangwu yinshuguan, 1934), pp. 5792–3. For another set of official guidelines, written mainly for government workers and covering not only national humiliation anniversary days but other anniversaries as well, see *Gezhong jinianri shilüe*. The front matter of this manual (pp. 1–9) discusses in fairly general terms the meaning, origin, and value of anniversaries, as well as the rituals and educational activities that should accompany them. See also Harrison, *The Making of the Republican Citizen*, p. 187.

42 Other strategies used by the Guomindang to place itself and Sun Yat-sen at the center of China's modern history are detailed in Harrison, *The Making of the*

Republican Citizen, pp. 151–64, and Robert Culp, " 'China – The Land and Its People': Fashioning Identity in Secondary School History Textbooks, 1911–37," *Twentieth-Century China* 26.2 (April 2001): 40–7.

43 For detailed information on Guomindang-managed commemorative activities (pertaining mainly but not exclusively to the May 9 anniversary) in Shanghai and other cities, see *Shenbao*, May 10, 1927, pp. 13–14; May 9, 1928, p. 8; May 10, 1928, pp. 6, 13; May 5, 1929, p. 13; May 10, 1929, p. 6; May 10, 1931, p. 13; May 6, 1933, p. 8; May 9, 1933, p. 8; May 10, 1933, pp. 6, 8. See also *North-China Herald*, May 14, 1927, p. 290 (Shanghai); May 5, 1928, p. 189 (Shanghai); May 11, 1929, p. 223 (Hankow); May 6, 1930, p. 229 (Shanghai); May 12, 1931, pp. 182 (Nanking), 194–5 (Shanghai); May 3, 1933, pp. 172 (Peking, Nanking), 177 (Shanghai); May 17, 1933, p. 243 (Shanghai); May 16, 1934, p. 224 (Shanghai); May 15, 1935, p. 262 (Shanghai); May 13, 1936, p. 277 (Shanghai, Nanking); May 5, 1937, p. 196 (Shanghai); May 12, 1937 (Shanghai), p. 234.

44 This is similar to, but not the same as, the polarity Hue-Tam Ho Tai establishes between hyper-mnemosis and willed amnesia. In the context of recent Vietnamese history, with particular reference to "totalitarian commemoration," Tai defines "hyper-mnemosis" as "the intensive, even obsessive, effort to keep...[the past] at the forefront of consciousness, to shape it and to exploit it for a variety of purposes." In these circumstances, she argues, "forgetting may be the only escape from the tyranny of enforced memory." The hyper-mnemosis portion of Tai's analysis seems to me eminently applicable in the republican Chinese case. The forgetting that took place in China, however, was not a "willed" form of resistance to state coercion but, rather, I would argue, an instinctive psychological response to an overload of identical or near-identical stimuli in the environment. See Tai's "Introduction: Situating Memory," in Hue-Tam Ho Tai, ed., *The Country of Memory: Remaking the Past in Late Socialist Vietnam* (Berkeley: University of California Press, 2001).

45 Zuming (pseud.), "Guochi jinianri ganyan" (Thoughts on National Humiliation Day), *Shenbao*, May 9, 1921, p. 18. For other complaints about the short-lived nature of Chinese enthusiasm or fervor, see *North-China Herald*, May 17, 1919, p. 416 (translation of Chinese circular); *Shenbao*, May 9, 1922, p. 17 (cartoon); Cao Wenhai, "Wujiu gantan" (Thoughts on May 9), *ibid.*, May 8, 1924, p. 17; Song (pseud.), "Guochi ri de jingyu" (Words of warning on National Humiliation Day), *ibid.*, May 9, 1924, p. 18; Feng Shuren, "Wu fenzhong redu de fenxi" (An analysis of enthusiasm that only lasts five minutes), *ibid.*; *North-China Herald*, May 17, 1924, p. 250; Li Dichen, "Xuechi" (Avenging humiliation), *Shenbao*, May 10, 1928, p. 17; *ibid.*, May 10, 1931, p. 13. A characteristic foreign view was articulated in the press on the eve of the May Fourth Movement:

> The peculiar Chinese brand of patriotism, which used to manifest itself in anti-dynastic and anti-foreign outbreaks of intense fury, has passed into decadence and is no longer practiced except by *the emotional young men who cut their fingers and write in blood on whitewashed walls, and then forget the whole matter before the cut is healed.*
> *North-China Herald*, May 3, 1919, p. 259 (emphasis supplied).

46 Yanyan, "Wuqi xuechao zahua," p. 28. The growing meaninglessness of the May 7 (or 9) anniversary observances is also noted in Na (pseud.), "Wujiu jinian" (The May 9 anniversary), *Shenbao*, May 9, 1921, p. 11; Zuming (pseud.), "Guochi jinianri ganyan"; Wu Lingyuan, "Guochi jinianri xiaoyan" (Trifling thoughts on the anniversary of the National Humiliation), *Shenbao*,

May 9, 1922, p. 17; Cao Wenhai, "Wujiu gantan"; Song (pseud.), "Guochi ri de jingyu"; Ji Lüshui (pseud.), "Sangxin bingkuang zhi guochi ri ji" (An account of an absurd National Humiliation Day), *Shenbao*, May 9, 1924, p. 18; Yaochang (pseud.), "Wuhu guochi ri na tian" (Alas, that National Humiliation Day), *ibid.*, May 9, 1928, p. 21; Li Dichen, "Xuechi"; Nian (pseud.), "Di ershi ci guochi jinian" (The twentieth anniversary of the National Humiliation), *Shenbao*, May 9, 1935, p. 5; Da haizi (pseud.), "Guochi jinian" (Commemorating the National Humiliation), *ibid.*, May 9, 1937, p. 18.

47 Lengguan [Wu Songgao], "Wujiu jinian zhi yizhong ganxiang," (A reflection on the anniversary of May 9), *Guowen zhoubao* 2.17 (May 10, 1925): 3; see also Bulei [Chen Bulei], "Wujiu jinian" (The anniversary of May 9), *ibid.*, 3.17 (May 9, 1926): 1.

48 [Wang] Yunsheng, "Guochi" (National humiliation), *ibid.* 12.18 (May 13, 1935): 1 (*yizhou jianping*). See also Congyu [Fan Zhongyun], "Guochi jinian yu Zhong-Ri jiaoshe" (The anniversary of the national humiliation and Sino-Japanese negotiations), *Dongfang zazhi* 21.10 (May 25, 1924): 1–2 (*shishi shuping*). According to an editorialist writing in May 1933, in the growing crisis then enveloping China the May 7 anniversary had become all but meaningless. Pu (pseud.), "'Wuqi guochi' yu guochi de jianglai" ("The May 7 national humiliation" and the future of national humiliation), *Shenbao*, May 7, 1933, p. 1 (Shanghai supplement). On May 7, 1940, the Nationalist government in Chongqing officially abolished the May 9 National Humiliation Day anniversary on the grounds that in the context of all-out war against Japan it had been overtaken by the anniversary of July 7, the date on which the Sino-Japanese War began, and was no longer meaningful. See the editorial (unsigned) "Feizhi wujiu jinian de yiyi" (The meaning of the abolition of the May 9 anniversary), *Shenbao*, May 8, 1940, p. 4. See also *ibid.*, May 9, 1940, p. 7. The growing meaninglessness of "May 9" is also pointed out in an editorial of the previous year (also unsigned): "Cong 'Ershiyi tiao' dao 'Dongya xin zhixu'" (From the "Twenty-One Demands" to the "New Order in East Asia"), *ibid.*, May 9, 1939, p. 4.

49 See, for example, Daniel L. Schacter, *Searching for Memory: The Brain, the Mind, and the Past* (New York: Basic Books, 1996).

50 Prasenjit Duara, "Response to Philip Huang's 'Biculturality in Modern China and in Chinese Studies'," *Modern China* 26.1 (January 2000): 32–7 (quotes from p. 35).

51 Luo, "National Humiliation and National Assertion," p. 314.

52 It was commonplace for writers to emphasize the fundamental building process China needed to engage in if it was to gain international respect and withstand its adversaries in the future. See, for example, Ping, "Jinri zhi ri" (The present time), *Shibao*, May 11, 1915, p. 5; Xiao, "Chujin er wai" (Aside from fundraising), *ibid.*, May 12, 1915, p. 2; Zizhu, "Neixiang yu waixiang" (Fundamental tendencies and superficial tendencies), *ibid.*, May 16, 1915, p. 2.

53 See, for example, Zizhu, "He wei buwang?"; Zizhu, "Neixiang yu waixiang"; Fu Youpu, *Zhongguo tongshi* (The painful history of China) (Shanghai: Xinhua shuju, 1927), pp. 2–3.

54 The legend of Old Lady Meng was derived from Buddhist folklore. See Schwarcz's *Bridge Across Broken Time: Chinese and Jewish Cultural Memory* (New Haven: Yale University Press, 1998), especially pp. 40–4. "The ability to forget the past," Lu Xun wrote, "enables people to free themselves gradually from the pain they once suffered; but it also often makes them repeat the mistakes of their predecessors." "What Happens after Nora Leaves Home?" (talk at Peking Women's Normal College, 1923), in Lu Xun, *Silent China:*

Selected Writings of Lu Xun, trans. Gladys Yang (London: Oxford University Press, 1973), p. 151.

55 Ba Jin, "We Must Never Forget" (August 6, 1979), in Ba Jin, *Random Thoughts*, trans. Geremie Barmé (Hong Kong: Joint Publishing Co., 1984), pp. 174–5. On Ba Jin's commitment to remembering the Cultural Revolution, see Schwarcz, *Bridge Across Broken Time*, pp. 109–10.

56 This was expressed in a variety of ways. On the more militant end of the spectrum was the explosive tract *China Can Say No* and a number of related works. See Song Qiang *et al.*, *Zhongguo keyi shuo bu: lengzhanhou shidai de zhengzhi yu qinggan jueze* (China can say no: politics and choice of sentiments in the post-Cold War era) (Beijing: Zhonghua gongsheng lianhe, 1996). For an insightful analysis of *China Can Say No* and the victimization-centered nationalism it embodies, see Toming Jun Liu, "Uses and Abuses of Sentimental Nationalism: Mnemonic Disquiet in *Heshang* and *Shuobu*," paper presented at the annual meeting of the Association for Asian Studies, Boston, March 1999. A useful recent commentary on this genre of writing is supplied in John W. Garver, "More from the 'Say No Club,'" *The China Journal* 45 (January 2001): 151–8.

57 Peter Gries notes that in the hours and days following the U.S. bombing of the Chinese embassy in Belgrade in May 1999 letters and poems sent to the *Guangming Daily* (two of whose reporters had been killed) frequently referred to the proverb *woxin changdan* (which he translates as "to undergo hardships and strengthen one's resolve to wipe away the national humiliation"). This proverb was directly derived from the Goujian saga. See his "Tears of Rage: Chinese Nationalist Reactions to the Belgrade Embassy Bombing," *China Journal* 46 (July 2001): 38.

58 Author's introduction, in Liang Yiqun *et al.*, *Yibai ge guochi jinian ri*, p. 11.

59 Two excellent accounts of the new nationalism of the 1990s are Yongnian Zheng, *Discovering Chinese Nationalism in China: Modernization, Identity, and International Relations* (Cambridge: Cambridge University Press, 1999), and Suisheng Zhao, "Chinese Intellectuals' Quest for National Greatness and Nationalistic Writing in the 1990s," *China Quarterly* 152 (December 1997): 725–45.

60 For an overview of the aims and content of the post-1989 emphasis on patriotic education, see Samuel Wang, "Teaching Patriotism in China," *China Strategic Review* 1.4 (July 5, 1996): 13–17.

61 For a fascinating account of the celebratory atmosphere surrounding the Hong Kong reversion and the meaning it had for the inhabitants of a small Sichuan city, see Peter Hessler, *River Town: Two Years on the Yangtze* (New York: HarperCollins Publishers, 2001), pp. 165–82, passim.

62 Many of these individuals did, of course, live during the period of hostile relations with the Soviet Union, when China regularly used the phrase "social imperialism" to refer to that country. But, partly (I suspect) because the emphasis in "social imperialism" was more on betrayal (of the socialist system and vision) than on victimization, and partly because Soviet actions against China took place after 1949, these actions were rarely if ever defined in terms of "national humiliation." The vocabulary of *guochi* in the People's Republic of China (PRC) has generally been reserved for actions taken against China prior to the establishment of Communist rule. The restoration of Chinese sovereignty over Hong Kong would thus clearly fall within the parameters of *guochi* because it corrected a wrong done to China at the time of the Opium War; Soviet anti-Chinese actions during the 1960s and 1970s, on the other hand, would not come under this heading.

63 Gong Shuduo, "Qianyan," in *Jindai Zhongguo bainian guochi ditu* (Maps of modern China's hundred years of national humiliation) (Beijing: Renmin chubanshe, 1997).

64 The series was published between 1991 and 1993 by Zhongguo huaqiao chubanshe in Beijing.

65 See, for example, Che Jixin, ed., *Guochi: Zhongguo renmin bugai wangji* (National humiliation: the Chinese people should not forget) (Jinan: Shandong youyi shushe, 1992); Liang Yiqun and Lu Zhenxiang, eds., *Bainian guochi* (A hundred years of national humiliation) (Beijing: Nongcun duwu, 1992).

66 Representative of the juvenile category is Zhou Shan and Zhang Chunbo, eds., *Tushuo Zhonghua bainian guochi lu* (An illustrated account of China's century of national humiliation) (Lanzhou: Gansu shaonian ertong chubanshe, 1998); examples of more scholarly works are Li Jichen and Chen Jialin, eds., *Guochi lu: Jiu Zhongguo yu lieqiang bupingdeng tiaoyue bianshi* (A record of national humiliation: a compilation and explication of unequal treaties between old China and the powers) (Chengdu: Sichuan renmin chubanshe, 1997), and Zhuang Jianping, ed., *Guochi shidian*.

67 Seven chapters in all are devoted to the War of Resistance. The postscript (*houji*) makes explicit the intent of the editors to memorialize China's victory with the book's publication. "Zhonghua minzu chiru shi" editorial committee, ed., *Women zen neng wangji? Zhonghua minzu chiru shi* (Beijing: Zhongguo guangbo dianshi chubanshe, 1995).

68 The following sources refer either to the importance of teaching youth about the century of humiliation or the leading role of the Communist Party in ending it, or both: "Bianzhe de hua" (Words from the compilers), in Zhuang Jianping, ed., *Guochi shidian*, p. 1; Gong Shuduo, "Qianyan," in *Jindai Zhongguo bainian guochi ditu*; Yu Xinyan, general preface (*zongxu*), in Liang Yiqun, Yang Jie, and Xiao Ye, eds., *Yibai ge guochi jinian ri*; Liang Yiqun's introduction (*qianyan*), in *ibid.*, p. 12; Zhonggong Beijing shiwei dangshi yanjiu shi (Party history research office of the Beijing municipal Party committee of the Communist Party of China), postface (*houji*), in Shao Rongchang and Wu Jialin, eds., *Wuwang bainian guochi* (Don't forget the hundred years of national humiliation), 2 vols. (Beijing: Zhongguo renmin daxue chubanshe, 1992), 2:361; Dai Yi, preface, in Liu Jishen, ed., *Guochi fen*, p. 3; "Wuwang guochi" (epilogue), in *ibid.*, pp. 269–73 (especially p. 273); An Zuozhang, preface, in Che Jixin, ed., *Guochi*, pp. 1–2; "Chuban congshu zongzhi" (General aim of the series), prefacing all volumes of the "Wuwang guochi lishi" series (see, for example, Lü Tao, ed., *Guochi de kaiduan* [The beginnings of national humiliation] [Beijing: Zhongguo huaqiao chubanshe, 1992]); Zhou Gucheng, preface, in *ibid.*; "Xie zai qianmian de hua" (Introductory words), in Zhang Zhi, ed., *Guochi, guohun, guowei: Bainian xingshuai hua aiguo* (National humiliation, national spirit, national dignity: talking about patriotism in a century of ups and downs) (Shanghai: Shanghai renmin chubanshe, 1995), pp. 2–3; postface (*xie zai houmian*), in Liang Zhanjun, *Jindai Zhonghua guochi lu* (An account of national humiliation in modern China) (Beijing: Beijing chubanshe, 1993), p. 108; and publisher's introduction (*qianyan*) and editor's postface, in Zhou Shan and Zhang Chunbo, eds., *Tushuo Zhonghua bainian guochi lu*, pp. 3, 157.

69 Among the first to make the point were Mary C. Wright, in the introduction to her *China in Revolution: The First Phase, 1900–1913* (New Haven: Yale University Press, 1968), and John Schrecker, in his *Imperialism and Chinese Nationalism: Germany in Shantung* (Cambridge: Harvard University Press, 1971). For a somewhat different view, which sees the anti-imperialist nationalism of the late Qing as being centered in gentry and regional opposition to

the central government, see Min Tu-ki, *National Polity and Local Power: The Transformation of Late Imperial China*, ed. Philip A. Kuhn and Timothy Brook (Cambridge: Council on East Asian Studies, Harvard University, 1989), especially pp. 207–11.

70 Rankin is particularly good on this. See her "Nationalistic Contestation and Mobilization Politics."

71 In his discussion of Ah Q's reaction to being beaten over the head by a man he had just insulted, Lu wrote:

> As far as Ah Q could remember, this was the second humiliation of his life. Fortunately after the thwacking stopped it seemed to him that the matter was closed, and he even felt somewhat relieved. Moreover, the precious "ability to forget" handed down by his ancestors stood him in good stead. He walked slowly away and by the time he was approaching the wine shop door he felt quite happy again.
>
> *The True Story of Ah Q*, in Lu Hsun [Xun], *Selected Works of Lu Hsun*, 4 vols. (Peking: Foreign Languages Press, 1956), 1: 92.

72 *Imagined Communities: Reflections on the Origin and Spread of Nationalism*, rev. edn. (London: Verso, 1991 [1983]), p. 159.

73 This tension also existed during the late Qing (as we have just seen) and the Yuan Shikai years. In regard to the latter, the *North-China Herald* in 1915 printed a translation of a telegram that the Yuan government sent to the provinces for the purpose of containing anti-Japanese activities in the aftermath of China's acceptance of the Twenty-One Demands. "Although we can have no reason to prohibit any declaration of patriotic feelings," the telegram read in part, "...yet, for fear of treacherous persons taking advantage of this opportunity, stringent measures should be taken to keep these matters within bounds." *North-China Herald*, May 22, 1915, p. 546. See also Gerth, "Consumption as Resistance," p. 135.

74 The difficult relationship between popular nationalism and official nationalism is explored in Yongnian Zheng, *Discovering Chinese Nationalism in China*, pp. 87–110, 123, 133–4.

75 The government's quandary in this area was illustrated in the immediate aftermath of the collision on April 1, 2001, between an American spy plane and a Chinese fighter jet in the air space between Hainan and the Paracel Islands. Government-monitored Internet chat rooms and bulletin boards, described (with some exaggeration) in the *New York Times* as "an easy barometer of opinion among the country's best-educated young people," were jammed with "furious denunciations of American imperialism" and calls for "retribution," but at the same time, the *Times* noted, "the most inflammatory comments were blocked or deleted." Still more telling, the Chinese leadership reportedly issued strict instructions to universities around the country that there were to be no student demonstrations. Craig S. Smith, "American Embassy Officials Wait to See Plane's Crew," *New York Times*, April 3, 2001, p. A6; Erik Eckholm, "U.S. Envoy to Meet Chinese Foreign Minister as Negotiations on Plane Crew Continue," *ibid.*, April 6, 2001, p. A10. A different sort of example was provided in the summer of 1991 when a small group of individuals met privately in Nanjing to commemorate the Nanjing Massacre of 1937. It was originally to have been a high-visibility conference, with many more delegates, held on the campus of Nanjing University. But the government had recently applied for a favorable loan from Tokyo and an unexpected visit by the Japanese prime minister appears to have persuaded Beijing that this was not the most opportune time for a large-scale, well-publicized conference on

Japanese war crimes. Ian Buruma, *The Wages of Guilt: Memories of War in Germany and Japan* (New York: Farrar, Straus, Giroux, 1994), p. 123.

76 Many writers have touched on this difference in one way or another. Halbwachs, for example, distinguished between autobiographical and historical memory, the former referring to events that have been personally experienced, the latter to events that have been experienced only indirectly, through books, commemorative rites, and the like. See Lewis A. Coser's introduction to Maurice Halbwachs, *On Collective Memory*, ed. and trans. by Lewis A. Coser (Chicago: University of Chicago Press, 1992), pp. 23–4, 29–30.

77 "Since context must, of necessity, constantly change," writes Israel Rosenfield, "there can never be a fixed, or absolute, memory. Memory without the present cannot exist." *The Invention of Memory: A New View of the Brain* (New York: Basic Books, 1988), p. 80. The point is nicely illustrated by the postwar experience of East and West Germany, where very different presents led to very different patterns of remembering and forgetting of the Nazi past. See Claudia Koonz, "Between Memory and Oblivion: Concentration Camps in German Memory," in John R. Gillis, ed., *Commemorations: The Politics of National Identity* (Princeton: Princeton University Press, 1994), pp. 258–80.

7 Revisiting *Discovering History in China*

It is now over a decade since the publication of *Discovering History in China*. Since it continues to be assigned in college courses not only in the United States but also (in translation) in Taiwan, mainland China, and Japan,[1] and has, I am told, become a favorite of nervous doctoral candidates on the eve of their oral exams, I thought it might be useful to supplement this reissue of the paperback edition with a brief overview of some of the (in my view) more important developments that have taken place since the early 1980s in the field of American historical writing on nineteenth- and twentieth-century China.[2] I also want to respond (nondefensively, of course) to some of the criticisms of the book[3] and indicate what parts of my analysis I would change if I were rewriting it today.

Throughout *Discovering History in China*, I operate on two levels: the level of the history that direct participants make and experience; and that of the history that historians write. The focus of the book is on the second level, in particular the intellectual constructs used by American historians in the post-World War II era to make sense of the recent Chinese past (by which, in the book, I mean specifically the nineteenth and twentieth centuries). I assume that, as historians, our aim is to do our utmost to understand and elucidate past reality.[4] At the same time, I of course recognize that, in pursuit of this goal, we must use ordering concepts and that these ordering concepts, precisely because of their quality of ordering, inevitably introduce an element of distortion. I believe that our task as historians is to choose concepts that combine a maximum of explanatory power with a minimum of distortional effect. In the book I argue:

1   that the conceptual frameworks that were most influential among American historians in the 1950s and 1960s – the *impact–response* and *tradition–modernity* approaches – and a third framework – the *imperialism* approach – that emerged in the late 1960s in criticism of the two earlier approaches were all heavily burdened with Western-centric assumptions;
2   that this burden of Western-centrism caused them to distort past Chinese reality to an excessive degree.

There is not much in my discussion of these three approaches (taking up the first three chapters of the original book) that I would change today, aside from an occasional modification of phrasing and the addition of new illustrative detail. The main substantive changes I would introduce would come in the fourth and final chapter, partly to address problems in this chapter that a number of reviewers have (I think correctly) identified,[5] and partly to bring up to date my account of the evolution of the field since the book's original appearance. The final chapter of *Discovering History in China* deals with an approach (more accurately described as a set of tendencies) that emerged in American China scholarship around 1970 and that challenged, sometimes explicitly, sometimes implicitly, the Western-centric biases of earlier approaches. The key feature of this approach, which I label "China-centered," is that its practitioners have striven empathetically to reconstruct the Chinese past as the Chinese themselves experienced it rather than in terms of an imported sense of historical problem. In addition to starting with Chinese problems set in a Chinese context, other features of the approach are that it attempts to cope with the size and complexity of the Chinese world by breaking it down into smaller, more manageable units; that it sees Chinese society as being arranged hierarchically in a number of different levels; and that it welcomes with enthusiasm theories, methodologies, and techniques developed in disciplines other than history (mostly, but not exclusively, the social sciences) and strives to integrate these into historical analysis.

One complaint leveled at my treatment of the China-centered approach, mainly by Michael Gasster, is that I am surprisingly uncritical of it, that I do not subject China-centered scholarship to the same kind of scrutiny that I apply to pre-1970 writing. The easy response to this complaint is that since the scholarship of the past few decades has in fact represented a decisive advance over that of the 1950s and 1960s there is therefore less to criticize. But, even if this is true, Gasster is right to point out that, at the very least, "all correctives tend to create their own distortions."[6] Certainly, the China-centered historiography of recent years has been no exception to this rule. Gasster's own recipe for righting the balance focuses on the need "to refine our methods of relating localities to China and China to the wider world."[7] He feels that if the new history continues in the directions outlined in my book it will not only overstate the autonomy of Chinese history at the very moment (the nineteenth and twentieth centuries) when links between China and the rest of the world were being forged on a stronger basis than ever before; it will also, in its exaggerated attention to local and lower-level history, cause us to lose sight of the national perspective. "What analytical tools are we developing," Gasster asks, to integrate all the local studies that have been done, "to accommodate our new picture of China's diversity to our old one of its unity and integrity?"[8] Dennis Grafflin, operating from a perspective quite different from Gasster's, poses essentially the same question: "Once we have disaggregated China over time, space, culture, society, etc., how can there be the China-centered historiography that Cohen is calling for? Don't we have to bind up China again?"[9]

In principle, I am not unsympathetic to the concerns raised by Gasster and Grafflin. If historical work centering on small-scale spatial units and/or on the lower reaches of society gets lost in specificities and fails to address broader analytical and interpretive issues, if it neglects to ask the question "so what?" it holds little interest for me either as a historian of China or as a student of human behavior and thought in general. On the other hand, it seems to me that in the case before us this criticism is premature. It is not so long, after all, since we got started on these smaller-scale, more focused studies. The scholarship of the first two decades after World War II bequeathed to the field an overabundance of generalizations pertaining to China as a whole, and the more bounded research that began to appear around 1970 or just before has played an important role in challenging and revising some of these earlier generalizations. Still more recently, starting in the mid-1980s, right around the time my book came out, we have been treated to a growing number of outstanding works that, although China-centered in the sense that they deal with changes of major significance that were taking place in China prior to or apart from the full onslaught of the West in the nineteenth century, are far more integrative than the earlier generation of China-centered studies and address major questions pertaining to Chinese history in general in the late imperial and republican periods.[10]

A very partial listing of these works might include Madeleine Zelin's book (1984) on the indigenous evolution of the eighteenth-century Chinese state, with particular attention to fiscal reform; William Rowe's study (1984) of the remarkable development of commerce in Hankou in the nineteenth century; Benjamin Elman's work (1984) on the critical changes in Chinese intellectual discourse that took place in the eighteenth century in the Lower Yangzi region; Philip Huang's book (1985) on long-term patterns of agrarian change in North China in the late imperial and republican eras; Mary Rankin's study (1986) of the growing mobilization and politicization of late Qing social elites, focusing on Zhejiang; Prasenjit Duara's inquiry (1988) into the impact of state-making on the social history of rural North China in the first half of the twentieth century; James Polachek's reconfiguration of the Opium War (1992), seen from the perspective of the internal Chinese political setting of the day; and Kathryn Bernhardt's analysis (1992) of the weakening of the landlord class in the Lower Yangzi area during the late imperial and republican periods, as a result of the increasing intrusiveness of state power coupled with China's growing commercialization.[11]

Most of these works are spatially delimited in subject matter, but this does not keep them from posing questions pertaining to the whole of China. Moreover, at least two of the studies cited, Rankin's and

Polachek's, although embodying all or most of the traits I describe as "China-centered," pay serious heed to the difference foreign imperialism made in the internal political evolution of China in the late Qing. The fact that these works are China-centered, in other words, not only does not imply a dismissive stance toward the importance of exogenous factors in Chinese history, but actually empowers them to illuminate the parts taken by these factors in special ways. Indeed, a number of writers have now taken the position that the China-centered approach has much to offer to the study of China's foreign relations in general.[12] [There are, on the other hand, a number of areas of recent scholarly interest – pertaining to China's regional and global links, Chinese migration overseas, non-Han ethnic groups within the Chinese realm, and so on – for which a China-centered approach is plainly not, or is at best only partially, appropriate. Some of these areas are discussed in the introduction to this volume.]

It has also been suggested, notably by the Chinese scholar Jiwei Ci, that, whatever the actual importance of the "foreign impact," the China-centered approach is especially well-suited to address Chinese *perceptions* of it. In the book I suggest that the Western impact, at least in nineteenth-century China, was overstated (and misstated) by an earlier generation of American historians. An especially egregious example of this, I argue, was American treatment of the Opium War, the objective importance of which was not nearly so great as we – and an almost unanimous corps of Chinese historians – have imagined. Jiwei Ci does not challenge what I have to say about the impact of the West at the time. But he insists, I think quite legitimately, that this impact became very important in subsequent Chinese consciousness, and undoubtedly, in that subjective form, had a very real shaping influence on later Chinese historical behavior of the most objective sort. If, he adds, I am to be true to my own injunction that the measure of the historical importance of a problem in Chinese history should be "a Chinese, rather than a Western, measure," Chinese consciousness with respect to the role of external agency must be taken with utmost seriousness in China-centered history, even if in my judgment as a historian this consciousness is substantially misguided.[13]

Jiwei Ci's criticism suggests a neat way of joining the China-centered approach and some of the tendencies of Maoist historiography (above all, the overstated importance of foreign imperialism) that, at first glance, seem to be challenged and perhaps undermined by it. Wang Xi, an economic historian, suggests a somewhat different way of integrating the China-centered approach and the impact of imperialism. Imperialism, for Wang Xi, was not just something in Chinese minds; it was real and had a critically important impact. This impact, however, was shaped in significant ways by internal factors, as emphasized by China-centered scholarship. If we are to gain a full and accurate understanding of modern Chinese history, therefore, we must see this history as the product of a complex interaction between both internal and external agencies.[14]

Still other Chinese scholars, it is important to note, have been basically unconcerned with the apparent (although not in my view real) problems the China-centered approach poses for the handling of foreign influences in recent Chinese history. These scholars, after having lived through years of past-bashing on the part not only of the Chinese Communist Party (and, in certain circumstances, the Guomindang) but also of Chinese intellectuals generally in the post-May Fourth era, have seemingly welcomed the opportunity to approach their own past as something alive and dynamic, as a viable source of growth and evolution, and not just an obstacle to be surmounted on the Chinese road to modernity. An unanticipated (and certainly unintended) consequence of the China-centered approach is that it appears to have licensed such individuals to see Chinese history prior to the twentieth century in a much more affirmative light.[15]

Although the particular criticisms of China-centered scholarship offered by Michael Gasster – that it fails to deal adequately either with China as a whole or with the exogenous factors shaping Chinese history in recent centuries – strike me as being wide of the mark, certainly there are other criticisms to which this scholarship is open. I will briefly note two of my own pet complaints. One is that as we have moved away from individual-centered history and event-centered history to the study of collectivities and long-term processes it sometimes seems as though we have jumped a stage or two in our historiographical development. We have gotten to levels of depth and sophistication that were unimaginable only a few decades ago. But we still don't have detailed, comprehensive studies of some of the major events of nineteenth- and twentieth-century Chinese history (for example the Sino-Japanese War of 1894); and we also lack strong, reliable biographies of several of the most important individual actors (such as Zeng Guofan, Cixi, and Chiang Kai-shek). Collectivities – lineages, social strata, religious sects, secret societies, guilds, and the rest – are enormously important, as are such long-term processes as population growth, commercialization, and state-building. But important individuals and major events also have terrific impacts, conscious and unconscious, on people's lives. It is understandable why these historiographical black holes exist. Partly it is because the study of big events and influential individuals has been out of fashion for some time; partly it is owing to the fact that the very scale of these subjects creates a daunting prospect for the solitary scholar. Perhaps this is a job for collaborative research – the sort of thing Mary Wright pioneered in her work on the 1911 Revolution.[16] But, one way or another, it is something that badly needs to be done.[17]

Another worry that I have, on a somewhat deeper level, pertains to the downside of what, in many respects, I see as a very wholesome development: namely, the increasing attention paid by American historians in recent years to Europe, coupled with a shift away from our earlier tendency to compare China, particularly in the nineteenth century, with Japan (almost invariably in the context of comparative modernization or comparative responses to the West). This shift has to do with changes in the kinds of questions we have been asking about late imperial and republican China and, accompanying these different questions, a much greater sensitivity to some of the crucial developments that were taking place in China during this time period. As historians of China have become interested in many of the same kinds of problems that historians of Europe have long been concerned with (commercialization, urbanization, demographic changes, social mobilization, state-making, the whole problem of the state–society relationship over time), we have been able to benefit from, at the same time as we have qualified and adjusted, the insights of Europeanists.

One consequence of this, hopefully, is that we are making China more interesting and less exotic to our Europeanist colleagues. We may actually be getting to the point where it will no longer suffice for historians of Europe to make mere polite bows in the direction of China, where they will have to become more familiar with Chinese history, on a serious level, in order to carry on with greater effectiveness their work in European history itself. [The exposure the recent work of R. Bin Wong and Kenneth Pomeranz, discussed in the introduction to this volume, has received in such mainstream historical journals as the *American Historical Review* is certainly a hopeful sign.]

For historians of China, on the other hand, I find in this newfound European connection a potential danger – or at least something we need to be continuously and assiduously watchful of. Until quite recently the main challenge for American historiography was getting beyond the view that China was incapable of making its own history, that it needed the West to do so for it. Now that we have made considerable headway in overcoming this earlier barrier to understanding we find ourselves face to face with another barrier that may be more difficult to surmount. A perusal of recent American scholarship on the Chinese past reveals that the history we have belatedly been discovering in that past has, ironically, often been marked by strong resonances with patterns of change that highlighted the West's own history on its march toward modernity. Thus American historians have documented China's flourishing scientific and technological traditions (Nathan Sivin), the high rates of literacy the Chinese reached in late imperial times (Evelyn Rawski), the growing urbanization, monetization, and commercialization of the Chinese economy from the late Ming (Ramon Myers, William Rowe, Susan Mann), and so on.[18] Individually, this scholarship is often highly sophisticated – its practitioners have been careful, for example, to point out differences from, as well as parallels to, the European experience. But collectively it raises a troubling question: In exploding one form of parochialism – that modernizing change could not be initiated by the Chinese themselves, that it could only be introduced by the West – have we inadvertently insinuated into Chinese history another form, to wit, that the only kind of change important enough to be worth looking for in the Chinese past is change leading toward modernity as defined by the Western historical experience?

This was the central problem, in my judgment, with Wm. Theodore de Bary's book on the "liberal tradition" in China (1983).[19] It is also a key problem in the controversy that has been taking place since the late 1980s in connection with two related concepts that were first applied to European history: *public sphere* and *civil society*. It would be extremely difficult to summarize, in short compass, the different facets of this discussion, which, despite the manifest intelligence of the participants, has been nothing if not confusing conceptually. Suffice it to say that the treatment of these concepts in European history has generally been tied explicitly or implicitly to such political developments as constitutionalism, the rise of liberal democracy, and/or the idea of an autonomous public realm separate and distinct both from the state and from the private world of familistic and parochial concerns. Those who have supported the view that something broadly akin to a public sphere (though not necessarily a civil society) began gradually to take shape in late imperial China (Rowe, Mary Rankin, David Strand) have been commendably cautious in the claims they have made and extremely sensitive to the potential problems involved in transferring value-laden concepts from European history to Chinese. But they have forged ahead nonetheless. A number of prominent scholarly voices have questioned their wisdom in doing so, some (such as Frederic Wakeman) disparaging the quality or interpretation of the data assembled, others (such as Philip Kuhn) questioning whether, by employing European concepts too mechanically, we may not end up with " 'sprouts of liberalism' – a political version of 'sprouts of capitalism,' a conception born from the compulsion to show that 'China had it, too.' "[20] There seems to be a degree of consensus that something new was indeed taking place in China beginning in the late imperial era. That is not the issue. The key question is whether it serves a useful purpose to give these fresh phenomena a name that, for all the cautionary qualifications, still is burdened by misleading associations from European history or whether we would not be better served with another name (or set of names) altogether.

Let me now turn to some of the newer developments in the field that strike me as being particularly important. Some of these represent further elaborations of tendencies that were already beginning to make their presence felt in the 1970s and early 1980s. A notable example is the study of popular culture, including how it both differed from and also interacted with elite culture. There has been a veritable explosion of writing within this subfield, beginning with the publication in 1985 of *Popular Culture in Late Imperial China*, a pioneering volume edited by David Johnson, Andrew J. Nathan, and Evelyn S. Rawski.[21] Subsequent highpoints have included, in the realm of labor history, work on groups as diverse as Shanghai prostitutes, Beijing rickshaw pullers, and factory workers in Shanghai and Tianjin[22]; and, in the area of popular communication, studies of almanacs, folk literature, operatic performance, and wartime propaganda.[23]

Another development that, although taken note of in *Discovering History in China*, has increased enormously in importance over the past decade (mirroring a trend in the historical profession generally in the United States) is the impact of the anthropology field on historical writing. Partly this comes from the fact that anthropologists have been studying Chinese folk religion for many years; as historians have turned more and more to the investigation of popular culture, we have found that popular culture is inseparable from popular religion and have leaned heavily on the work of our anthropologist colleagues.[24] Partly, also, the impact of anthropology has assumed new forms, as symbolic anthropology in particular has begun to exert a significant influence on historical scholarship. The writings of Prasenjit Duara and James Hevia come quickly to mind as examples. Duara, in an article on the Chinese God of War (Guandi), takes an almost archeological approach to the cultural symbols embedded in important myths. Although allowing, certainly, for the possibility of the total disappearance of a given symbol, central to Duara's understanding is the notion of layers of symbolic meaning, the latest such meaning being "superscribed" on earlier ones in stratigraphic fashion.[25] Hevia's work has focused on the realm of ceremony, ritual, and ritualized behavior, mostly in the context of Sino-Western interactions (foreign embassies to the Chinese court, Sino-foreign negotiations, missionary retribution against China in the post-Boxer period, and so forth). One of its great strengths is its careful contextualization of the behaviors (Western and Chinese) brought under scrutiny. Hevia takes great pain, for example, in his analysis of the conflicts attending the Macartney Embassy of 1793 to steer clear of "modernist" constructions of the roles of ceremony and ritual on either side and to attempt to understand what ceremonial and ritual meant to Chinese/Manchus and British at the time.[26]

Insofar as the China scholarship of Hevia, Duara, and others is concerned with the excavation of "original" meanings, before such meanings suffer from the inevitable distortion of being "represented" by a nonparticipant "other," it may legitimately claim to be "China-centered," in the most pristine sense. But insofar as, like all intellectual inquiry, it is "positioned," in the sense that it reflects (necessarily and inevitably) the concerns and biases of the inquirer, it cannot help but result in knowledge that is, in important respects, reconfigured – and hence, to a greater or lesser extent, *not* China-centered.

The work of Hevia and Duara forms a bridge to another development of major consequence for the field. Both scholars are members of the editorial board of the journal *positions: east asia cultures critique*, which began publishing in spring 1993. The geocultural focus of this journal is East Asia and the Asian diaspora. Its central concern, as noted in its

Statement of Purpose, is to place "cultural critique at the center of historical and theoretical practice."

The diverse theoretical concerns that have appeared in the contents of the first several issues of *positions* – among them gender, class, feminism, deconstructionism, various forms of Marxism, anticolonialism and the nature of the postcolonial world, the relationship between knowledge and power and more specifically between scholarship and the fates of the people scholars study – are far too varied and complex to survey here. As I examine the work of people who appear sympathetic to all, or at least many, of these strands of what for lack of a generally agreed-on term I will loosely refer to as "postmodern" scholarship, I am struck by a number of things. First, its practitioners, in their impassioned critique of colonialism and the parts taken by the West in general and the United States in particular (including American scholars) in the shaping of the colonial and postcolonial orders, are clearly the spiritual descendants of the graduate students and young academics who formed the Committee of Concerned Asian Scholars (CCAS) a generation ago. A major difference between the two is that, where the CCAS in the late 1960s and early 1970s targeted the "hard" colonialism of guns and bombs (we were, of course, still engaged at the time in the war in Indochina), the postmodern scholarship of the early 1990s seems mainly concerned with the "soft" colonialism of the mind. Second, individuals engaged in postmodern scholarship are more overtly concerned with theory than the CCAS scholars and, unlike the latter,[27] are involved not only in criticism of the defective scholarly approaches of the past but also in the development of new approaches (much influenced by symbolic anthropology and postmodernist literary criticism) that they believe will foster a future scholarship that is less distortive, less oppressive, more self-aware and self-critical. The downside of this is that in the process these scholars have shown a deplorable tendency, through the unchecked use of abstract conceptual formulations and neologisms, to build intellectual walls around themselves and what they are up to. James Peck may have been less theoretically informed than today's postmodernists. But at least you always knew exactly what he was saying.

Although a major concern of postmodernist scholarship is with gender and women's studies, the latter clearly have a life of their own and cannot be subsumed under the former. These are approaches that were just beginning to attract attention when my book first appeared. In the ensuing decade they have burgeoned in significance. No longer dismissible as exotic subfields or treatable as species of historiographical affirmative action, gender and women's studies are now seen as strategic approaches that, even more than analyses focused on class, have the potential to inform – and transform – our understanding of past human society in its entirety. As the editors of the landmark work *Engendering China: Women, Culture, and the State* put it: "China viewed through the lens of gender is not just more inclusive; it is different."[28]

I want to conclude this discussion by returning once again to the valuable commentary of Michael Gasster. One of Gasster's criticisms that I find very much to the point is his identification of my failure in *Discovering History in China* to recognize what Tongqi Lin, in a similar criticism, refers to as "the advantage of the 'outsider's perspective'."[29] "It is well to remind ourselves," Gasster notes

> that both our time perspective and our Westernness are advantages as well as disadvantages. Here…Cohen is too onesided. He performs a service in reminding us to be alert to our twentieth-century and Western biases, but he writes as if our perspectives as latecomer-outsiders are only liabilities and in no sense assets.[30]

This is a criticism that runs deep. It gets at a problem that I thought about a good deal while writing the book and that since then has moved to the forefront of my concern as a historian.

The emphasis in the book is, as Gasster correctly states, almost entirely on the negative, distortional consequences of a particular kind of outsideness, which I label variously as "ethnocentric" (*not* "ethnic bias"),[31] Western-centered, Europocentric, and so forth. I describe the China-centered historiography that became increasingly prominent in the field after 1970 as a wholesome corrective to this earlier form of outsideness, insofar as it adopted, in a number of senses, a more interior perspective on recent Chinese history. At the same time, in my account of this later stage in our historiographical evolution I also take note, at several points, of the problem of residual Western-centric bias. (I do this, in particular, in my discussion in the final chapter of the application of social science theory to Chinese historical data.) And in the concluding pages of the book I address the more general problem of "outsideness" faced by *all* historians in our efforts "to retrieve the truth about the past."

In other words, although I allow for different forms of outsideness and clearly regard some forms as less damaging than others, I consistently portray outsideness as a *problem*, as a burden upon the historical enterprise, rather than an asset. The possibility, raised by Gasster and Lin, that American historians of the Chinese past may actually have an advantage over Chinese historians (or, for that matter, that historians in general may have an advantage over the direct participants in history) is a very real one and deserves the most serious attention. Our outsideness, after all, is a major part of what makes us different from the immediate experiencers of the past and enables us, as historians, to render the past intelligible and meaningful in ways that simply are not available to the direct participants in history. Outsideness, in other words, whether that of Americans addressing the Chinese past or that of historians in general addressing the past in general, does not just distort; it also illuminates. Which means that the central task facing historians, to paraphrase what I said earlier, is to find ways of exploiting our outsideness that maximize the illumination and minimize the distortion.

If the historian's outsideness is viewed not as a necessary evil but, in more positive terms, as one of the very qualities that defines the historian as a historian, the most basic questions are raised about the entire historical enterprise – questions that, because they touch on our ultimate goals, are bound to be not a little unsettling. Is it really true, for example, that our aim as historians is in some sense to recapture past reality, "to retrieve the truth about the past?" If so, what do "past reality" and "the truth about the past" mean? How does the historian's understanding of "reality" and "truth" differ – as most surely it does – from that of the direct participant? And what implications does this difference have for what we do as historians? It is not likely that questions of this sort will ever be finally answered.[32] Yet, clearly, they are in the category of questions that we must keep asking if we are to maintain the highest levels of honesty and self-awareness concerning what it is we are about as historians.

Notes

This chapter is a reprint, with minor changes, of the preface to the second paperback edition (1997) of *Discovering History in China: American Historical Writing on the Recent Chinese Past*, originally published in 1984 (New York: Columbia University Press).

1   A Korean edition is also currently being prepared, to be brought out by Jontong and Hyundae Publishers in 2003. As of the time of the original publication of this preface (1997), the following translations had appeared: *Chi no teikokushugi: Orientarizumu to Chūgoku zō* (Intellectual imperialism: orientalism and the image of China), trans. Satō Shin'ichi (Tokyo: Heibonsha, 1988); *Zai Zhongguo faxian lishi: Zhongguo zhongxinguan zai Meiguo de xingqi* (Discovering history in China: the rise of the China-centered view in America), trans. Lin Tongqi (Beijing: Zhonghua shuju, 1989); Taiwan reprint (with same title) of Zhonghua shuju edition (Taibei: Daoxiang chubanshe, 1991); *Meiguo de Zhongguo jindaishi yanjiu: Huigu yu qianzhan* (American study of modern Chinese history: retrospect and prospect), trans. Li Rongtai *et al*. (Taibei: Lianjing, 1991). (In the last-named version my name as author is given as Ke Baoan.)
2   Two excellent reviews of the literature that appeared after my book, both of them focusing on social history, are William T. Rowe, "Approaches to Modern Chinese Social History," in Olivier Zunz, ed., *Reliving the Past: The Worlds of Social History* (Chapel Hill: University of North Carolina Press, 1985), pp. 236–96; and Jeffrey N. Wasserstrom, "Towards a Social History of the Chinese Revolution: A Review," *Social History* 17.1 (January 1992): 1–21, and 17.2 (May 1992): 289–317. For two more theoretically oriented critiques of postwar American China historiography, both informed by the new culture criticism approach, see Tani E. Barlow, "Colonialism's Career in Postwar China Studies," *positions: east asia cultures critique* 1.1 (Spring 1993): 224–67; and Judith B. Farquhar and James L. Hevia, "Culture and Postwar American Historiography of China," *ibid*., 1.2 (Autumn 1993): 486–525.

3 For two earlier efforts to do so, see Paul A. Cohen, " 'State' Domination of the China Field: Reality or Fantasy? A Reply to Robert Marks," *Modern China* 11.4 (October 1985): 510–18; Cohen, "Our Proper Concerns as Historians of China: A Reply to Michael Gasster," *American Asian Review* 6.1 (Spring 1988): 1–24. Portions of the present preface are adapted from the latter essay.

4 For a probing examination of this and other of the book's assumptions, see the review essay by Tongqi Lin, "The China-Centered Approach: Traits, Tendencies, and Tensions," *Bulletin of Concerned Asian Scholars* 18.4 (October–December 1986): 49–59; also the Chinese version: "Ke Wen xin zhu *Zai Zhongguo faxian lishi* pingjie," *Lishi yanjiu* 1 (1986): 60–70.

5 Reviewers who have adopted a critical stance toward the book have tended to focus almost exclusively on the final chapter; two exceptions are Robert Marks, "The State of the China Field, or the China Field and the State," *Modern China* 11.4 (October 1985): 461–509; Michael Gasster, "Discovering China in History: Some Comments on Paul Cohen's *Discovering History in China*," *American Asian Review* 5.2 (Summer 1987): 121–53.

6 Gasster, "Discovering China in History," p. 145.

7 *Ibid.*, p. 151.

8 *Ibid.*, p. 145.

9 Grafflin, "Bound China," p. 22, unpublished paper, presented at Harvard University, April 5, 1985.

10 This was true of some of the earlier China-centered scholarship as well, a notable example being Kuhn's discussion of the implications of his study for the boundaries of modern Chinese history. See Philip A. Kuhn, *Rebellion and Its Enemies in Late Imperial China: Militarization and Social Structure, 1796–1864* (Cambridge: Harvard University Press, 1970), pp. 1–10.

11 Madeleine Zelin, *The Magistrate's Tael: Rationalizing Fiscal Reform in Eighteenth-Century Ch'ing China* (Berkeley: University of California Press, 1984); William T. Rowe, *Hankow: Commerce and Society in a Chinese City, 1796–1889* (Stanford: Stanford University Press, 1984); Benjamin A. Elman, *From Philosophy to Philology: Intellectual and Social Aspects of Change in Late Imperial China* (Cambridge: Council on East Asian Studies, Harvard University, 1984); Philip C.C. Huang, *The Peasant Economy and Social Change in North China* (Stanford: Stanford University Press, 1985); Mary Backus Rankin, *Elite Activism and Political Transformation in China: Zhejiang Province, 1865–1911* (Stanford: Stanford University Press, 1986); Prasenjit Duara, *Culture, Power, and the State: Rural North China, 1900–1942* (Stanford: Stanford University Press, 1988); James M. Polachek, *The Inner Opium War* (Cambridge: Council on East Asian Studies, Harvard University, 1992); Kathryn Bernhardt, *Rents, Taxes, and Peasant Resistance: The Lower Yangzi Region, 1840–1950* (Stanford: Stanford University Press, 1992). One could, of course, from the perspective of the year 2003, add many other books to this group. I will content myself with naming only one: Susan Naquin's monumental study of the wide-ranging (and changing) parts that temples played not only in the religious but also in the social and cultural life of Beijing during the final five centuries of the imperial era, *Peking: Temples and City Life, 1400–1900* (Berkeley: University of California Press, 2000).

12 Andrew J. Nathan, "Implications for Foreign Relations of Some Recent Trends in the Western Historiography of Republican China," paper presented at a meeting of the Association for Asian Studies, Boston, April 1987; Michael Hunt, "The Study of the History of Chinese Foreign Relations in the United States: Problems and Prospects," unpublished paper, 1987, p. 6. See also the published Chinese version of Hunt's piece: Hengte [Hunt], "Meiguo guanyu Zhongguo duiwai guanxi shi yanjiu de wenti yu qianjing," *Lishi yanjiu* 3

(1988): 152. In his recent book *The Genesis of Chinese Communist Foreign Policy* (New York: Columbia University Press, 1996), Hunt, while acknowledging the tendency of historians who have embraced a China-centered approach to turn a critical eye on the external-relations emphasis of much earlier Western historical writing (p. 239), also makes a persuasive case for the importance of "China-centered and China-sensitive perspectives" in furthering our understanding of China's "beliefs and behavior in international affairs" (p. 248).

13 Letter to author, August 22, 1992. See also Jiwei Ci, *Dialectic of the Chinese Revolution: From Utopianism to Hedonism* (Stanford: Stanford University Press, 1994), pp. 248–9, n. 1. The quoted phrase is from *Discovering History in China*, p. 154.

14 "Approaches to the Study of Modern Chinese History: External versus Internal Causation," paper presented at U.S.–China conference on "China's Quest for Modernization: Historical Studies on Issues concerning the Evolution of Modern Chinese Society," Fudan University, May 1992. This paper (with minor changes) was published as an article in Chinese: "Yanjiu Zhongguo jindaishi de quxiang wenti: Waiyin, neiyin huo neiwaiyin jiehe" (The problem of approach in the study of modern Chinese history: external factors, internal factors, or internal and external factors combined), *Lishi yanjiu* 5 (1993): 61–73. For an interesting effort (in reference to American cultural influences on China during the Deng Xiaoping era) to recast the impact–response approach by integrating it explicitly with China-centered analysis, see Zhu Shida, "Zhong-Mei wenhua chongji-huiying pianlun" (A brief discussion of Sino-American culture in terms of the impact–response approach), *Meiguo yanjiu* (America studies) 2 (1993): 76–93.

15 See the very interesting review essay by Xu Jilin, "Cong bentu tanxun lishi" (Looking for history in one's own country), *Dushu* 11 (1991): 30–7; see also Chen Pingyuan, "Xin wenxue: Chuantong wenxue de chuangzaoxing zhuanhua" (New literature: the creative transformation of traditional literature), *Ershiyi shiji* 10 (April 1992): 89.

16 A more recent example is the series of conferences Ezra Vogel and others are engaged in planning, focusing on different aspects of the Sino-Japanese segment of World War II. The first of these conferences, "Wartime China: Regional Regimes and Conditions, 1937–45," was held at Harvard University, June 27–9, 2002.

17 Joseph Esherick's superb study of the early stages of the Boxer movement points us in the right direction. Although China-centered in approach, Esherick's book (like those of Rankin and Polachek cited earlier) pays ample attention to the impact of imperialism. See his *The Origins of the Boxer Uprising* (Berkeley: University of California Press, 1987).

18 See, for example, Sivin, "Science and Medicine in Chinese History," in Paul S. Ropp, ed., *Heritage of China: Contemporary Perspectives on Chinese Civilization* (Berkeley: University of California Press, 1990), pp. 164–96, and his "Why the Scientific Revolution Did Not Take Place in China – Or Didn't It?" *Chinese Science* 5 (1982): 45–66; Rawski, *Education and Popular Literacy in Ch'ing China* (Ann Arbor: University of Michigan Press, 1979); Myers, "Tranformation and Continuity in Chinese Economic and Social History," *Journal of Asian Studies* 33.2 (February 1974): 274, and his "On the Future of Ch'ing Studies," *Ch'ing-shih wen-t'i* 4.1 (June 1979): 107–9; Rowe, *Hankow: Commerce and Society in a Chinese City, 1796–1889*, and the companion volume, *Hankow: Conflict and Community in a Chinese City, 1796–1895* (Stanford: Stanford University Press, 1989); Mann, *Local Merchants and the Chinese Bureaucracy, 1750–1950* (Stanford: Stanford University Press, 1987).

19 *The Liberal Tradition in China* (New York: Columbia University Press, 1983). For an exchange I had with de Bary in connection with the book, see Cohen, "The Quest for Liberalism in the Chinese Past: Stepping Stone to a Cosmopolitan World or the Last Stand of Western Parochialism? A Review of *The Liberal Tradition in China*," *Philosophy East and West* 35.3 (July 1985): 305–10; de Bary, "Confucian Liberalism and Western Parochialism: A Response to Paul A. Cohen," *ibid.*, 35.4 (October 1985): 399–412; Cohen, "A Reply to Professor Wm. Theodore de Bary," *ibid.*, pp. 413–17.

20 The literature on this controversy has quickly become unmanageable and I will make no attempt to cover it comprehensively here. The major books that have argued in one way or another for application of the term *public sphere* to China are: Rankin, *Elite Activism*; Rowe, *Hankow: Commerce and Society*; Rowe, *Hankow: Conflict and Community*; David Strand, *Rickshaw Beijing: City People and Politics in the 1920s* (Berkeley: University of California Press, 1989). Important article-length contributions to the discussion include: William T. Rowe, "The Public Sphere in Modern China," *Modern China* 16.3 (July 1990): 309–29; Frederic Wakeman, Jr., "The Civil Society and Public Sphere Debate: Western Reflections on Chinese Political Culture," *ibid.*, 19.2 (April 1993): 108–38; Rowe, "The Problem of 'Civil Society' in Late Imperial China," *ibid.*, pp. 139–57; Mary Backus Rankin, "Some Observations on a Chinese Public Sphere," *ibid.*, pp. 158–82; Richard Madsen, "The Public Sphere, Civil Society and Moral Community: A Research Agenda for Contemporary China Studies," *ibid.*, pp. 183–98; Heath B. Chamberlain, "On the Search for Civil Society in China," *ibid.*, pp. 199–215; Philip C.C. Huang, " 'Public Sphere'/'Civil Society' in China? The Third Realm between State and Society," *ibid.*, pp. 216–40; Rankin, "The Origins of a Chinese Public Sphere: Local Elites and Community Affairs in the Late-Imperial Period," *Études chinoises* 9.2 (Fall 1990): 13–60; Philip A. Kuhn, "Civil Society and Constitutional Development," in Léon Vandermeersch, comp., *La Société civile face à l'état dans les traditions chinoise, japonaise, coréenne et vietnamienne* (Paris: École Française d'Extrême-Orient, 1994), p. 307.

21 Johnson, Nathan, and Rawski, eds., *Popular Culture in Late Imperial China* (Berkeley: University of California Press, 1985).

22 Gail Hershatter has written several articles on prostitution in Shanghai, including "The Hierarchy of Shanghai Prostitution, 1919–1949," *Modern China* 15.4 (October 1989): 463–97, and "Courtesans and Streetworkers: The Changing Discourses on Shanghai Prostitution, 1890–1949," *Journal of the History of Sexuality* 3.2 (October 1992): 245–69; these are now largely superceded by her book *Dangerous Pleasures: Prostitution and Modernity in Twentieth-Century Shanghai* (Berkeley: University of California Press, 1997). On the culture and lives of rickshaw pullers in twentieth-century Beijing, see Strand, *Rickshaw Beijing*, especially pp. 38–64; on factory workers in Tianjin and Shanghai, see Gail Hershatter, *The Workers of Tianjin, 1900–1949* (Stanford: Stanford University Press, 1986), Emily Honig, *Sisters and Strangers: Women in the Shanghai Cotton Mills, 1919–1949* (Stanford: Stanford University Press, 1986), and Elizabeth J. Perry, *Shanghai on Strike: The Politics of Chinese Labor* (Stanford: Stanford University Press, 1993).

23 Richard J. Smith, *Chinese Almanacs* (New York: Oxford University Press, 1992); David Johnson, ed., *Ritual Opera, Operatic Ritual: "Mu-lien Rescues His Mother" in Chinese Popular Culture* (Berkeley: Chinese Popular Culture Project, University of California, 1989); Chang-tai Hung, *Going to the People: Chinese Intellectuals and Folk Literature, 1918–1937* (Cambridge: Council on East Asian Studies, Harvard University, 1985); Chang-tai Hung, *War and*

Popular Culture: Resistance in Modern China, 1937–1945 (Berkeley: University of California Press, 1994).

24 In my own work on the religious world of the Boxers at the end of the nineteenth century I have drawn heavily on the writing of such anthropologists as Emily M. Ahern, Ann S. Anagnost, Alan J.A. Elliott, David K. Jordan, Arthur Kleinman, Jack M. Potter, Gary Seaman, Robert P. Weller, Arthur P. Wolf, and Margery Wolf. See Paul A. Cohen, *History in Three Keys: The Boxers as Event, Experience, and Myth* (New York: Columbia University Press, 1997), especially chaps. 3–4; also Chapter 3 of the present volume.

25 "Superscribing Symbols: The Myth of Guandi, Chinese God of War," *Journal of Asian Studies* 47.4 (November 1988): 778–95.

26 See his "Making China 'Perfectly Equal,'" *Journal of Historical Sociology* 3.4 (December 1990): 380–401; also his book *Cherishing Men from Afar: Qing Guest Ritual and the Macartney Embassy of 1793* (Durham: Duke University Press, 1995). Another example of Hevia's approach is his article "Leaving a Brand on China: Missionary Discourse in the Wake of the Boxer Movement," *Modern China* 18.3 (July 1992): 304–32, in which he treats missionary discourse at the turn of the century as the product of "a historically specific culture rather than as a natural or commonsense response to a transparent situation" (p. 324). By closely examining the symbolism embedded in the retributive acts taken by missionaries and foreign soldiers in the post-Boxer months, Hevia gives us new insight into what Westerners were attempting to do in – and to – China via these actions.

27 I refer specifically to the CCAS generation of the 1960s and 1970s; certainly the editors of *Critical Asian Studies*, the successor to the original CCAS journal (the *Bulletin of Concerned Asian Scholars*), include individuals who are very much concerned with theory. Some of the theoretical failings of the CCAS in its early years are limned in Barlow, "Colonialism's Career in Postwar China Studies," pp. 248–50.

28 Christina K. Gilmartin, Gail Hershatter, Lisa Rofel, and Tyrene White, "Introduction," in Gilmartin *et al.*, eds., *Engendering China: Women, Culture, and the State* (Cambridge, Mass.: Harvard University Press, 1994), p. 2. This book grew out of a conference of the same title held at Harvard University, Wellesley College, and MIT in February 1992. Another recent volume that, although primarily about twentieth-century Chinese literature, also has much insight into the parts played by gender in the history of this period is Tani E. Barlow, ed., *Gender Politics in Modern China: Writing and Feminism* (Durham: Duke University Press, 1993).

29 Lin, "The China-Centered Approach," p. 55.

30 Gasster, "Discovering China in History," p. 148.

31 This is the phrase Gasster sometimes uses in his review (for example pp. 123, 131). I don't in fact use it anywhere in my book. My understanding of "ethnic," rightly or wrongly, is quite different from my understanding of "ethnocentric," by which I mean little more than "placing ourselves at the center of things."

32 For a sustained effort at grappling with them, see my *History in Three Keys*, passim; also Chapter 8 of the present book.

8 Three ways of knowing the past

Philosophers have written lengthy theoretical treatises on what historians do. In my book *History in Three Keys: The Boxers as Event, Experience, and Myth* (1997), as a practicing historian I explore the issue through an actual historical case, the Boxer uprising in China at the turn of the twentieth century. When I first began to study history, my idea of what historians "did" was very different from what it is now. I used to think of the past as, in some sense, a fixed body of factual material which it was the historian's job to unearth and elucidate. I still think of the historian as a person whose main object is to understand and explain the past. But I now have a far less innocent view of the processes – and problems – involved. I now see the reconstructive work of the historian as in constant tension with two other ways of "knowing" the past – experience and myth – that, in terms of their bearing on people's lives, are far more pervasive and influential.

Plotted at a certain level of abstraction, the Boxer uprising formed a major chapter in the narrative structure of the final years of the Qing era. It was the largest-scale armed conflict to occur between the rebellions of the mid-nineteenth century and the 1911 Revolution, and as such reflected the increasingly tenuous political position of the dynasty. Seen as a social movement, the Boxers, many of them young farm boys made destitute by the successive natural disasters that had battered North China since the early 1890s, were a striking expression of the more general breakdown of the agrarian order in China at the end of the nineteenth century. This breakdown, characterized in many parts of the empire by high levels of popular unrest, was also reflected in the religious beliefs of the Boxers, in particular their practice of spirit possession and frequent recourse to magic. The antiforeign dimension of the Boxer phenomenon, expressed most dramatically in the attacks on native Christians and foreign missionaries, created a profound crisis in Sino-foreign relations and eventually led to direct foreign military intervention and a Chinese declaration of war against all the powers. Finally, the lifting of the siege of the legations in Beijing in August 1900, the flight of the court to Xi'an in the northwest, the foreign occupation of the capital, and the diplomatic settlement (including a huge indemnity) imposed on China by the victorious powers brought a decisive shift in Qing government policy, which in the first years of the twentieth century became increasingly (if reluctantly) wedded to far-reaching reform. It is small wonder, taking all of these different aspects of the Boxer episode together, that Mary Wright should have begun her widely read essay on the background of the 1911 Revolution with the ringing pronouncement: "Rarely in history has a single year marked as dramatic a watershed as did 1900 in China."[1]

In addition to being an event, tightly woven into the larger tapestry of events comprising this period of Chinese history, the Boxers also gave rise to a potent set of myths in the popular imaginations of both Chinese and Westerners. In the West in the early decades of the twentieth century, the Boxers were widely viewed as "the Yellow Peril personified[,]...the very word Boxerism conjur[ing] up visions of danger, xenophobia, irrationality and barbarism."[2] Chinese intellectuals prior to the early 1920s – people like Lu Xun, Hu Shi, and the early Chen Duxiu – often shared this negative perception of the Boxers, adding to the foregoing list of attributes "superstitiousness" and "backwardness." Then, during the period of heightened nationalism and antiforeignism that marked the 1920s, while many Westerners sought to discredit Chinese nationalism by branding it a revival of "Boxerism" (Figure 8.1), Chinese revolutionaries began to rework the Boxers into a more positive myth, centering on the qualities of "patriotism" and "anti-imperialism." This more affirmative vision of the Boxers as heroic battlers against foreign aggression reached a high-water mark among Chinese on the mainland (and some persons of Chinese ancestry abroad) in the Cultural Revolution years (1966–76) (Figure 8.2),[3] at the very moment that Chinese on Taiwan (as well as many Westerners) were resurrecting the more lurid image of the Boxers as fanatical, uncivilized xenophobes and pinning it on the Red Guards.[4] During the Cultural Revolution, under the spirited oversight of Mao Zedong's wife Jiang Qing, praise was also lavished on the Boxers' female counterparts, the Red Lanterns, in particular for their alleged rebellion against the subordinate status of women in the old society[5] (Figure 8.3).

The Boxers as *event* represent a particular reading of the past, while the Boxers as *myth* represent a pressing of the past into the service of a particular reading of the present. Either way a dynamic interaction is set up between present and past, in which the past is continually being reshaped, either consciously or unconsciously, in accordance with the diverse and shifting preoccupations of people in the present. What happens to the past – or, to be more exact, the *lived* or *experienced* past – when we perform this feat of redefinition? What happens to the experiential world of the original creators of the past when, for purposes of clarity and exposition, historians structure it in the form of "events," or mythologizers, for altogether different reasons, distill from it a particular

Figure 8.1 Sapajou, "Making things move. The Boxer with the match: 'Ah ha! Something's going to happen now!'." In the 1920s the treaty-port press resorted to Bolshevik as well as Boxer imagery to denigrate Chinese nationalism, which is here equated with mob violence.

Source: *North-China Daily News*, January 27, 1927.

symbolic message? If it is true, to paraphrase the French philosopher Paul Veyne, that events never coincide with the perceptions of their participants and witnesses and that it is the historian who carves out of the evidence and the documents the event he or she has chosen to make,[6] what are the implications of this for historical understanding? Are historians, too, ultimately fashioners of myth? Finally, if we were to unravel an event, to break it down into smaller, more discrete mini-events or units of

Figure 8.2 Cheng Shifa, "Boxers heroically resisting the invading army." The theme of primitively armed Boxers fighting against powerfully armed foreign aggressors was not confined to the Cultural Revolution years.

Source: This illustration is from a booklet, published in 1956, that was written for upper-level primary school students and farmers and factory workers of low literacy attainment: Bao Cun, *Yihetuan* (Shanghai: Shanghai Renmin Chubanshe).

human experience – the tedium and physical wretchedness of life in the trenches rather than the grand order of battle – what would we be left with? Just a messy and meaningless pile of data? Or, on a more optimistic note, a closer approximation of what the past was actually like and what exactly happens to this "real past" when historians attempt to explain it or mythologizers to exploit it for its symbolic content?

Figure 8.3 Cultural Revolution depiction of a Red Lantern. The only thing this Red Lantern has in common with Red Lantern representations of the Boxer era is the quality of youth. The clothing and hairstyle have been modernized and the feet unbound. Most important, the Cultural Revolution Red Lantern has exchanged the reserve of her forebears for the persona of a fiercely rebellious warrior, who, sword in hand, takes her place side by side with male Boxers in the fight against the foreigner.

Source: *Hongdengzhao* (Shanghai, 1967).

These questions illustrate but do not exhaust the range of issues I am concerned with in *History in Three Keys*. The first part of the book tells the "story" of the Boxer uprising, as later narrated by historians – people with foreknowledge of how things turned out, a wide-angle picture of the entire event (that is, the capacity to discern how the experiences of different individuals in the past related to one another and how a profusion of small-scale events widely distributed in space interconnected to form event-structures of broader compass), and the goal of explaining not only the Boxer phenomenon itself but how it fitted into a mosaic of prior and subsequent historical developments. The second part probes the thought, feelings, and behavior of the immediate participants in different phases of the Boxer experience – Chinese peasant youths who often for reasons of survival joined Boxer units in their villages, anxious missionaries scattered across the drought-parched North China plain at the height of the uprising, Chinese and foreign inhabitants of Tianjin trapped in that city during the battle that raged there in the early summer of 1900 – individuals, in short, who didn't know whether they would emerge from their respective ordeals dead or alive, who did not have the entire "event" pre-inscribed in their heads, and who therefore conceptualized what was happening to them in ways that differed in the most fundamental way from the retrospective, backward-reading constructions of historians. The third part of the book explores the myths surrounding the Boxers and "Boxerism" that were fashioned in twentieth-century China – symbolic representations designed less to elucidate the Boxer past than to draw energy from it and score points, often (but not always) of a political or overtly propagandistic nature, in the post-Boxer present.

My aim in scrutinizing – and juxtaposing – these different zones of consciousness is to convey something of the elusiveness of the historical enterprise in general, to illuminate the tension between the history that people make, which is indeed in some sense fixed, and the histories that historians write and mythologizers use, which seem forever to be changing. This is really quite different from the well-known "Rashomon" effect, referring to the famous Kurosawa film about a rape-murder in eleventh-century Japan and the different accounts the four people who witnessed it supplied of what happened.[7] "Rashomon," at least as it has come to be used in English, refers to the different points of view different people have of an event (different versions of the "truth") depending on where they are situated, either literally or figuratively, in relationship to that event. The different ways of knowing the past that I'm interested in certainly encompass differences in perspective. But they also go beyond this and address differences of a more substantive nature. Experiencers of the past are *incapable* of knowing the past that historians know, and mythologizers of the past, although sharing with historians the advantage of afterknowledge, are *uninterested* in knowing the past as its makers experienced it. In other words, although the lines separating these three ways of knowing the past are not always clear (historians do, as we are well aware, engage in mythologization, and the makers of the past are entirely capable, after the fact, of turning their own experiences into history), as ways of knowing they are analytically distinct.

There are a number of issues that are raised implicitly in *History in Three Keys* which I address explicitly in the book's conclusion. One has to do with the matter of representativeness. In the book, in an effort to gain a clearer picture of what historians do, I examine the distinctive characteristics of event, experience, and myth in reference to a single – and in many ways quite singular – episode out of the past, the Boxer movement and uprising at the turn of the century. I assume, of course, that buried in the particularity of the Boxers are universals that are applicable to other historical events. This assumption, however, needs to be looked at more closely.

Let me begin with a clarification. In the book I am not interested in all aspects of the past, only in those aspects directly engaging the *consciousness* not only of the historian but also of the experiencer and mythmaker. This leaves out a whole category of historical writing, which is focused on long-term, impersonal developments (frequently but not necessarily social

or economic) that, however important, are generally too incremental to be
noticed and therefore rarely, if ever, engage people's passions. The writing
that encompasses such developments assumes, like all historical writing, a
narrative form,[8] expressing the consciousness of the historian-narrator
(historians never lose *their* consciousness). But it leaves little or no room
for the consciousness of the agents of history, the individuals who make
and experience the past, and it is doubtful anyone would ever set out to
mythologize price inflation in eighteenth-century China or agricultural
change in northern Europe during the late feudal era.

If we omit those aspects of the past that, whatever their cumulative
effect on people's lives, are so slow-changing as to go undetected and train
our attention instead exclusively on the aspects that individual human
beings experience on a conscious level, there is a lot still left. In fact virtually everything is left that people ordinarily think of when they
contemplate the past as an arena in which "things happened." The real
question for us, then, is whether the Boxers, for all their distinctiveness,
may still be taken as illustrative of the consciously apprehended past in
general. My answer to this question is strongly in the affirmative.

When viewed as an event, reconstructed after the fact by historians,
with the goal of understanding and elucidating what happened and why,
the Boxers, I would argue, are as appropriate for illustrative purposes as
any other phase of the past. (Indeed, since the focus, in all such reconstructive effort, is on the consciousness of the historian, rather than that of the
direct participant or mythologizer, there is no reason why historical reconstructions even of the more impersonal parts of the past – as opposed to
"events" and "individuals" – cannot be used to exemplify what historians
do.) The contents of every historical event are, of course, unique.
Moreover, some events, like the Boxer movement, are complex, occurring
over great stretches of time and space, while others, such as the first
performance of a new Broadway play or the death of a national political
leader, are relatively simple (although their ramifications may not be). But
the historian's structuring of these events – the narratives we tell about
them – operates according to a fairly distinctive set of principles regardless.
One of these principles, which is absolutely fundamental, is that, unlike
the mythologizer, the historian seeks to understand and explain the past in
accordance with a socially agreed-upon and enforced set of professional
guidelines. Although as human beings we are subject to the same spectrum
of emotional requirements as anyone else, in our capacity as historians our
efforts to understand the past are guided by a conscious commitment
(never fully realized in practice) to accuracy and truth. This commitment
defines us as historians. If the other commitments to which we also owe
allegiance – say, a feminist historian's desire to give voice to women who
have previously been silent and, by so doing, contribute to the empowerment and liberation of women in the present and future – take precedence
over the goal of understanding and explaining what happened in the past

in accordance with generally accepted standards, we abdicate our responsibility as historians and move in the direction of mythologization.[9] Another principle, no less important (though admittedly far less controversial), is that, in contrast to the participant/experiencer, historians know in advance the outcomes of the events they seek to reconstruct. Like Merlin the magician, we know what is coming next; indeed, it is precisely this knowledge, J.H. Hexter observes, that enables us to "adapt the proportions" of the stories we tell "to the actual historical tempo."[10] A third principle, again distinguishing the historian from the immediate participant, is the former's freedom from the constraint of spatial location; that is, unlike the original agents of history the historian is endowed with what I earlier referred to as wide-angle vision.

The suitability of the Boxers as an illustrative case when the past is viewed as experience is somewhat less straightforward. Here, after all, the spotlight is trained not on the consciousness of the historian-reconstructor but on that of the historical agent, and while we may argue with confidence that *historians*, regardless of their subject matter, always do more or less the same thing, surely the same cannot be said of the people who made the past in the first place and directly experienced it. Wars, election campaigns, baseball games, first loves, and final exams all refer to intrinsically different kinds of experience. The number of different kinds is infinite, and the individual experience is always unique. How, then, can an event like the Boxer episode, in which the key areas of experience included such things as drought, spirit possession, magic, rumor, and death, be taken as illustrative of the experienced past in general? Indeed, isn't the very notion of experience "in general" a contradiction in terms?

The answer, like that to the question of the representativeness of the Boxers *qua* event, has several levels. At its most concrete and particular, the experience of those involved in the Boxer summer was, like the experience of participants in any phase of the past, unique and nonreplicable. Here, for example, are two wish rumors (one of them incorporating Boxer magical claims) that circulated in Tianjin at the time of the fighting there in the early summer of 1900, along with my analysis of their meaning for Chinese contemporaries. The Boxers were said to have told people in Tianjin on July 4 that their teacher, after rendering himself invisible, had entered the foreign concession (Zizhulin), where he came upon a tall building that was vacant. Making himself visible again, he went inside. The building had four stories. There was nothing on the first two floors. But the third floor was filled with gold, silver, pearls, and precious gems, and on the fourth floor he encountered an elderly foreign couple seated facing each other. The couple performed the *koutou* (a ubiquitous Chinese ritual denoting respect for a superior) before the teacher. They said that they were husband and wife and were over 100 years of age. Suddenly bursting into tears, they said they knew that the teacher's magic was very powerful and also knew that he was to come on that day. Therefore they were waiting for him. They said that the foreign countries had only firearms to rely on. Today the foreigners were to be destroyed. Heavenly soldiers had come into the world. The firearms would not fire. The foreign countries had therefore resigned themselves to being extinguished. They invited the teacher to go to the lower floor and help himself to the gold, silver, pearls, and jewels. They then announced that they were going to die. When they had finished talking, they both seized pistols and shot themselves in the chests.

"The Boxers," we are told by a contemporary Chinese chronicler,

> took much pleasure in telling this story and the people of Tianjin were convinced it was true. Suddenly, they spread the word that the government forces and Boxers had repulsed the foreign armies and that the Chinese had taken Zizhulin.... The news circulated noisily through the streets of Tianjin. Only after a long time had passed did people discover that it had no basis in fact.

A related rumor that circulated at the same time asserted that the foreigners had fled Zizhulin, that the government forces and Boxers had entered the area and quartered themselves there, and that within the concession they had found forty crates, each containing 280,000 *liang* of gold (1 *liang* = 50 grams). Neither the government troops nor the Boxers took the gold; instead they presented it to the governor-general's *yamen* (office) to be used for relief purposes.[11]

There were a number of wishes symbolized in these rumors, and they had to do with people's deepest and most pressing concerns. On the most obvious level, of course, there was the wish, shared by both the Boxers and the population at large, that the Chinese side would be victorious in the Battle of Tianjin and the foreigners go down to defeat. (This wish was also given expression in the woodcut art of the day, which frequently showed the foreigners being overwhelmed by the Chinese in military encounters or humiliated by them in some other way; see Figures 8.4 and 8.5.) In an area suffering from the effects of protracted drought, there was also the wish, expressed in the second rumor (and implying a possible divergence of interest between the Boxers and the general population), that ordinary people (not the Boxers or the government soldiers) would be the beneficiaries of the precious-metal windfall discovered in the foreign concession. Finally, and perhaps least obvious, the first rumor incorporated the fantasy that the foreigners (as represented by the truth-telling elderly couple) accepted the efficacy of Boxer magical claims and had bought into the master narrative of the heavenly nature of the Boxer movement and its mission, thereby confirming in the most powerful way the validity of the Boxer cause.

Experience on this level of particularity, while enormously helpful in advancing our understanding of the psychological climate prevailing

Figure 8.4 Battle of Tianjin. This is a detail from a larger, full-color patriotic print depicting the use of a variety of weapons (including explosives) by glowering Chinese troops in a victory over the foreigners.

Source: By permission of the British Library.

during the spring and summer of 1900 in the northern Chinese city of Tianjin, doesn't tell us much about events occurring in other places and other historical eras. On a somewhat more general level, on the other hand, world history is full of popular movements in which, as with the

Figure 8.5 Execution of Russian and Japanese soldiers. This print, originally in full color, shows Russian and Japanese prisoners being hauled before Prince Duan and Dong Fuxiang (two strong Boxer supporters) for judgment (upper right), and their subsequent execution (upper left).

Source: H.C. Thomson, *China and the Powers: A Narrative of the Outbreak of 1900* (London: Longmans, Green, 1902).

Boxers, religion and magical rituals played a key part, antiforeign feeling was a driving force, rumor and incredulity were pervasive, and war, blood-shed, and dying predominated. And on the most general (or abstract) level, there are a number of phenomena that appear to characterize all human experience, regardless of the specific, concrete forms in which it is expressed. I have in mind here such things as indeterminacy (or outcome-blindness), emotional engagement, multiple motivation, cultural construction, and biographical consciousness (as distinct from historical consciousness).[12]

The kinds of historical data available for the reconstruction of different experiential worlds will, of course, vary according to the idiosyncrasies of historical circumstance. Except at the most superficial level, for example, it is impossible to explore the consciousness of individual Boxers because very few Boxers were literate and, although we have a good deal of oral history material collected from former Boxers over a half-century later, no Boxers at the time left detailed accounts of their experience.[13] There is a profusion of documentation, on the other hand, relating to such facets of the Boxer experience as the high levels of anxiety occasioned by the uncer-tainties attending prolonged drought and premature death and the pervasive tendency of Chinese and foreigners alike to interpret their expe-riences in terms of prior cultural patterning (see Chapters 3 and 4 of this volume). While we obviously cannot reconstruct the Boxer experience in its entirety, therefore, we can certainly gain access to significant portions of it, and, at a certain level of generality, in so doing we can gain insight into the experienced past more broadly considered.

The problem of the Boxers' representativeness as myth is different, but not fundamentally so. The main difference is that many parts of the past – and I refer here expressly to the consciously experienced past – do not survive, in any significant way, as myth. To live on as myth, an event or person must embody characteristics or themes that seem especially perti-nent to the concerns of particular groups of people and/or governments in later times. Columbus is important to Italian-Americans because when viewed as the discoverer of America he is emblematic of the contribution people of Italian ancestry have made to American life. In a quite different way, Columbus is also important to African-Americans and Native Americans, who, focusing on his involvement in the slave trade and his brutal treatment of the Indian populations of the Caribbean, have refash-ioned him into a powerful symbol of the oppression and racist exploitation these groups have suffered throughout their history at the hands of Americans of European ancestry.[14]

On the Chinese side, to take an example very different from the Boxers, the Taiping movement and uprising have been mythologized in a wide variety of ways. In the last years of the Qing, the radical journal *Minbao* hailed the Taiping founder, Hong Xiuquan, as one of China's great nation-alist revolutionaries (along with the first emperor of the Ming dynasty and

Sun Yat-sen).[15] The Guomindang in the early 1920s and the Chinese Communists throughout the period of Maoist dominance also identified with and saw themselves as carrying on the Taiping revolutionary tradition.[16] Individual Taiping leaders, in heavily mythologized form, have figured centrally in Chinese Communist political wars. After being sumptuously praised in the historiography of the 1950s, for example, the able commander Li Xiucheng, because of the confession he made (following torture) to Zeng Guofan after the Taipings' defeat, was reviled during the 1960s as a traitor to his class and regularly deployed as a negative symbol in Cultural Revolution attacks on revisionists.[17] And Chinese historians in the late 1970s and early 1980s, in their attacks on "feudal despotism" in general and (more guardedly) the "patriarchal despotism" of Mao Zedong in particular, regularly drew parallels between Mao's slide into increasingly autocratic leadership after 1958 and that of such past political leaders as Hong Xiuquan.[18]

The Taipings, as one might expect, have also been a favorite source of local-level mythmaking, especially in the area of their origin in the Pearl River delta. Sun Yat-sen, who came from the same part of southern Guangdong as Hong Xiuquan, is said to have admired and identified with the Taiping leader ever since his childhood days.[19] Refugees in Hong Kong reported that in the mid-1950s Guangdong peasants, viewing Hong as an all-purpose spokesman for popular resistance to the coercive power of the state, looked for him to return from the dead to lead them in opposing the cooperativization of their land.[20] Recent work on the Hakka minority of southern China shows how Christian members of this ethnic group have integrated a positive vision of the Taiping movement (whose founders were Christian-influenced Hakkas) into the invented traditions that form part of their definition of themselves as a community.[21]

The Boxers, too, as we have seen, have been mythologized by later Chinese in sharply conflicting ways over the years, depending on what aspect of modern Chinese cultural identity – condemnation of foreign imperialist aggression or emulation of foreign-inspired models of modernity – has been uppermost in the mind of the mythologizer. But, although the particularities of one or another example of mythologization will differ greatly (the Taiping experience does not, for example, like that of the Boxers, resonate in a special way with the issue of modern cultural identity), the underlying processes involved do not. Whether it is the Boxers or Columbus or the Taipings or the French Revolution or Martin Luther King, in all instances of mythologization of the past the emphasis is less on what actually happened than on how what happened is transformed and recast by later people for their own purposes. Invariably, particular themes from the past are identified, simplified, magnified, and highlighted, to the point where they become sources of energy in the present, making it possible for present and past to affirm and validate one another, sometimes in extremely powerful ways. The themes so used may or may not be part of the actual historical past – it isn't clear, for example, that real Red Lanterns ever saw themselves as rebelling against the Confucian social conventions that hobbled Chinese women at the end of the nineteenth century (as alleged by Cultural Revolution mythmakers) – but they must, if they are to work effectively as myths, possess at least a degree of plausibility. They must be believable, even if not true.

On the matter of the Boxers' representativeness, to summarize, I would draw essentially the same conclusion with respect to each of the alternative avenues of access to the past that I explore in *History in Three Keys*. At the most concrete and specific level, the Boxers, whether viewed as event, experience, or myth, are undeniably unique. This uniqueness, however, has embedded within it broad recurrent patterns encountered in all phases of the consciously experienced past, making it perfectly feasible, at a more general level, to appropriate the Boxers – or, for that matter, any other historical episode – for illustrative purposes. We don't study lions in order to learn about giraffes, but we can study either lions or giraffes to enrich our understanding of the animal kingdom.

Another issue that invites further comment has to do with the comparative validity of event, experience, and myth as ways of knowing the past. Are we to understand the experienced past as being privileged over the historically reconstructed one because it is more real? Or the historically reconstructed past as preferable to the mythologized one because it is truer, a more accurate reflection of what happened? Although at one point in my career as a historian I would not have hesitated to answer "yes" to both of these questions, my growing conviction is that each of the three approaches, despite manifest tensions among them, possesses a solid kind of legitimacy within its sphere.

The case is perhaps hardest to make with respect to the polarity between the experienced and the historically reconstructed pasts. Although we see the ways in which they differ, the value we attach to the one is difficult to cordon off and keep from being affected by the value we attach to the other. We may, for example, in certain circumstances, delight in confronting, for the first time, the historical recounting of a part of the past – a war, say, or a political campaign or a social movement – in which we ourselves have directly participated, marveling in the new information and perspectives it supplies. But in other circumstances our earlier participatory role may, in the light of later historical understanding, become a source of far greater pain or guilt or emotional conflict than we originally experienced. Reading about the history that we ourselves have lived, in other words, invariably touches it, affecting for better or worse our memory of the actions we engaged in and the thoughts and feelings we had at the time. But the original experience, I would insist, however much reframed and redefined by subsequent reconstructive efforts, retains a special place in our minds and hearts, as something that happened to us. Bob Kerrey could never have written his memoir *When I Was a Young*

Man if it had been not him but someone else who had been involved in the killing of women and children in a Vietnamese village in 1969.[22]

The situation with respect to the value of myth is also complicated and potentially problematic, although perhaps less so in regard to the relationship between myth and experience than that between myth and history. Experience does not take place within a cultural void. As people encounter "life" they instantly "process" it in terms of the myths – or cultural assumptions – that have formed a vital part of their socialization. Boxers do not hesitate to identify the gods who possess them as the historical and literary figures they have learned about from early childhood or to understand the failure of their magic in battle situations in terms of deep-seated cultural beliefs about female pollution. Christian missionaries almost instinctively interpret the Boxer movement as the work of Satan, and their own actions (and fate) as reflections of God's will. Such mythic constructions are ubiquitous in the world of experience and form an inseparable part of it. But, as merged as they seem – and perhaps are – at the moment an experience is first registered (the immediate past) they remain analytically distinct. This distinctness, moreover, becomes a lot clearer (at least to others) when in reviewing the personally experienced past from a more remote point in time we inadvertently mythologize it. The process of constantly reworking one's own experienced past, which I call autobiographical mythologization, obviously does violence to the "purity" (not to mention the accurate remembering) of the original experience. "However honest we try to be in our recollections," a character in Robertson Davies' *World of Wonders* cautions, "we cannot help falsifying them in terms of later knowledge."[23] But, at the same time, as a number of writers have argued compellingly, autobiographical mythmaking has a clear value, in that it helps to preserve a sense of psychological coherence and personal integrity over time.[24]

The value of myth in the context of the relationship between myth and history is still more complicated. Most professional historians see it as part of their responsibility to distance their reconstructions of the past from the relatively crude, mythologized understandings of the general population. We shrink, for example, from accepting a simple, idealized vision of Abraham Lincoln as "the great emancipator" and feel in duty bound to point out that, despite his personal conviction that slavery was wrong, Lincoln's priority, from start to finish, was not to free the slaves but to save the Union.[25] Similarly, historians today (although not always in the past) challenge the simple American view of World War II as "the good war" and insist on pointing out that, although many Americans believed the war was waged, at least in part, to vanquish an ideology based on racial difference, the United States government, in addition to fielding a military force segregated along racial lines, also in the name of wartime exigency systematically incarcerated well over 100,000 persons residing on the West Coast for no other reason than their Japanese ancestry.[26]

Nevertheless, despite our best efforts, the mythic power of a Lincoln or of a World War II – the emotional investment in an essentialized understanding of certain individuals and events that isolates out one strand from a complex picture and emphasizes *it* to the exclusion of all else – remains serenely intact. And this is true even for historians when we're not behaving as historians. The most disciplined purists among us will perhaps always do their utmost to substitute empirically demonstrated truths for long-cherished myths. But the majority of historians, I think it's fair to say, are happiest when laying siege to other people's mythologized understandings, not their own.

Indeed, the very notion that the truth about the past – what historians seek to attain[27] – is necessarily and always of greater value than what people want to *believe* is true about the past may itself be little more than a myth. Gabriel García Márquez's fictional portrayal of Simón Bolívar as a foul-mouthed, flatulent hypochondriac "capable of crossing the Andes barefooted, naked, and unprotected, just to go to bed with a woman" threatened to deprive Latin Americans of one of their few genuine heroes. Although García Márquez insisted that *The General in His Labyrinth* captured "the way Bolívar really was," Belisario Betancour, the former president of Colombia, said the book left him feeling "an immense desolation" as well as "an impression of anguish and infinite sadness" that would force readers to "rethink the world, amidst sobs."[28] There are, in short, as García Márquez's account and Betancour's reaction plainly suggest, several different kinds of value – moral, intellectual, emotional, political, aesthetic – and an assertion about the past that ranks high in respect to one of them may not rank very high at all in respect to the others.

One last issue, related to but distinct from the one just discussed, bears scrutiny. This concerns my own role, as author, in the several parts of *History in Three Keys*. Each part, after all, explores a different realm of consciousness: the consciousness of the historian in the first part, that of the participant experiencer (or historical agent) in the second part, and that of the mythologizer in the third. And, yet, in all three parts my own consciousness, as historian-narrator, is also at work. This presents no problem in the first part of the book, since the consciousness of the author and that of the historian-reconstructor of the Boxer episode are one and the same. But what about the second and third parts, where this is not so?

In the experience portion of the book, I, as historian-author, select the specific themes to be presented: drought, spirit possession, magic, and so forth. I also explore analytical issues that it would never have occurred to the Boxers themselves to raise – issues such as the role of youth and hunger (and hunger anxiety) in the rapid spread of the Boxers' possession ritual in the spring and summer of 1900, or of prepubescence in the collective fantasies that existed concerning the exceptional magical powers of the Red Lanterns. Similarly, in the myth section, in addition to identifying how the Boxers were mythologized in different time periods, I analyze the process or dynamic of mythologization in ways that the mythologizers themselves would likely resist. In both parts, in other words, in the course of playing the conventional historian's role of reconstructor of the past – in this instance the experienced and mythologized pasts – I also introduce a consciousness, my own, that is certainly different from and may well run counter to that of the people whose consciousness I am probing.

It would be foolish to maintain that this is not a problem. The question is: how debilitating a problem is it? The answer hinges partly on what as a historian one is *capable* of doing and partly on what one *aspires* to do. Although it is clearly not within the bounds of the historian's capability to resurrect the experienced past in its pristine form (if, indeed, such a thing ever existed), it is certainly possible, in the case of both the experienced and the mythologized pasts, to reproduce live voices from those pasts (although not necessarily the voices one might ideally wish to reproduce), and this is as good a way as we have of evoking what the people we are studying (whether experiencers or mythmakers) themselves thought and felt. I do this repeatedly in the second and third parts of the book. But to do only this would have been to do only a portion of what I initially set out to accomplish. Since from the outset it was my hope not merely to present examples of event, experience, and myth but to scrutinize analytically their distinctiveness as ways of knowing the past, it was essential to introduce my own intelligence as a historian into the scrutinizing process. It may well be that in so doing I have created a situation in which different consciousnesses, the scrutinizer's as well as the scrutinized's, are in a state of tension with one another. But, apart from being unavoidable, it occurs to me that there is a palpable benefit, in terms of greater historical understanding, to be derived from this very tension.

Essentially, the problem I am addressing here is that of the historian's "outsideness." This outsideness can take a variety of specific forms: European or American (or Japanese or Southeast Asian) historians writing about the Chinese past, male historians reconstructing the experience of women, white historians probing Black history. It can also – indeed must always – take the more general form of people in the present attempting to elucidate the experience of people in the (sometimes remote) past. In all of these cases, the historian's outsideness, precisely because it is outside, has the potential to misconstrue and distort, to introduce meanings alien to the material under examination. And it is in this respect, clearly, that outsideness can be a problem.[29]

But the historian's outsideness can also be an asset. It is an essential part of what makes us different both from the immediate experiencers of the past and from the past's mythologizers, enabling us, in our capacity as historians, to render the past intelligible and meaningful in ways unavailable to either. In addition to attempting, with all the attendant risks, to recreate the consciousness of the experiencer and/or the mythologizer of the past, in other words, we also seek to form a bridge between those worlds and the world of the people of our own day, making possible some degree of useful communication between the two. Akin to the translator, whose job is to render a text not only faithfully but also meaningfully from one language into another, historians act as mediators between present and past. In the complex process of negotiation that ensues, we must curb our outsideness as we try to understand the consciousness of the people we are studying (in the past). But we cannot curb it – on the contrary we must capitalize on it – in the effort to explain this consciousness meaningfully to the people for whom we are writing (in the present). Historians, in short, not unlike translators, must be acquainted with two languages, in our case those of the present and of the past, and it is the need to navigate back and forth between these two very different realms, incessantly, sensitively, and with as much honesty as possible, that is the ultimate source of the tension in our work.

Notes

Parts of this chapter are adapted from the preface and conclusion of *History in Three Keys: The Boxers as Event, Experience, and Myth* (New York: Columbia University Press, 1997); originally a talk given at the University of Charleston and Columbia University, it is here substantially revised.

1 Mary C. Wright, "Introduction: The Rising Tide of Change," in Wright, ed., *China in Revolution: The First Phase, 1900–1913* (New Haven: Yale University Press, 1968), p. 1.
2 Jeffrey Wasserstrom, "The Boxers as Symbol: The Use and Abuse of the Yi He Tuan," unpublished paper (1984), pp. 10–11.
3 In the United States the Boxers and Red Lanterns came in for warm praise from radical Chinese-Americans in New York and San Francisco. A Red Guard party was formed in the latter city. In New York, an organization calling itself I Wor Kuen (Cantonese for Yihequan or "Boxers") started publishing a bimonthly (sometimes monthly) bilingual magazine called *Getting Together* (*Tuanjiebao* in Mandarin) in February 1970. An editorial entitled "I Wor Kuen" in the second number clearly indicated the group's stance:

> I Wor Kuen fighters were not frightened away by the foreigners' weapons because they believed that spiritual understanding and unity among people were more important than weapons in deciding the outcome of a war.... Tens of thousands of liberated women fought against foreigners alongside of the men in units such as the Red Lantern Brigade.... The patriotic rebels of the Taipings and I Wor Kuen lit the spark which started the gigantic fire for the liberation of Chinese [*sic*] and world's peoples.
> *Getting Together* 1.2 (April 1970): 2 (English-language section).

4 The "murderous Boxer Uprising" loomed large in Part 1 of *Life*'s three-part pictorial survey of the historical background to the emergence of "the young fanatics of the Communist Red Guard." See "Behind Mao's Red Rule: The 100 Violent Years," *Life*, September 23, September 30, and October 7, 1966.
5 See Paul A. Cohen, "Imagining the Red Lanterns," *Berliner China-Hefte* 12 (May 1997): 88–95.

6 Paul Veyne, *Writing History: Essay on Epistemology*, trans. Mina Moore-Rinvolucri (Middletown, Conn.: Wesleyan University Press, 1984 [original French edn. published 1971]), p. 40.

7 The film, in turn, was partly based on a short story, also entitled "Rashōmon," by the early twentieth-century Japanese writer, Akutagawa Ryūnosuke.

8 Paul Ricoeur argues forcefully that even the work of Braudel and other members of the Annales school, although proclaiming itself to be nonnarrative in character, has embedded in it a concealed narrative structure. See, especially, Ricoeur, *Time and Narrative*, trans. Kathleen McLaughlin and David Pellauer (Chicago: University of Chicago Press, 1984), vol. 1, chap. 6, on "Historical Intentionality." See also David Carr, *Time, Narrative, and History* (Bloomington: Indiana University Press, 1986), pp. 8–9, 175–7.

9 This problem is encountered in all historical scholarship. It is posed most conspicuously by scholars who are candid about their extraprofessional social and political commitments. See, for example, Gail Hershatter, "The Subaltern Talks Back: Reflections on Subaltern Theory and Chinese History," *positions: east asian cultures critique* 1.1 (Spring 1993): 103–30. Hershatter, a first-rate social historian, raises the problem implicitly but does not actually address it in her article.

10 J.H. Hexter, as quoted in David Lowenthal, *The Past is a Foreign Country* (Cambridge: Cambridge University Press, 1985), p. 218.

11 Anon., *Tianjin yiyue ji* (An account of one month in Tianjin), in Jian Bozan *et al.*, eds., *Yihetuan* (The Boxers), 4 vols. (Shanghai: Shenzhou guoguang she, 1951), 2: 153–4.

12 The distinction between biographical (or autobiographical) and historical consciousness is elaborated in Cohen, *History in Three Keys*, pp. 65–7. It is illustrated in an account Shen Tong, one of the student leaders in Beijing in the spring of 1989, gave of his participation in the demonstrations. Shen observed that, for him, there were "two Tiananmen Squares," the one he personally experienced, which was full of confusion and excitement and remained an ongoing part of his consciousness, and the one created by the Western media, which quickly faded from view after the June 4 crackdown. Likening his experience to a "voyage" or "journey," Shen noted that, although Tiananmen as an *event* was "over," his own sense of involvement in the movement that resulted in it began before the spring of 1989 and continued after it. Talk, Harvard University, October 24, 1990.

13 The oral history materials, which give us the fullest Boxer evocations of their own experience, clearly are inadequate for this purpose, both because they are not contemporary and because they are structured to a substantial extent by the consciousness not of the respondents but of their interrogators. None of these materials, in any case, comes close to supplying us with the kind of intimate biographical tracking (including pre-Boxer or post-Boxer life experience or both) that is readily available for foreign participants in the Boxer events in Richard A. Steel, *Through Peking's Sewer Gate: Relief of the Boxer Siege, 1900–1901*, edited by George W. Carrington (New York: Vantage, 1985), Eva Jane Price, *China Journal, 1889–1900: An American Missionary Family During the Boxer Rebellion* (New York: Scribner's, 1989), and numerous other published and unpublished accounts.

14 John Noble Wilford, *The Mysterious History of Columbus: An Exploration of the Man, the Myth, the Legacy* (New York: Knopf, 1991), pp. 249–62. The emotions aroused by competing mythologizations of Columbus were very much in evidence in the summer of 1991 in Philadelphia when, to mark the 500th anniversary of Columbus's landing in America, the City Council voted to change the name of Delaware Avenue (almost 4 miles long) to Christopher

Columbus Boulevard. Italian-American groups had pushed for the change. But an Apache Indian active in the Stop the Name Change coalition said his group did not wish to honor a man who stood for "the enslavement of people of color." *New York Times*, August 25, 1991, p. 27L. A year later, a group of Native American protesters in Boston elicited the following response from the grand marshal of the planned Columbus Day parade: "We're Italian-Americans, and they've taken all our heroes away from us.... Columbus is the last hero we have.... He discovered America. Why don't they leave the guy alone?" *Ibid.*, October 11, 1992, p. 18.

15 Don C. Price, "Popular and Elite Heterodoxy toward the End of the Ch'ing," forthcoming in Kwang-Ching Liu and Richard Shek, eds., *Heterodoxy in Late Imperial China* (Honolulu: University of Hawaii Press).

16 In the case of the Guomindang, Mary C. Wright discusses the growing shift away from this identification with the Taipings as, under the leadership of Chiang Kai-shek, the party in the course of the 1920s became more and more wedded to stability and order and less and less to revolutionary change. "From Revolution to Restoration: The Transformation of Kuomintang Ideology," *Far Eastern Quarterly* 14.4 (August 1955): 515–32.

17 Stephen Uhalley, Jr., "The Controversy over Li Hsiu-ch'eng: An Ill-Timed Centenary," *Journal of Asian Studies* 25.2 (February 1966): 305–17; James P. Harrison, *The Communists and Chinese Peasant Rebellions: A Study in the Rewriting of Chinese History* (New York: Atheneum, 1971), p. 128.

18 Lawrence R. Sullivan, "The Controversy over 'Feudal Despotism': Politics and Historiography in China, 1978–82," *Australian Journal of Chinese Affairs* 23 (January 1990): 2–3, 14.

19 Harold Z. Schiffrin, *Sun Yat-sen and the Origins of the Chinese Revolution* (Berkeley: University of California Press, 1970), p. 23; see also Marie-Claire Bergère, *Sun Yat-sen*, trans. Janet Lloyd (Stanford: Stanford University Press, 1998), pp. 33–4.

20 Harrison, *The Communists and Chinese Peasant Rebellions*, p. 260.

21 Nicole Constable, "Christianity and Hakka Identity," in Daniel H. Bays, ed., *Christianity in China: The Eighteenth Century to the Present* (Stanford: Stanford University Press, 1996).

22 Bob Kerrey, *When I Was a Young Man: A Memoir* (New York: Harcourt, 2002).

23 Robertson Davies, *World of Wonders* (New York: Penguin, 1981), p. 58.

24 In her moving ethnography of an elderly Jewish community in Venice, California, Barbara Myerhoff writes that in her subjects' quest for "the integrity of the person over time" the creation of "personal myths" often took precedence over "truth and completeness." *Number Our Days* (New York: Simon and Schuster, 1978), pp. 37, 222. On a more general level, Shelley E. Taylor argues that, to a significant degree, the operations of the healthy mind are marked less by a concern for accuracy than by the ability to engage in "creative self-deception." *Positive Illusions: Creative Self-Deception and the Healthy Mind* (New York: Basic Books, 1989). David Carr, while acknowledging that individuals in the course of "composing and constantly revising" their autobiographies are much concerned with coherence, is less willing than either Myerhoff or Taylor to yield on the governing importance of truth and truthfulness to people so engaged. *Time, Narrative, and History*, pp. 75–8, 98–9, 171–2.

25 "My paramount object in this struggle," Lincoln wrote Horace Greeley on August 22, 1862, "*is* to save the Union and is *not* either to save or destroy slavery. If I could save the Union without freeing *any* slave, I would do it." *The*

People Shall Judge: Readings in the Formation of American Policy, 2 vols. (Chicago: University of Chicago Press, 1949), 1: 768–9.

26 Almost 75 per cent of those interned were American citizens. German-Americans, Italian-Americans, and German or Italian nationals living in the United States encountered difficulties only when there were specific grounds for believing them to be enemy agents.

27 History, according to Roger Chartier, while "one among many forms of narration,...is nevertheless singular in that it maintains a special relationship to truth. More precisely its narrative constructions aim at reconstructing a past that really was." Chartier's remarks, made in a paper delivered at the International Congress of Historical Sciences in Montreal in 1995, are quoted in Georg G. Iggers, *Historiography in the Twentieth Century: From Scientific Objectivity to the Postmodern Challenge* (Hanover and London: Wesleyan University Press, 1997), p. 12.

28 *New York Times*, June 26, 1989, pp. C13, C17.

29 For a discussion of the many sides of this issue, see Lowenthal, *The Past is a Foreign Country*, especially pp. 210–38.

Index